THE OTHER CIVIL WAR

THE OTHER CIVIL WAR

American Women in the Nineteenth Century

Catherine Clinton
Consulting Editor: Eric Foner

American Century Series

HILL AND WANG • NEW YORK
A division of Farrar, Straus and Giroux

First printing, 1984
Printed in the United States of America
Published simultaneously in Canada by Collins Publishers, Toronto
Designed by Nancy Dale Muldoon

Library of Congress Cataloging in Publication Data
Clinton, Catherine.
The other civil war.
(American century series)
Bibliography: p.
Includes index.
1. Women—United States—History—19th century.
2. Feminism—United States—History—19th century.
I. Title. II. Series.
HQ1410.C44 1984 305.4'0973 84-525
ISBN 0-8090-7460-5
ISBN 0-8090-0156-X (pbk)

For Daniel L. Colbert

Preface

PROTEST sparked my commitment to this topic. While I was a teaching assistant for an undergraduate lecture course on nineteenth-century America at an Ivy League university, I complained bitterly that none of the readings or lectures dealt with women. The professor in charge, my dissertation director, who had listened to my railings for many years, responded sympathetically by asking me to prepare and deliver a lecture on women for the course. I realized the absurdity of trying to cover women's experiences in the nineteenth century in one presentation out of twenty-six, but tokenism seemed better than nothing at all. My interest in the topic has grown, as has the literature over the past few years. This book is testimony to my optimism, combining my enthusiasm for undergraduate teaching with my commitment to scholarship in women's history.

As a teacher of women's history, as well as a scholar and student in the field during the past decade, I wrote this book to be completely self-serving. I wanted a comprehensive treatment which would incorporate the recent specialized literature on nineteenth-century women while providing a general social-history overview of the era. After several years of research, I realized my task was easier to envision than to accomplish.

It is striking to me that I was unable to fill in many of the gaps I found in the general literature on American women. Searching through bibliographies and indices for material on native American women, black women, and other women of color is a dispiriting endeavor. The literature is on the increase, but scholars in women's history should tackle these subjects, as well as the especially difficult task of integrating neglected females into general surveys. For those who are dedicated to making women visible in American history, the failure to include these forgotten women seems even more discouraging. Our work will speak louder than rhetoric.

Despite these drawbacks, the field affords more optimism than pessimism. Women's history can no longer be dismissed as fad or trend or any of the other diminutives critics employed to try to wish it away. Rather, this burgeoning field has become a dynamic force within the profession, demanding that we remember what has not been lost but forgotten.

This volume, divided into ten chapters, uses a chronological framework. Certain aspects of the text lend themselves to thematic exposition, so I have tried to let the events of the century unfold in order. But at certain junctures I was forced to organize my material in a manner which did not fit a time line. I also employ the terms "feminism" and "feminist" throughout the text, although these labels are clearly modern usage, identifying ideas and activists who wished to advance women's progress within society, to provide women more power and autonomy within the culture.

The opening chapter, "Edging toward Equality," puts into perspective some of the topics I explore. Colonial women remain a diverse and relatively unknown group within American history. We are only just beginning to understand their lives through use of demographics, anthropology, archaeology, and other reconstructions of their experiences. Yet what few sources we have on colonial women remain underexploited, especially for regions outside New England.

The American Revolution wrought great changes in the lives of women as well as men. The consequences of the Revolution and the dimensions of the transformation are examined briefly so that we may understand women's lives at the opening of the century. The amount of available material on women as well as the historical literature on the period increase dramatically following the Revolution.

The second chapter, "Women's Work and the Cotton Revolution," deals with an era traditionally called the Age of Jackson. In discussing this era, in which white males were granted unprecedented political freedoms, I try to explore some of the concurrent developments for women. First, I examine the growth and expansion of the factory system in the North and women's central role in industrial development. Then I outline the lives of women on southern plantations during these years. The expansion of the frontier, the founding of the mills, and the explosion of the cotton economy had dire consequences for women, slave and free. The transformations of the period might well be "the cotton revolution."

The majority of women were not involved directly in this revolution—although most suffered or profited from the production of cotton. By far, most females during the antebellum era were concerned with their roles in the home and the expanding realm of "domesticity," which was increasingly regarded as women's domain. Females formed networks which had social and political repercussions. An ideological split between women's sphere and the public, male world forged even stronger bonds of womanhood. Female responses to sex-segregated responsibilities and their increasingly gender-identified roles within society are examined in Chapter 3. Art, religion, and education combined to shape female identity and culture during the antebellum era.

The next chapter, "Organization and Resistance," deals with women's collective political responses to their cultural roles. I look at the various reform movements which developed during the first half of the century. How and why women joined evangelical crusades, moral reform campaigns, temperance and purity drives, and finally the abolitionist movement, provide a critical perspective on women's enormous contributions. At the same time, I explore the issues which led women to wage an independent crusade for their own rights which created a feminist revival at mid-century.

The struggle for women's rights accelerated as women started their own grass-roots campaigns. Feminists rallied behind a barrage of demands ranging from custody of children in divorce suits to the vote. But with the outbreak of war, females joined the home front: northern women supported the Union, while southern women were divided: most white women favored the Confederacy, while black women opposed it. The ways in which women coped with the prolonged turmoil varied. War required women to assume new duties, to accept larger responsibilities in wartime. Some shrank from their burdens, but the vast majority met the challenge. The triumph of the Union not only signaled the defeat of Confederate women, but even northern women lost what few feminist gains they had made during wartime. Slave women provided the exception; emancipation was undeniably an improvement in status.

Feminists were frustrated by events during Reconstruction. Although Radical Republicans mobilized to free the slaves, the majority opposed granting women the vote. Many women believed the time was ripe to effect reform, but the political climate remained hostile to feminist demands. Suffrage advocates split over the best way to achieve their goal, and rival organizations sprang up to mobilize support for votes for women.

While women were caught up in the war and their own battles, other events were shaping the nineteenth century. Migration westward and large-scale immigration had a permanent impact, as described in "Natives and Immigrants." Thousands of families made their way across the plains during the middle decades of the century, which created urban centers and white communities where only "wilderness" had been before. Of course, the natives who inhabited this wilderness were casualties of this settlement. The impact on women was enormous, and so, too, was women's influence on the process.

Before migrants exploded onto the frontier, immigrants had flooded eastern cities during the 1840s. The Civil War discouraged immigration, but it increased rapidly after the war. Women immigrants played an important role in the wage-earning force, and the face of the nation changed.

By the middle of the century, women were campaigning vigorously for equal access to education. "Pathbreaking and Backlash" discusses the feminist crusades that created improved opportunities in the last half of the century, and the setbacks that often followed the initial gains. With the establishment of women's colleges and the sexual integration of many previously all-male institutions, females created an impressive record of achievement. These accomplishments, especially in the professions, are testimony to women's steadfast commitment to self-improvement and autonomy. Women's battles for equality during the last quarter of the century provide us with a legacy of feminist reform, just as the backlash reminds us of ferocious resistance.

Women reformers, expanding their activities into an ever-widening sphere by the end of the century, began to focus on issues of primary importance to women; sexual and reproductive concerns attracted powerful critics as well as widespread interest and support. Women's health and women's bodies, their sexual natures, disorders, and activities became topics of intellectual as well as medical discourse. Birth control, abortion, sexual attitudes and acts provide challenging topics for women's history, subjects which are addressed in "Sexuality and Stereotypes."

The last two sections cover a wide range of issues which come under the general heading of women's political culture. "Networks and Reform" examines women's prodigious efforts to expand female influence in the public domain—the formation of women's clubs, temperance organizations, and other activities geared to improve society at large. Female reformers believed the imposition of feminine values and concerns might halt the decline of America they felt they were witnessing.

Women organized to fight the deterioration so apparent within the cities, ills which threatened social order. Female participation in settlement houses and urban reform crusades was overwhelming; here women far outnumbered their male comrades.

In addition to female-dominated reform crusades, by century's end women were contributing to all the major political reform campaigns: Progressivism, Populism, Socialism, Nationalism, and the fight for black civil rights. These contributions are dealt with in "Divided and United." Sometimes women could only participate as "auxiliaries," since they were denied equal status in male-dominated political movements. But whether women formed separate societies or worked within men's organizations, they raised consciousness about women. Feminist ideology was a force with which most, if not all, political reformers were forced to contend by the turn of the century.

The feminist impact on other political campaigns was overshadowed by the enormous strength of the crusade of women's suffrage. The final stages of the seventy-year battle (from Seneca Falls to the Nineteenth Amendment) are described briefly in the last chapter. Assuredly, this is one of the most significant achievements for modern American women. The franchise guaranteed women no privileges beyond the vote. But by obtaining this most basic civil right, the American woman moved closer to liberty and autonomy.

Women spent a great deal of the century being pioneers: in the mills, on the frontiers, in the professions, battling for reform in political crusades. Female activists were a force for change in every decade, from the converts of the Second Great Awakening to those who organized against lynching during the 1890s. Individual leaders and outstanding achievers will be discussed in some detail. More important, countless women without notoriety who participated in economic shifts, political crusades, and social movements will be chronicled.

A number of women have appeared rarely, if ever, in traditional histories: black women, poor women, native American women, lesbians, women prisoners, and others. Wherever possible, I integrate the lives of such forgotten women into the fabric of America's past. Because this study derives largely from secondary sources, the scarcity of literature contributes to their marginality. Yet the prognosis is hopeful.

Barely twenty years ago, the literature available on nineteenth-century American women would hardly warrant a full-scale historical synthesis. Following the explosion in women's history in the past two decades, this book appears a foolishly ambitious undertaking, but it is one which will contribute, I hope, to the ongoing process of historical rediscovery and revision.

The completion of this project was helped by a number of people. First and foremost, a patient and encouraging publisher, Arthur Wang, and my insightful and supportive editor, Eric Foner, made this book possible. Their vision and guidance were invaluable to me over the years. Second, I wish to thank both my students at Union College and the Humanities Faculty Development Committee of that institution for their contributions, which enabled me to finish my research and to complete the bulk of my writing during my four years there. I am also extremely grateful to Zack Deal and the staff of the Harvard University Office for Information Technology, whose advice and assistance immeasurably eased the delivery of my manuscript.

My labors have afforded me countless pleasures. More than I can express, I have appreciated the hundreds of books and articles, dissertations and unpublished papers on women's history which have poured forth during the past decade. This book has been made possible by the work of scores of committed scholars whose research enriches this growing body of literature.

I was warned by male mentors in graduate school that I should expand my interest beyond women's history. But feminist historians whose scholarship and careers inspired me provided the examples which pressed me onward: Mary Beth Norton, Linda Gordon, Ellen Dubois, Mary Jo Buhle, and Jacquelyn Hall. It has been my good fortune that two who have become friends, Norton and Hall, read drafts of my manuscript. In addition, other generous scholars have afforded me advice and invaluable support, most especially Ben Barker-Benfield and Rosalind Rosenberg. However, I must accept sole responsibility for any errors and shortcomings.

C.C.

Cambridge, Massachusetts
September 1983

Contents

THE OTHER CIVIL WAR

1
Edging toward Equality

THE American Revolution created unprecedented opportunities for women as well as men. With the founding of the United States of America, females of the former British colonies—at least the free, white women of the new nation—had the greatest potential for political and economic equality, and indeed some enjoyed privileges not extended to the female sex anywhere else in the world. Mary Wollstonecraft's influential *Vindication of the Rights of Women* (1792), considered by many to mark the beginning of the modern women's rights movement, appeared two years after females in one of the new American states—New Jersey—explicitly were granted the right to vote. Many women who had supported the Revolution—the Daughters of Liberty, for example—anticipated an expanded civic role for females in the new nation. They believed that women's talents and energies, which proved so crucial in the struggle for independence, would be put to better use in the new republic.

Although in principle women were indeed granted power and influence, in practice their hopes for equality were shattered: statesmen's acknowledgment of the importance of women was too often shallow rhetoric rather than an expression of willingness to grant them a substantial role in the public domain. At the same time, however, some women improved their status dramatically in the early years of the republic, with liberalization of divorce, with favor in the courts of equity, and even with female suffrage (documented in the case of New Jersey).

This transformation was not merely based on roles and responsibilities which developed during the Revolution but stemmed in part from the evolution of female status during the colonial era. Economic necessity and political conflicts created more flexible roles for women in the New World. Many women in the seventeenth and eighteenth centuries were able to exploit the potential for increased influence and autonomy, a potential which grew alongside the religious and political ferment of pre-Revolutionary America.

During the seventeenth century, women were a desperately required commodity for the New World—to supply settlements with much needed labor, domestic influence, and the power of natural increase. The founders of the American colonies believed settlements would prosper only through the introduction of European women. Perhaps they had learned this lesson from British outposts in the West Indies, where the lack of female colonists caused many communities to languish. Lord Baltimore held that the success of his colony depended on the importation of white women. Females became essential for the survival and prosperity of colonizing ventures. Proprietors and entrepreneurs lured women abroad; many were offered their passage money in exchange for a term of service as "indentured servants."

Women, like men, journeyed to the New World for many different reasons. Most hoped to improve their economic status. Judith Giton and her husband were Huguenot refugees who fled their native France in 1685, settling in Charleston. Life in Carolina was extremely harsh, and she wrote: "I have been six months without tasting bread, working like a ground slave; and I have even passed three and four years without having food when I wanted it." When her first husband died, she married a distiller named Manigault and they jointly struggled to build a prosperous life for themselves and their family. Judith Giton Manigault's grandson became one of the most successful entrepreneurs in the colony and an influential politician in the post-Revolutionary government. So, throughout the eighteenth century, the rags-to-riches folklore of the New World lured women westward across the sea.

During the seventeenth and eighteenth centuries many women left the Old World fleeing religious intolerance. Anne Hutchinson left her native England seeking a community where she and her family might worship without fear of interference. Hutchinson found Massachusetts authorities equally inhospitable, and in 1638 she was faced with a public trial, where examiners determined: "You have stepped out of your place, you have rather been a husband than a wife and a preacher than a hearer; and a magistrate rather than a subject." She was banished from the Bay Colony for her heretical beliefs and behavior. She did not, however, die on the gallows, as Mary Dyer, a Quaker, did—hanged for her repeated defiance of the law.

Despite incidents of religious persecution, America afforded dissenting religions relative freedom to practice, proselytize, and prosper. In the late eighteenth century, "Mother" Ann Lee founded a Shaker community in upstate New York, and branches soon sprang up across New England, the Middle Atlantic, and the old Northwest. The Moravians established model communities North and South. The continent also attracted traditional religious institutions. Communities of Jews founded synagogues in Truro, Rhode Island, in 1763 and as far afield as Port Gibson, Mississippi, a generation later. Ursuline nuns established a convent and academy in New Orleans in 1727. Despite the fact that a number of women who came to the New World for religious freedom suffered persecution, many more found North America fertile soil for their spiritual flowering.

In addition to those women who were bribed or cajoled into emigrating, there were those who made the crossing with little or no say in the matter. Females put on trial might be given the choice of prison or service in the New World. Many preferred being "barbadoed" (the popular expression for the custom in seventeenth- and eighteenth-century England) to spending time in British jails.

Women from Africa—like their brothers, fathers, husbands, and sons—were stolen and shipped across the Atlantic to be sold. In 1648 there were only three hundred blacks out of a population of fifteen thousand in the colonies, but by 1671 this proportion had grown to two thousand blacks out of forty thousand settlers. By the 1770s, half the population of Virginia and two-thirds of South Carolina were black. Because births as well as importation increased the number of slaves, women's role in the system was central to its flourishing.

Female chattel were subjected to the worst indignities. White indentured servants, unlike slaves, had some small room to maneuver within the system. It might be argued that female contract workers were equally deprived: servant women were not allowed to marry, and were sexually abused by co-workers and masters alike, and indentured mothers were required to serve longer terms and apprentice their "bastard" offspring. Serving maids generally were at the mercy of men who owned their contracts, but the contractual nature of indentured servitude set it apart from the absolute thrall of slavery. Blacks were forced to serve for life, and the children of slave women had the same chattel status.

Not surprisingly, Indian women, too, were exploited by European settlers. Throughout the colonial period, transplanted European males outnumbered females—with a greater sexual imbalance in the South than in the North. Some colonists, denied emigrant women, lived with native females. Often these arrangements were sanctioned neither by the white community nor by the Indian tribes. Many liaisons were not solemnized by civil or religious marriage ceremonies. There were, however, notable exceptions: Pocahontas, daughter of a chief, who married John Rolfe; and Tame Doe, sister of a chief, who married Sir Francis Ward. The underlying rationale for these unions was a desire for closer bonds between reds and whites, but these intermarriages were limited and largely symbolic. Because women were viewed as more susceptible to religion and moral coercion, the white clergy invested an enormous amount of time and energy trying to convert native women. It was assumed that these females would convert the men in their families and their tribes, not turn themselves into suitable wives for white men.

One of the most successful spiritual conquests was that of the Indian woman Tekakawitha (Lily of the Mohawks). Born in 1656, the native girl joined the Catholic Church at the age of eighteen, despite the fact that her conversion made her a pariah among her people and earned her the enmity of tribal leaders. She was forced to move to Sault Sainte Marie in Canada, where she lived with French nuns and took the name Katherine. She was a prize trophy for the Catholic clergy. When she died prematurely at the age of twenty-four, she became a celebrated figure, dubbed the "Genevieve of New France."

Saints and native brides did little to alter the course of European conquest during the colonial era. Although Indian women often served as mediators and peacemakers, the tides of political and economic greed swept the invaders inland. Their "manifest destiny" resulted in disruption and disintegration of the native peoples of the continent.

Scholars have argued that, ironically, for some Indian women the introduction of "civilization"—European influence—brought about a decline in female status within their tribe. For example, in the Iroquois nation, a select group of elder women determined who served as sachems on the council, the most powerful ruling body within their governance system. Whites frowned on this custom, which gave women, in some measure, dominance over men. Side by side with their disapproval of strong roles for women, whites promoted the notion of "squaw passivity" and of the "subjugation" women suffered among "savages." Europeans distorted images of Indian women as well as men to support their own political and economic drives to dominate and, in the end, drain Indian cultures. By painting the natives as "barbarous" and "savage," whites could justify their own imposition and brutality.

Women (native, black, and white) were the key to the survival of settlements in North America. They were "keepers of the culture"; they gave birth to future generations and provided this tenuous mixture of peoples with a promise of domestic order and family stability. Women held homes together and enabled their families and their people to survive and flourish on the frontier.

Women played vital roles in the colonial economy. Because of the shortage of labor, male colonists allowed white females to fill positions which were traditionally accorded males. When a tavernkeeper or shopkeeper died, his wife often took over and ran the business. Widows maintained their late husbands' enterprises, relatively unhampered by colonial authorities. A steady supply of goods and services was essential to a fragile colonial community.

New England's colonial records indicate that commerce was abustle with industrious and enterprising women. Jane Mecom, Benjamin Franklin's sister, ran a shop in Boston during the 1760s. Elizabeth Murray Smith ran a successful business in Boston, as did Margaret Hutchinson in Philadelphia and Elizabeth Thompson in Charleston. In addition, some women were able to make their mark as artisans and artists: Patience Lovell Wright became a successful artist in her native America before she emigrated to England in 1771. Like many colonial women who became self-supporting, Wright did not start with a career in mind. When her husband died in 1769, leaving her with four children and another one on the way, she turned her energies to sculpting wax figures, and developed a "traveling waxworks," which she took on tour from Boston to Charleston. Disillusioned by her prospects in the colonies, she emigrated to London, where she joined a small circle of American artists in residence and in vogue such as Jonathan Copley and Benjamin West.

Still, legal discrimination hampered women's efforts to advance within the colonial economy. English common law was a tremendous stumbling block: a single woman was under the protection of her father and was designated *feme sole*, granted all the rights of man but voting, while a married woman turned over all her rights of person and property to her husband and became *feme covert*. In colonial America there were, in fact, two competing systems: common law and courts of equity. Common law held that a married woman's legal status was wholly subsumed in her husband's, but judges in equity courts could rule against this principle, granting wives control over their own land, chattel, and even funds. Marriage settlements and trusts were honored in these colonial courts, allowing a woman separate administration of her property. Widows especially were able to gain some measure of autonomy. Most colonies required the courts to grant them one-third of their deceased husbands' estates. Men, disturbed by women's increasing freedom in the New World, moved against liberalization. Maryland legislators attempted to prevent a single woman's control over her rightful property by introducing a statute in 1634 declaring that any female inheriting land must marry (or remarry) within seven years of possession or forfeit her claim. Margaret Brent, a Maryland executrix, was trusted and skilled at the management of business for absentee landlords. But she got into trouble with the authorities when she attempted to take a seat on the council, due her by virtue of her power of attorney. She was denied the privilege, despite staunch support from males impressed by her talents and abilities.

Men and women shared the responsibility for turning colonial outposts into thriving communities, for profit to both the Old World and the New. Some scholars contend that this common task reduced gender differentials, but in any case, female influence was visibly increasing in the English colonies. Mary Katherine Goddard edited her brother William's newspaper when he became preoccupied with the political opposition to Britain during 1773. Indeed, Mary Goddard was one of the printers and distributors of the Declaration of Independence, and maintained a successful business throughout the Revolution.

This New World provided challenging opportunities to women as well as men. In general, free colonial women had more opportunity to attain better economic positions in society than they had ever been afforded in Europe.

Tensions remained, nevertheless, because even in New England women were still politically inferior. But, by and large, women seemed content with their greater freedom and influence. Divorces were granted in Massachusetts and Connecticut. Property-owning women were better able to circumvent male domination—in the North much more than in the South. In this expanding society, increasing urbanization and the growth of an increasingly complex and diversified market economy created unparalleled opportunities for women, opportunities which many seized and exploited.

At the same time, housewives' daily burdens remained depressingly similar to those in the Old World. A composite excerpt from a farm girl's diary of 1775 reveals domestic routine:

> Fix'd gown for Prude—Mend Mother's Riding-hood, Spun short thread, —Fix'd two gowns for Welsh girls, —Carded tow,—Spun linen—Worked on Cheese-basket —Hachel'd flax with Hannah, we did 51 lbs. apiece, —Pleated and ironed, —Read a sermon of Dodridge's —Spooled a piece, —Milked the Cows, —Spun linen, did 50 knots —Made a Broom of Guinea wheat straw —spun thread to whiten —Set a red dye —Had two scholars from Mrs. Taylor's —I carded two pounds of whole wool and felt —Spun harness twine —Scoured pewter —Ague in my face . . .

This female, like many white women in colonial America, was literate, so she could read if she wished. But her hectic schedule could not have allowed her much time for reflection and leisure.

Wealthier women enjoyed the luxury of a servant to assist them in their domestic chores. An advertisement in the *Pennsylvania Packet* in 1780 shows the hardiness required for such a position: "Wanted . . . a Single Woman of unsullied Reputation, an affable, cheerful, active and amiable Disposition; cleanly, industrious, perfectly qualified to direct and manage the female concerns of country business, as raising small stock, dairying, marketing, combing, carding, spinning, knitting, sewing, pickling and preserving, etc." The numerous advertisements for domestic help in colonial periodicals testify to the dullness and drudgery of domestic responsibilities for women.

Despite a temporary laxity due to the shortage of women, colonial society generally adhered to strict gender differentiation which favored males. Pre-Revolutionary America was no golden age for women. One school of historical thought contends that during the colonial years circumstances combined to improve the status of women: a woman's economic contributions to the household were "equal"; sex roles were less rigid during frontier years, and the enforcement of legal constraints was lax. Recent research challenges this claim. Careful analysis of colonial law by Marylynn Salmon disputes any interpretation of women's legal status as "liberal" during the first hundred years of the colonies. Colonists, she maintains, adhered to a strict code of "marital unity," a married woman's legal personality as defined by that of her husband. Also, in a family-obsessed culture, a daughter's interests were further subsumed in those of the colonial patriarch. Carol Karlsen's work on witchcraft in seventeenth-century New England demonstrates that women who exercised any influence in the economic realm—widows or wives who participated in commerce, who carved out for themselves a greater measure of independence than other women in the community—were more likely to become victims of a witch-hunt. And Mary Beth Norton's work on colonial women refutes the myth of the golden age by demonstrating that colonial women labored under debilitating, rigid gender restrictions.

To appreciate the complex reality, we must explore the ways in which women's lives evolved and were transformed during the many generations between the colonization of the New World and the declaration of a new nation. Rank ordering of all these changes, labeling each new phase as an advance or decline, may add little to our understanding of the patterns of women's experiences. Revisionist scholars of women's history seek rather to pinpoint events or forces which brought about perceptible transformations in women's social status and roles.

Developments in eighteenth-century America were slow but recognizable departures from seventeenth-century patterns. First and foremost, the colonies developed an identity separate from Europe. Immigrants from a variety of nations created a cosmopolitan and hybrid colonial culture, especially in seaport cities such as Boston, Philadelphia, Baltimore, and Charleston. By the mid-eighteenth century, American colonists were a unique mixture, with their disparate economies ranging from the fur traders in New York to the tobacco planters in Virginia, and with the considerable contrast between Puritan New England and Carolina backwoods culture. For all this diversity, however, many colonists found that their interests were discernibly different from those of the royal government abroad. The War for Independence itself and the enormous enterprise of organizing and imposing a new system of government absorbed the colonies during the last quarter of the eighteenth century. What were the changes wrought in women's lives during this significant period?

Some of the important transformations stemmed from cultural shifts which appear before the break with Britain. Certainly the Great Awakening of the 1740s must be considered a landmark. During this decade and in the years to follow, colonists reevaluated their relationship to the church and to their God. Divines roamed the countryside preaching a new doctrine which celebrated the individual. Radical evangelicalism encouraged people to abandon old faiths and strict adherence to the teachings of Puritan fathers, to venture into untrodden territory with those dubbed the "New Lights." This challenge to patriarchal and hierarchical church authority provided colonial ministers with a new spiritual climate. Women responded most fervently to the call. Indeed, they were widely lauded for their "special" ability to spread religion, particularly to children. Sermons began to promote the image of women as spiritually pure and more religious than their male brethren.

Women's role within the family emerged as a popular theme in ministerial literature. Even a generation before the Great Awakening, females dominated congregation membership. Preachers increasingly acknowledged the importance of woman's familial role and praised female piety. The rise in female church membership and women's increasing influence in the spiritual realm created a "feminization" of religion. This major transformation in the nineteenth century had its foundations in pre-Revolutionary revivals. This was also the case in another major transition for American women: the limitation of the family.

Scholars are unclear as to how and why American women began to decrease family size during the eighteenth century and into the nineteenth. But the results are impressive. Birth rates, of course, vary according to class, region, and color throughout American history—but there is a steady pattern of overall decline starting with the Revolutionary generation. This decline is startling in light of the fact that preceptors and statesmen of the new nation proposed that patriots be fruitful and multiply, to cover the continent with American citizens. Yet many factors combined to create an opposite development. Generations of colonists had adopted attitudes which produced a new pattern of affective relations within the family. Fewer children meant the quality of life might improve. Mortality rates, concurrently, were declining; this varied dramatically according to region, but a larger proportion of those born after the Revolution than those born in the British colonies survived to maturity. Most methods of contraception employed at this time required the cooperation of both partners. Studies of Quaker families indicate that mutual cooperation and mutual benefit were a growing concern for married couples, one that shortly would become the norm for white middle-class Americans.

The most glaring exceptions to this rule were the masters and slaves of the colonial South. Planters required numerous heirs to maintain dynastic control over their lands, and they also wanted a large and increasing slave population to supply plantation labor. We have no internal evidence from the slave community concerning their reasons for large families. Evidence, admittedly fragmentary, indicates that the white South diverged from northern patterns until much later.

The Revolution, of course, was one of the most vital catalysts for women's changing roles. The political crisis provided women with new and essential tasks and paved the way for accelerated changes. During the war, women were left alone on the home front, forced to cope with their husbands' households, estates, and businesses, with little or no guidance and limited managerial expertise. Documents demonstrate that scores of women underwent dramatic transformation during the prolonged separations from their husbands and fathers. Initially, women shrank from the tremendous burdens men expected them to shoulder during the Revolution. They believed themselves incapable of coping with the tedious and intricate business which men had claimed so long as solely a male domain. But slowly and surely women found the strength and capability not only to endure but to master these responsibilities. Because of the emergency nature of the situation, men were not only willing but eager that females display such "masculine" talents.

However, when men returned from war, women soon found that their assumption of masculine pursuits was only temporary. Even though wives enabled their husbands' estates and businesses to survive the war, returning patriarchs expected women submissively to relinquish the reins of power. Some women had relished their tenures: they valued the independence and control war allowed them, however harsh this fate had seemed at the outset. Indeed, the conflicting perceptions of women's wartime role created no small tension between many couples following the British defeat.

Women had gained, in some measure, confidence and pride in their abilities, both collectively and as individuals. During the Revolution, women had formed numerous war-relief organizations. The female counterpart of the Sons of Liberty attained ideological as well as material gains for the patriotic cause. Women organized tea boycotts and assembled large quantities of food and clothing for troops at the front. Women patriots encouraged female industry on behalf of the Revolutionary campaign: spinning societies were not merely social convention, they allowed colonists to supply themselves with much needed cloth in the face of a boycott of British goods. Homespun was not merely handy or profitable, it had its political purpose, as one Revolutionary editor indicated: "The industry and frugality of the American ladies must exalt their character in the eyes of the World and serve to show how greatly they are contributing to bring about the political salvation of a whole Continent." Many women bridled at remarks critical of frivolous feminine pursuits. During the war, women were seasoned to the harsh realities of building a democracy, and they sought acknowledgment of their abilities and contributions to the patriotic cause.

Women were but one of the many oppressed groups seeking recognition during this critical time. Blacks, native Americans, artisans, and others excluded from the public spheres of power took to the platform, to the streets, and served in battle to win the Revolution. Many, if not most, hoped their contributions would be repaid with concessions following the Revolution. Artisans hoped to smash the aristocracy which allowed birthright to substitute for advancement by merit. Blacks believed that patriotic diatribes against the tyranny of the British, the "slavery" to which the colonists were subjected, might move the new regime to abolish the labor system which held the majority of blacks in bondage. Native Americans wanted access to their homelands. Some natives fought alongside the British, and others served in the Continental Army; Indians on both sides sought autonomy for their tribes. Finally, women wished to receive their due, after holding the country together during a prolonged and difficult war.

Recognition of women's patriotic and pivotal role in winning independence from Britain was reflected in post-Revolutionary rhetoric. Rhetoric was far from satisfying to many women, however. Some women resented husbands and statesmen alike who consigned them to dependent status after such a display of female ability. Outspoken women lobbied for legal and political rights. Following the Revolution, many widows railed against the new governments, as when Mary Willing Byrd of Virginia proclaimed: "As a female, as the parent of eight children, as a virtuous citizen, as a friend to my Country, and as a person, who never violated the laws of her country . . . I have paid my taxes and have not been Personally or Virtually represented. My property is taken from me and I have no redress." Despite the fact that Byrd (like other women in her situation) couched her plea in the language which patriots had employed to implore English authorities to desist their tyrannical rule, women were denied equal status. However, seeking to disengage themselves from the Old World and establish a new and more democratic order, patriot leaders allowed women what they proclaimed was an equivalent role in the new nation.

This new role was not reflected in the laws or statutes of the land. Women were not even mentioned in the Constitution. This is in stark contrast to the prominent inclusion of Indians (who were granted a special role) and slaves (who were accorded the mythical status of "three-fifths a person"—for the purposes of representational apportionment). It was not until the Fourteenth Amendment (1866) that the Constitution made any specific reference to gender. Statesmen in the early republic often explicitly excluded women from definitions of citizenship. Nevertheless, in at least one state this was evidently not the case. Revolutionary leaders of New Jersey not only assumed women should have suffrage within their newly founded state; the laws reflected this sentiment.

We know that the franchise was a privilege granted by the states, and therefore each individual state government determined voter eligibility for its inhabitants. During the colonial era the term "freemen" was used frequently in connection with legal rights; evidence indicates that women in many colonies possessed all the rights of "freemen" except voting, and women could function as proprietors. Quakers granted women more equitable status within their religion, and this liberalizing influence might have encouraged New Jersey officials—elected from communities where Friends dominated local politics—to take a more advanced attitude toward women's role in the newly founded state.

As early as 1783 a New Jersey statute granted the franchise to "all inhabitants of this state, of full age, who are worth fifty pounds proclamation money, clear in the same . . ." A Burlington, New Jersey, poll list from October 1787 reveals that women were voting. Although only two of the 258 votes cast were by women, financial hardship and some initial confusion over eligibility during the early years of the new government rather than gender may have been primary factors in this poor showing by females. The election law of 1790 very clearly refers to voters as "he or she"; a member of the committee which drafted this statute, Joseph Cooper, a Quaker, openly advocated women's rights. We have little evidence of how many others endorsed the principle, but we do know that women voted in local elections.

In a heated contest in October 1797 over an Essex County representative to the state legislature, women voters turned out in large numbers to support the Federalist candidate—although his Republican rival, John Condict, won. One observer declared in a Newark paper: "The *Rights of Man* have been warmly insisted on by Tom Paine and other democrats, but we outstrip them in the science of government and not only preach the *Rights of Women*, but boldly push it into practice." (The author of the article later makes reference to Mary Wollstonecraft, indicating the sophistication of local politics at this time.) Reports of this event were widely circulated in the press throughout the state, along with a few humorous poems and satirical essays. This was not an isolated incident; in 1798 another journalist in the state capital lamented: "Many important election contests have been terminated at least by these auxiliaries [women voters]."

By the turn of the century, local politicians frequently deplored the practice of women voting. Newspapers and taverns were full of ridicule, with men arguing that women must be prevented from voting, lest the legislature be "filled with petticoats." But the principle was upheld repeatedly in the (all-male) legislature. A state representative declared in 1800 during debates over eligibility for voting in congressional elections: "Our Constitution gives this right to maids or widows, black or white." When a bill was introduced to prohibit all but free white males from voting, the proposal was soundly defeated.

Critics complained that married women defied the law when they cast ballots. Conservatives argued that wives were never intended to vote because the law clearly stated only those who had a sum of money free and clear were eligible; with *feme covert* still in force, no married woman could lay claim to independent income. During this same period, many attacks on female suffrage were coupled with charges that slaves were admitted illegally to the polls—the lumping together of women and blacks as perpetrators of election fraud.

The problem of voter eligibility plagued local New Jersey contests, and the state was out of step with the rest of the country. In 1806 events came to a boil with a fierce battle over relocation of the Essex County courthouse. The election became a carnival, with reports of women as well as men, blacks and whites, moving from poll to poll to cast multiple ballots. Abuses were so flagrant that the legislature had little trouble declaring the results null and void. But the incident had far-reaching consequences when a state committee appointed to look into the matter proposed revision of the election law to eliminate "problems."

This new statute, enacted in 1807, was clearly aimed at denying women and other "undesirables" the vote. Although many challenged the bill when it was introduced, John Condict, the Republican representative from Essex (the very same man who nearly lost his seat because of the large turnout of women voters who cast ballots against him in 1797), spoke eloquently in favor of restricting eligibility. His speeches turned the tide and the legislature endorsed the measure. The preamble makes clear the intent of the lawmakers: "Whereas doubts have been raised and great diversities in practice obtained throughout the state in regard to the admission of aliens, females and persons of color, or negroes to vote in elections . . . it is highly necessary to the safety, quiet, good order and dignity of the state, to clear up said doubts by an act of the representatives of the people . . ." And so voting became limited to white male adults of property.

Women obviously wielded very little political clout, even with the vote. Despite their active role in local contests, New Jersey women failed to petition the legislature to restore their franchise. There is no evidence of any protest in the press. However, opponents of female suffrage were jubilant. A local paper reported in November 1807: "Election bill met better fate,/On every hand defended,/To check confusion through the State,/The female's voting ended."

Although we should not exaggerate the importance of the New Jersey case, the fact remains that women were granted the vote as part of their political rights in this new democratic experiment. Even if it was calculated that only a handful of women would be able to vote if the franchise was guaranteed only to women with *feme sole* status, that does not diminish the fact that rigid gender differential was abandoned in this volatile realm of voting rights. And although this temporary suspension of the rule of sex discrimination lasted longer than northern

Reconstruction in the post-Civil War South, it was an impermanent and less significant departure. Not only because this aberration can be found in only one state, but because it is clear that women neither sought nor fully grasped the political significance of this measure. However, when women began to exercise their right to vote, to exploit their potential, men responded with alarm; this pattern continues throughout the century. The episode may tell us very little about women's struggle for equality, but it affords insights into male attitudes toward sex roles and female status.

It would appear that the majority of females, content to accept the flattery of orators and flowery authors, pressed for greater influence, not in the forbidden realm of electoral politics, but in a more suitable sphere, the home. Since most women's lives were spent confined to the household, and the public domain was unwilling to welcome women, this compromise seemed reasonable to the majority of Americans. Females hoped that they might effect reform in critical matters such as divorce, child custody, and property rights.

During the early years of the republic, rhetoric celebrating women's value to the new nation was lavish. Statesmen and ministers believed families were vital to the success of the country. Women attached great significance to their emerging role. The bearing and rearing of "liberty-loving sons" was a political priority, and one to which women could devote their lives. Despite being denied the right to vote, women were encouraged and indeed expected to fulfill a civic role.

Women who sought their rights struck a very ambiguous bargain with men during this period. It is clear that full participation for women in political affairs was unwelcome and threatening. Yet women's fervor was fired by Revolutionary slogans during the war with Britain. And so, enterprising and spirited women pleaded for basic privileges, which men were willing to grant in exchange for women's withdrawal from their wartime positions as surrogate males. Women wanted education above all else.

Daughters had long been denied access to schooling in favor of their brothers, and now they, too, sought intellectual improvement. Statesmen had to justify granting such a valuable commodity to women, whom they claimed were inferiors. It was within this context that the cult of republican motherhood was developed. Elite women were granted the right to obtain some education but not to overcome their legal disabilities or in any way alter their political or economic status. Rather, their demands for education were linked to their roles as mothers. Women argued that, as they were the first educators of children, they required better educations themselves. If women had tied their campaign for female academies to suffrage—because men argued women's ignorance was at the root of male objections to female voting—the crusade for women's education would surely have been doomed.

Not only were American statesmen generally unhappy at the prospect of female participation in politics, but by the end of the 1790s Federalist politicians decried the specter of decadence following France's recent political turmoil. "The excesses of the French Revolution" conveyed a myriad of evils to newly independent Americans, conjuring up images of conniving mistresses and courtesans plotting for their own advantage at the expense of their enemies most certainly, but perhaps also of their country. Women who meddled in politics might become indecorous, at the very least, and, in all likelihood, indecent. Debauchery and decline would follow for any country which allowed such a development.

Male theorists wanted to spare American womanhood this unworthy fate. They denied women participation in the public realm allegedly to protect them. And thus men consigned women to the private sphere, a haven in a heartless world, the home.

During this transitional post-Revolutionary phase, production increasingly shifted out of the home. One of the most heralded developments after the turn of the century was the growth of centralized manufacturing. Scholars maintain that a "division of spheres" resulted from the economic restructuring of American society—although indeed this transition was primarily a northern phenomenon. The expansion of manufacturing and the growth of urban populations had dramatic impact during this period. Prescriptive literature on the new roles of the family and education reflected this shift; the household was no longer the central economic unit. Within this new reworking of domestic ideology, the household acquired a supposedly enhanced social status and image: the home, the female domain, the woman's sphere.

In this new mythological kingdom, woman reigned from within the comfortable confines of the home. The hearth was her throne. Men ventured out of the household and into the workplace, which was increasingly perceived as the "real world." Although males were forced into competition and conflict outside the domestic household, every man could return to his own unchallenged rule: his home was his castle. In this new ideological schema, work was also assigned a new meaning. Prior to the development of commercial markets, work was productive activity which contributed to the economy: household labor was the mainstay of the agrarian and even the commercial colonial economy. With the boom in manufacturing, notably cloth and shoe-making, with the shift from household industry to factories, work was also divided into spheres. Wage-earning became even more important within an increasingly capitalist American society.

Manufacturers needed workers reoriented to wholly new notions of work and the workplace. Capitalists preferred to pay for the worker's time—an hourly wage—rather than for the worker's skill or product, ushering in the concept of a "living wage" (the amount needed to support a family). Domestic labor within the home was excluded in calculating production, resulting in a devaluation of women's labor. "Women's work" had always had an inferior status, but with the onset of industrialization, traditional female domestic labor was even more discounted. The invisibility of household work, within calculations of economic productivity, remains a problem throughout the nineteenth century and well into the modern era.

Female economic status was lowered by separating women's labor into a different and inferior category. Even today housework generally remains women's unpaid responsibility. This segregation creates a hardship both by demoting female productivity within the home to a non-status and by consigning female labor in the market economy to an equally abysmal devaluation. Throughout the nineteenth century, although females often worked at the same jobs and their hours were made up of the same sixty minutes as men's, the pay scale for women was often half what men earned.

So the abstract division of spheres had very concrete consequences for women. Within the increasingly commercializing American economy, females experienced numerous and complex role changes. New responsibilities devolved upon them even as new opportunities opened up. Women accepted the challenge of designing innovative models of womanhood for the new nation, ideals which met standards that fulfilled the needs of the expanding culture.

During the nineteenth century the transformation of women's roles, the several and subtle shifts in women's status, the division, intersection, and collision of spheres (public and private, male and female, home and work) created a myriad of permutations and opportunities for women. Females in nineteenth-century America were affected by their class, their color, their vocations and skills. But black or white, rich or poor, educated or illiterate, single or married, homebound or wage earner, all women encountered the handicap of gender. Although the great majority of women labored under this burden with limited appreciation of the possibilities of change for themselves or their daughters, the first generation of American women gave birth to a new breed of female pioneer determined to explore her own talents and make new contributions despite restrictive roles and limited political status. A few women were determined to turn this division of spheres into an asset, almost champions of female differentials. Other committed women were equally eager to break down these artificial barriers which they believed worked against female achievement. In either case, a hardy group of pathbreakers began the slow but steady march on the road toward autonomy. A road American women continue to travel.

2
Women's Work and the Cotton Revolution

MAJOR shifts in the economy, both North and South, in the first half of the nineteenth century had a dramatic effect on women's lives. Although the nation was splitting into two regional economies (the plantation South and the industrializing North), cotton was a key factor in the expansion of both systems. The literature is extensive on the growth of the plantation economy in the South and the development of the textile industry in the North, but until very recently little if any attention has been paid to the significant role of women in what may be termed the cotton revolution.

Historians have concentrated on the ideological conflicts between the two systems, the titanic rivalry between Lords of the Loom, as factory operators were called, and Lords of the Lash, the slaveowners. Despite the alleged competition between free enterprise and slave labor, both systems managed for a long time to work profitably side by side in the production and processing of cotton. After the invention of the cotton gin in 1793 and the consequent expansion of the southern frontier, planters believed slave labor was the most expeditious means of supplying the necessary field force to grow cotton. During the early days of the factory system, textiles were the foundation of what was to become America's industrial and manufacturing empire. Women played a major part in the creation of both systems.

Slave women may have been disproportionately represented in the cotton fields as a result of men's promotions into artisan and skilled positions. Slave men generally filled posts on plantations reserved for trained workers: coopers, blacksmiths, stonemasons, carpenters, and most trades, with the exception of spinning. Also, men were more likely to be rented out (slaves for hire in town), further reducing their numbers in the field. Thus, ironically, while the fragility and delicacy of white women were celebrated by the master class, they exploited female slave labor in the backbreaking work of the cotton fields. Most of the cotton was exported to England, but an increasing amount was processed in the growing factory system of the North.

In rural New England, young women flocked to the mill towns. White single women constituted the overwhelming majority of the early textile work force. By 1831, women comprised nearly forty thousand of the fifty-eight thousand workers in this industry. As late as 1850—despite the large influx of male immigrants—women represented 24 percent of the total number of all manufacturing workers because of cotton's first rank among American industries. While the West siphoned off able-bodied men, young women supplied the factories with a seemingly endless supply of cheap laborers. Thus, however marginally women have been represented in the historical accounts of the era, they played a major role in the development of the antebellum economy. The wealth of the nation (60 percent of the export economy in 1860) relied—to a great extent—upon cotton, which was harvested by black women (and men) in the South and processed by white women in the North.

Obviously, the women in the fields and the women in the mills constituted a small proportion of the American female population. Yet these two groups were significant contributors to the American economy during a crucial take-off era. While the majority of free women remained housekeepers within the home (and they will be dealt with at length in the following chapters), modeling themselves on the ladylike behavior prescribed in the dozens of periodicals published for the predominantly female audience of the era, lower-class women were afforded no such luxury.

Quite clearly, society designated domesticity and the household as women's domain. Most deviations from this narrow role met with stern disapproval. Nevertheless, many young, single women were encouraged to earn pay outside the home as a temporary measure, to tide them over until marriage. Lower- and middle-class females were expected to supplement, instead of draining, family incomes before they wed. These young women slipped into wage-earning roles (albeit within paternalistic mill towns where factory owners served as surrogate fathers) and then back again into dependent status as wives.

The vast majority of women in antebellum America did not work "outside the home." Some scholars estimate as few as 10 percent of wives brought cash into the household. (This statistic, however, excludes the two million or more slave women who toiled in production positions in the South.) And, of course, all women worked, producing goods and services of value within the household.

Before the factory system replaced household production, home industry allowed workers greater control over their hours, conditions, and craft. Work and home, as in the agricultural economy, were integrated spheres. But with the introduction of modern methods of manufacture (task specialization, manufacturers' contribution of tools as well as materials, and other developments), these spheres began to separate. The two worlds of household and workplace were moving apart. This was not a swift and tidy division, but rather a slow and tangled disengagement.

The shift to industrial production has been dissected and debated in numerous historical studies. Until recently, both labor and business history have scrupulously ignored the contributions of women; indeed, "ghettoized" women's work into a separate and unequal category for analysis. This fragmentation distorts the past. If historians filter out women from their formulas, they totally miscalculate family and household income strategies for the working class, as well as neglect women's dynamic contributions to labor history. In both Britain and America, textiles paved the way for the growth of factory manufacturing. The success of the New England cotton industry provided the basis for industrial dominance within the nation as a whole.

In 1813 Francis Cabot Lowell's Boston Manufacturing Company established the first textile mill in America. This operation, located at Waltham, Massachusetts, produced a standardized, coarse cotton cloth. Lowell recruited young, unmarried women fresh from New England farms for work in his plant. Females were rapidly incorporated into this labor force for three major reasons. First, clothmaking was traditionally women's work. The term "spinster" originated in the fact that unmarried women within the household were drafted to do the tedious chores associated with the processing of raw materials into cloth. Second, as women were not the traditional "breadwinners," they could be hired for substandard or "supplemental" wages, making them attractive to manufacturers. And finally, during the first quarter of the century—with westward migration on the increase and before large-scale European migration—there was a male labor shortage on the eastern seaboard. At this time factory work was viewed as degrading: men refused to work in the mills until economic necessity forced immigrant men into the textile work force.

In 1822 mills were founded in what became Lowell, Massachusetts. Besides moving all elements of production under one roof, the Lowell system introduced numerous innovations designed to maintain tight control over the workers. The women who flocked to Lowell lived in spare but adequate dormitories. Mill owners provided these company lodgings to keep the workers under disciplined supervision. The Lowell Manufacturing Company rules required all persons in their employ "to give information at the Counting-Room, of the place where they board, when they begin; and also give notice whenever they change their boarding place . . . the Company will not continue to employ any person . . . who shall smoke within the Company's premises, or be guilty of inebriety, or other improper conduct . . . The doors must be closed at ten o'clock in the evening, and no person admitted after that time without reasonable excuse." These regulations provided a model for mill towns. Throughout New England, workers were required to lodge in company boardinghouses (non-employees could not board at these dormitories), to conduct themselves properly, and to observe the Sabbath. Additionally, keepers of the boardinghouses would lose their boarders if they did not enforce the rules and report any worker's impropriety to her employer. Mill hands were literally under company scrutiny for most of their waking hours; they accepted rigid company routine and curfew or risked losing their jobs.

This rigid regimen and strict enforcement allowed mill workers little or no freedom. However, women had few alternatives. Rather than remain in equally restricted positions within the household, as "unproductive" drains on the family, young women had the opportunity to be self-supporting. Thus, despite the drawbacks of the Lowell system, females sought employment in the cotton industry as a means to improve their lot in life.

Women on the average spent less than two years working in the factory. One verse composed by the factory girls described the poor conditions: "Amidst the clashing noise and din/Of the ever beating loom/Stood a fair young girl with throbbing brow/Working her way to the tomb." Perhaps most ignored the confining mill conditions, since they anticipated a brief tenure. Most women left wage earning to marry, while others found positions as teachers or, more commonly, in domestic service (if they persisted in earning cash). Quite clearly, the pattern of hiring temporary (unskilled) factory workers favored the manufacturers. Mill owners put little effort into recruitment, trusting word of mouth to keep the factory well stocked with workers. Some workers came only for a few months, to earn enough to buy a trousseau or set up a household; a woman from a poor family would ostensibly earn her own dowry. The few records left by former "factory girls" indicate a variety of reasons for working in the mills. Two women who published their impressions, Harriet Robinson and Lucy Larcom, were anomalies in that they both spent years, instead of the usual period of months, in the mills. Their views, however, vividly illuminate the era.

Lucy Larcom was an exemplary mill worker, spending her time—if one accepts her nostalgic memoirs—quite happily at Lowell: "It was a rigid code of morality under which we lived. Nobody complained of it, however, and we were doubtless better off for its strictness, in the end . . ." Larcom wrote glowingly of the bonds shared by these women. She believed this community inspired intellectual attainment and high morals: "I regard it as one of the privileges of my youth that I was permitted to grow up among those active, interesting girls, whose lives were not mere echoes of other lives, but had principle and purpose distinctly their own." Larcom left the mills to pursue her education, teaching at Wheaton Seminary after completing her training. She never advocated unionization, as did her fellow author and mill worker Harriet Robinson.

Robinson was the daughter of a poor carpenter. At the mills she was an active force, leading a strike against the mill owners in 1836. She left factory work in the 1840s, married, and dedicated her talents to reform—antislavery and women's rights. She, too, lauded the circulating libraries and cultivated society afforded by Lowell. But she condemned the laws which forced women to assume false names when they ran away from husbands to work at the mills: "I have seen more than one poor woman skulk behind her loom or her frame when visitors were approaching the end of the aisle where she worked." Married women who worked feared that their wages, like those of children (under the age of fourteen), could be "trusteed" to husbands. But the sufferings of workers rather than the "wrongs against women" drove mill workers to agitate for better conditions.

By the second quarter of the century, factories were unhealthy for workers. In 1845 a woman testified before a Massachusetts legislative committee hearing about her experience in the mills. She reported that summer hours were 5 a.m. to 7 p.m. In the early mornings or evenings when it was dark, 293 small lamps and 61 large lamps lit a single workroom, while 130 females and a handful of men and children spent twelve to fourteen hours a day manufacturing cotton. Lunch hours and dinner breaks were brief and regimented. Women were not allowed to bring reading material into the workrooms. Sickness was common and wages for women were a mere $20–$25 per month. Female workers had a variety of complaints about these oppressive conditions. In 1828 women launched a "turn out" (as strikes were called) in Paterson, New Jersey, protesting against the company's arbitrary shift of workers' lunch hour from noon to one o'clock. It may appear a small matter, but this company imposition was symbolic of the total and harsh control mill owners exerted over workers' lives. Since factory operatives had so little power, they clung to those aspects of their lives over which they could exert some (however small) influence. Generally, women workers did not organize a systematic direct-action program to seek better conditions: more commonly, their protests were spontaneous.

Most strikes, walkouts, and shutdowns failed to secure permanent improvements. There was a lack of well-developed strategies and coordinated campaigns: a ready supply of strikebreakers and other obstacles hampered labor protests. Although protesters won a ten-hour day in New Hampshire in 1847, bids for higher wages and other demands failed repeatedly. Strikes were short-lived because workers attempted these mobilizations during hard times, during periods when it was easier to find scabs and more difficult for women to stop working if their families were dependent on their wages. Economic necessity forced females to stay in the shop despite adverse working conditions. The first decade of manufacturing was alluring for women; the factory system seemed to open a whole new world for them. But by the 1830s factory conditions deteriorated to the extent that many women were willing to strike for better conditions, if not for themselves, then for their daughters, who might one day enter the mills.

Many historians wrongly have assumed that the influx of immigrant labor—foreign-born workers more desperate and therefore more docile in the face of company demands—worsened the situation for factory workers. However, long before the Irish outnumbered the Yankee daughters in the mills, the status of mill operatives had declined. Manufacturers instituted severe practices to counter what they perceived as imperiled profits during the 1830s. "Speed-ups" (forced increases in productivity) combined with wage cuts reduced both the morale and the rewards of factory workers. The Lowell Company in particular was often devious with its few concessions. If the manufacturer agreed to pay hikes, they would be followed by a raise in rent at the company boardinghouses; the result was no net increase for the employees. The mill owners had the upper hand, and workers suffered increasingly under the lash of "wage-slavery."

The operatives did not resign themselves to this fate. The factory girls at Lowell had a journal, *The Lowell Offering*, which voiced their views. Besides publishing the poems and other literary efforts of the working women, the magazine (partially financed by the company) provided them an outlet for political opinions, on women's issues only. For when the women workers began to organize in earnest, founding the Lowell Female Labor Reform Association in 1845, the company withdrew its support. Indeed, the *Offering* exercised censorship, refusing to print a spirited attack upon "the evils of factory life" by "Julianna." In 1845 she ended her plea of justice for her sisters with a rousing indictment:

> . . . producers of all the luxuries and comforts of life will you not wake up on this subject? Will you sit supinely down and let the drones in society fasten the yoke of tyranny, which is already fitted to your necks that you do not feel it but slightly—will you I say suffer them to rivet that yoke upon you, which has crushed and is crushing its millions in the old world to earth; yea, to starvation and death? Now is the time to answer this all important question. Shall we not hear the response from every hill and vale, "EQUAL RIGHTS, or death to the corporations"?

Sarah Bagley, a leader of the reform association, collected signatures to petition the state for a ten-hour-day law. Although her write-in campaign failed to bring about remedy through legislation, these efforts demonstrated that factory women could exert influence beyond their limited sphere. The Lowell petitions prodded the Massachusetts legislature to hold hearings on industrial conditions—the first governmental inquiry of its kind. Further, the women circumvented company censorship by taking over the leading local labor weekly, the *Voice of Industry*, to spread their propaganda. They organized lyceums, sent representatives to the New England Workingmen's Association, and even more importantly called widespread attention to their organization.

These campaigns at Lowell were not isolated incidents. In 1828 three hundred to four hundred women went out on strike in Dover, New Hampshire. Their protest was well publicized in the press throughout the country. During this initial period of labor militance, women's efforts were mocked; a Philadelphia wag warned: "By and by the governor may have to call out the militia to prevent a gynecocracy." But the protests were not silenced by ridicule. Reductions in pay at Dover in 1834 mobilized eight hundred women to strike and form a union. The company fought back by hiring new recruits, forcing these scabs to sign an agreement "not to be engaged in any combination" which impeded company welfare. This broke the back of the organization.

Cotton workers in Allegheny and Pittsburgh launched an offensive against mill owners in 1844. By September 1845, workers banded with women from the Manchester mills, threatening to declare their "independence" if a ten-hour day was denied them. They vowed to wage "war" on the following Fourth of July if their demands were not met. Employers blackballed these agitators, closing their doors to those who refused to work a twelve-hour day.

On October 20, 1845, a riot broke out at a Pittsburgh mill when militants protested against scab workers. Authorities—trying to protect their interests—intervened with muscle. The operatives triumphed in the face of physical force, outnumbering their opposition and taking over the plant. They were able to bargain for a ten-hour day, winning out over the manufacturer. The mill owners, however, got their revenge by a one-sixth reduction of wages. Many women wanted another strike to maintain higher pay equivalents, but the majority settled for reduced hours.

At Dover in 1834, mill girls sang lyrics such as who among them "could bear the shocking fate of slaves to share"? The parallel with slaves appeared in verses chanted at Lowell in 1836 as well. The drudgery and oppression of life in the factory transformed these industrial experiments from model businesses into laboratories for exploitation. How much could the manufacturer increase productivity? How much could the employer squeeze the workers? How little could the employer pay? How high could company rents escalate before the workers would rebel? Thus, worsening mill conditions and economic hard times created "wage slavery" for hundreds and thousands of women in northern industry. At Lowell in 1836, factory women complained: "As our fathers resisted unto blood the lordly avarice of the British ministry, so we, their daughters, never will wear the yoke which has been prepared for us."

By the 1840s the better-educated Yankee daughters were creating powerful ripples of militance within the labor force. This restless element threatened mill owners' stability. Women traditionally moved quickly through the system, indeed so rapidly that a case study of one mill in 1836 shows only eighteen women employed for six years or longer out of the 233 female employees. However, by 1860, the mean years at the company, for women, almost doubled. In 1836 women's mean years of employment were 1.8, and by 1860 the mean had risen to 3.6 years. Another significant development transformed the work force at this time. The proportion of Irish mill workers rose from 8 percent in 1845 to 47 percent in 1860. However, historian Thomas Dublin argues, "the increasing permanence of the work force was not due simply to the influx of immigrant operatives in this period after 1845. Yankee workers had even longer careers in this period than did immigrant newcomers."

Although Dublin effectively makes his case that female persistence within the mill work force could win women better positions and higher pay, these gains were generally negligible. Especially when the evidence also demonstrates that the few men who were employed in cotton manufacture generally enjoyed supervisory positions and better pay. All overseer posts were held by men—the surrogate fathers of mill girls, and stern patriarchal bosses for immigrants. With large blocs of immigrants moving into cotton centers, women faced stiff resistance and the threat of replacement if they tried to organize for better conditions—or, as the employer would call it, "against the mill."

Women—like men—were concerned about issues central to labor.

Two of the many myths about women in labor have been disabused by recent work. First, women have been labor militants from the beginning of their participation in industry. Their involvement in direct-action campaigns and mobilization of the work force throughout the antebellum years belies assumptions to the contrary. In 1825 New York City witnessed a strike of women workers in the tailoring trade. Women led numerous strikes and walkouts in the cotton mills as well. Second, in those industries where women outnumbered males, it is apparent that worker solidarity rather than division along gender lines prevailed. In 1824, women in the cotton mills at Pawtucket, Rhode Island, struck with their male co-workers.

However, the growth of the factory system contributed to the division of work along gender lines. In the shoemaking trade, for example, men gathered in shops, while the women remained at home, stitching and binding the uppers. The introduction of the sewing machine in 1855 pushed women out of shoe manufacturing (until the end of the century, when they returned in large numbers). But until the 1850s females comprised one-third of the workers in the shoe industry. (Their proportion dipped to 14 percent by 1870.) In the beginning of industrialization, daughters and wives did the binding for male shoemaker "heads of household." But gradually shop bosses in towns like Lynn, Massachusetts (one of the shoe centers of the country), dealt directly with women. This home "piece work" (pay by the item rather than the hour) was also a staple of women's contributions to garment manufacturing throughout the century. Women in the home, as a rule, did not organize. They were isolated in their separate workplaces, without any bargaining power, and perhaps the most alienated as well as atomized of the work force.

Some women, especially in factory towns, turned to boarding to supplement family incomes. This was an especially common means of income for widows. Boarders in the nineteenth century not only demanded food and shelter, but most expected women to serve as their servants, if not take on the role of surrogate wife-mothers. Women had to mend and launder boarders' clothes, keep their rooms clean, and tend to details which we today could only expect from a fleet of personal attendants. Often one woman was drafted into this cycle of chores for a half dozen or more paid lodgers. Because of their obligation to remain within the home, widows and married women with children were likely to take on this responsibility more out of need than choice.

Mothers remained in the home, at least until their children could be put out to work (from age eight), when they might join them in the factories. Children in agricultural economies from an early age had always participated in production, as did all members of the farm household, each according to his or her abilities. When America moved into the factory age, women and children were among the first recruits. Indeed, whole families transferred from farms into rural towns and later to factories.

Some manufacturers took advantage of this trend. Instead of the barracks-like lodgings of Lowell, in mill towns such as Slatersville, Rhode Island, and Webster, Massachusetts, company owners preferred to let their mill hands live in single-family dwellings. The company purchased tracts for male heads of household to farm, while the daughters and children worked at the factory. Mothers were able to stay at home and care for their families to maintain the semblance of domesticity and preserve republican values. Some men entered the mills, although none but adolescent males worked on loom or spindle. Adult men held better-paying positions with authority. This, too, reinforced traditional patterns. The values transmitted within these homes created a disciplined and orderly work force, which the mill owners cherished during times of labor unrest. This system, however, crumbled along with the others, but not so rapidly as at Lowell and other sites with non-family households for workers.

While immigrant women flocked to the mills in the 1840s, just as Yankee girls had done in the quarter century before, these impoverished unskilled females often filled more exploited work roles in urban areas as laundresses, domestic servants, and seamstresses. In 1846, of the twelve thousand servants in New York City, almost eight thousand were born in Ireland, two thousand in Germany, and many of the remainder were from other ethnic minorities. Despite the advantage of piecework in the home, by which a woman could earn wages and remain in the household to supervise her family, the seamstress was among the most exploited of the working class. Immigrant women in fact remained the most vulnerable and abused in the garment industry.

The antebellum seamstress earned next to nothing for her long hours of labor. If a woman tried to supplement her husband's inadequate pay by taking in sewing, she might work as long and hard as the head of household did in the mill, but her earnings were less than $2 per week (compared to his $10–$15). These females paid a high price for their lack of opportunity. The needle trades were so poorly paid, reformers of the era complained, that many seamstresses were driven to part-time prostitution to survive in urban centers.

Many wives of the immigrant working class, like most poorer women in the decades to come, were caught in a double bind. They needed to earn money to help support their families, but women were shackled to the home by child care. Since they could neither find nor afford proper "day care" for their offspring, females trapped in the household had to perform long and arduous labor at negligible pay.

By 1855 only one-third of New York City garment workers (dressmakers, milliners, shirt and collar makers, embroiderers, and other fancy workers) were native-born. Again, two-thirds of the foreign-born were Irish. The preponderance of Irish females in the tailoring trades was not particularly due to their skill as seamstresses but was the result of a backlash against women in jobs where the poorest and least educated could earn wages: domestic service.

Protestant mothers feared to have their children exposed to the "evils" of Catholicism. Vicious anti-Irish sentiment was rampant in cities where large numbers of Irish immigrants had settled. Hostilities sharpened in competitive urban environments. Despite the pressing need for servants, "No Irish Need Apply" was a common line in advertisements for help wanted. This scorn was so widespread that an archetypal "Paddy" was often accompanied by the incompetent serving maid "Bridget"—a stock character for ridicule in the popular press. Despite these prejudices, household workers were predominantly Irish. In 1846, of the ten thousand to twelve thousand domestic servants in New York City, over seven thousand were Irish.

Ironically, during the antebellum period, white northern housekeepers sought black servants, thinking them docile and suitable for domestic work. Black women, denied so many other options, had few wage-earning opportunities besides domestic service. Indeed, no black women were hired in northern mills. Black women with families were reduced to sewing for pay, like immigrant women, but more often they found employment in trades they had learned as slaves, hiring themselves out as washerwomen and cooks. Women who took in laundry were forced into the same pattern of economic exploitation as seamstresses. During the antebellum era, when black women in northern towns took in shirts for washing, they charged the going rate of less than thirteen cents per dozen.

Black women who hired themselves out as cooks and maids were usually forced to live in. In essence, white householders saw free blacks as servants who would serve as surrogate slaves, and many unskilled and uneducated black women were exploited as such. Of the eighteen thousand free blacks in Philadelphia in 1838, the Pennsylvania Abolitionist Society discovered five thousand were live-in servants for white families. However, some black women were able to earn a living at other trades. Hairdressing, flower selling, and hat cleaning were some of their pursuits. Black women, like black men, were best able to improve their economic position within this racist society by catering to whites in a service trade. Cooks, maids, and laundresses earned enough in some cases to escape to a higher station within society (or at least to allow their children some mobility). Owning a boarding establishment was a step up for black women—shifting them into the role of property owners, moving them further away from exploited slave sisters who could not even own themselves.

Although by looking at these women we learn only about a minority of black women and certainly only a small fraction of American women, this particular segment of the female population affords us a rare and significant insight. Free black women—by necessity as much as choice—were pathbreakers. Emancipation in the North threw many of them on their own. Even if husbands bought their freedom for them, few black women were guaranteed economic comfort or security. They had to seek wages—and many had to achieve economic independence, because of their peculiar position within society. Because of the extreme racism in nineteenth-century America, black women were sought out as employees mainly because they could be so poorly paid and exploited. Whites were well aware that black female labor was the cheapest on the market and insured their continued availability by maintaining the handicaps of racism and sexism. The kinds of positions that women filled were extensions of their domestic roles; indeed, analogous to those that women in industry occupied.

The conflict between myth and reality concerning women's role was most apparent for black women. The majority were slaves, subjected to physical, psychological, and sexual exploitation. Even black females emancipated from slavery were disproportionately employed outside the home as domestic servants—"wage slaves." In or out of slavery, black women were confronted by the irony of their status within a culture which celebrated a feminine model of domestic gentility.

This irony is dramatically highlighted in Sojourner Truth's remarks at an Ohio Women's Rights Convention in 1851. This majestic-looking black woman, despite opposition, rose to speak: "That man over there says that women need to be helped into carriages and lifted over ditches and to have the best place everywhere. Nobody ever helps me into carriages, or over mud-puddles, or gives me any best place . . . And ain't I a woman? Look at me. Look at my arm . . . I have ploughed and planted and gathered into barns, and no man could head me. And ain't I a woman? I could work as much and eat as much as a man—when I could get it—and bear the lash as well. And ain't I a woman?" Her words stunned the crowd. Truth's stirring call to action (to mobilize for women's rights) moved the audience to cheers.

In this moment of crisis, Sojourner Truth rose to challenge the hypocritical ideal by which society measured women. Although society applied a double standard—i.e., black and working-class women were denied any vestiges of ladyhood—the extreme gap between prescription and reality exacerbated rather than eliminated tensions over women's role. While the cult of domesticity promoted a doctrine of gentility and refinement for women, it was not realized by the majority of American women. Even those upper- and middle-class females who aspired to idealized visions of the lady were not wholly exempt from domestic labor, and those who were simply substituted other women's labor for their own. Somebody had to do the dirty domestic chores, and it was always labeled "women's work."

In nineteenth-century America, all black women identified slavery as an enemy. Even though all slaves suffered, females had particular handicaps as chattel. Even emancipated females could not escape the side effects of this brutal and oppressive system. Racism still created a virtual ward system for all blacks within American society. Slavery nurtured race and class prejudice in both the North and the South.

Women were emancipated more often than men before the close of the slave trade in 1807. Further, free black women in the South (who outnumbered free black men) seemed better able to support themselves with their domestic talents without posing an ostensible threat to whites. Black women fared well in service occupations and running boarding establishments. So much so that many of the free blacks who were able to leave property to their children—especially in the border states—were mothers, rather than fathers. But only a small proportion of blacks were free in antebellum America—North or South. Of the two million blacks in 1820, only 13 percent were free, and by 1860 this proportion had declined to 11 percent, despite the near doubling of the free black population. The rest were more directly subjected to oppression—as slaves.

Slavery took its toll on both men and women, but the exploitation of the female labor force was extraordinary. Not only were women subject to field and household work equal to that of men, but black women on plantations were coerced and encouraged into reproductive roles to provide more slaves/workers for the planter. Without slave women's steady fulfillment of reproductive as well as production roles in southern society, the system could not continue. With the end of the slave trade in 1807, planters were wholly dependent on natural increase to create a labor supply for their cotton economy. Throughout the antebellum years, the demand for slaves outstripped the supply.

Masters sought profit and expansion of their system, both contingent upon black women's contributions. Herbert Gutman, in his study of the black family, describes the fecundity of two female slaves owned by a Virginia planter named Cohoon by tracing the two women's seventy-three blood descendants living on Cohoon family estates. This "talent" for keeping the master supplied with workers had its cruel price. One ex-slave's account reveals the plight of a Texan slave woman who "was sold four times. Being considered an excellent breeder, she always brought large prices and was always well cared for, was never whipped; but was with a broken heart constantly..."

Black women's equivalent role in the slave work force should not be misconstrued as equality. Rather, slave owners simply extracted as much work from their investments as they could. Further, slave females were not exempted from household duties by their participation in field labor. Rather, slave women, like free women wage earners, were subject to double burdens. After a grueling day's work in the fields, slave women returned to their cabins to face the numerous cares which burdened all wives and mothers. In addition, recent mothers had to nurse their infants in the cotton fields. Slave cooks were charged with food preparation for the field hands, as well as tasks in the dairy and the barnyard. Older and pregnant women might be assigned less physically exhausting tasks, but planters demanded participation of all females in the work force. Females were wholly integrated into most aspects of labor and production on the plantation.

Some slaves escaped the heavy burdens of field work. Those of the "middle stratum"—the artisans—possessed skills which they parlayed into a preferential status. Masters could rent out skilled slaves as blacksmiths, carpenters, coopers, and sometimes even spinners and seamstresses. But because of women's childbearing capacity, slaveowners were loath to send female property off the estate, preferring to keep them under patriarchal scrutiny. Skilled slave women such as nurses and healers on occasion were loaned out to nearby neighbors; slave midwives were often sent off the plantation, especially to aid family (either planter relatives or black kin on neighboring plantations). But generally slave women were too valuable to be allowed "abroad": their reproductive value outweighed their production skills and they remained confined to the master's estate. So males dominated the artisan slave class.

In the Big House, however, female slaves had equal numbers and influence. A few slaves escaped the cotton field to serve as cooks, butlers, maids, dressers, launderers, carriage drivers, and personal servants. Even very young slaves were assigned as companions to the children of the master. Also, slave children were required to perform the most mindless and trivial tasks, such as fanning flies from the table. Owners hoped to instill in slave children the values of obedience and submissiveness, by keeping them occupied at all times with tasks, however demeaning, which provided for the white family's comfort.

It is a testimony to black women as well as men that a counterculture of values, including many African survivals, was preserved by these people held in bondage. Many slave children robbed of or separated from their families developed "fictive kin" to maintain a strong sense of cultural heritage. Slave mothers not only insured that their children adopted manners to survive under their owner's watchful eyes, but slave women were able, against great odds, to instill in offspring a sense of pride in the customs and traditions of their native people.

This tension between two worlds (black and white, slave and free, European and African) not only made for friction but fused these two cultures in the Old South. The identity if not the destiny of planter and slave were entwined. Slave women could not often give their children legal freedom, but they could provide sons and daughters with a sense of self and heritage which might transcend the alienation fostered by slave owners.

House slaves were perceived by the majority of the masters and slaves as "privileged," as the elite of the chattel class. Only during the height of the harvest were house slaves required to do field labor. This attitude was reinforced by the "banishment" of uncooperative house slaves to the fields when masters or mistresses were displeased with their performance of household duties. Not all house slaves had less demanding chores, but many had less back-breaking physical labor and most had better food and improved material conditions. However, these "privileges" were not without a price.

Blacks who served in the house were hampered by a more frequent contact with whites—they were subject to closer watch and to more frequent punishment for minor infractions. Although white planter families made "confidantes" of these black servants, paternalism crippled them. They were caught in the web of the Big House. And despite any creature comforts and any personal relationships which developed between owner and owned, slaves lived with the threat of a return to the fields. Blacks in the house had less contact with their family and friends—cut off by their long hours serving white masters' whims. Slaves in the fields had long hours, but they developed camaraderie in the workplace. House slaves were under whites' constant watch. Often young or female blacks were required to sleep on the floor by the bedside of their owner (or outside the door) so they could tend to the needs of the whites throughout the night, forced to serve as "domestic pets" for members of the planter class. In addition, slave women in the house were much more subject to harassment by the male white planters.

Southern slaveholders maintained that their system was Christian and "civilizing" for the blacks. Although white mistresses might try to measure up to this moral idealism, many men were not so dedicated. A variety of light-skinned slaves on southern plantations testified to the transgressions of white owners with black females. Mulatto offspring created but one of many conundrums within slave society.

Miscegenation caused anxiety, pain, and frustration for all women in the South. Primarily, the women subject to sexual coercion were rightfully enraged by their subjugation. Unfortunately, many of the children produced by these liaisons received less than welcome treatment by either parent. Some black women believed that a mulatto infant was a badge of shame, while other slave mothers hoped their child's lighter skin might assure preferential treatment (and in many cases, the less black a slave, the more likely he or she would serve in the house). This theory could and did backfire. White women on plantations frequently resented mulattoes as constant reminders of male infidelities, and believed that lighter-skinned black women presented greater sexual temptation. Mistresses could and did take out their frustrations with the system by callous or cruel treatment of slaves. Thus, slavery disrupted family life for both white and black women.

Although it has not been widely recognized, wives of slave owners often identified slavery as an enemy. Until recently, very little but stereotypes were found in southern history on the role of white women. Now we are better able to understand both their functions within the system of slavery and their contradictory behavior and attitudes. But most were so confused by their roles that they attacked slaves as inferior and immoral rather than pinning the blame for moral trespass on their own class. Planters expected their wives to minister to the basic needs of their "black family"—the generic term employed by planters for all slaves, whether the connection was biological or simply economic. Mistresses had fivefold functions in caring for their own family as well as all the slaves on the plantation: food, clothing, shelter, medical care, and religious instruction. Overseers might have had full charge of slaves in the field, but plantation mistresses ruled within the household—and the household extended from the slave cabins to the Big House, from the barnyard to the sick ward to the slaughtering pen. Instead of the alleged "relief" from drudgery which planters claimed their system afforded, slavery also brought with it physical and managerial burdens. These burdens were shouldered by the wives of planter-owners.

White women found themselves saddled with an exhaustive round of care and a ceaseless cycle of chores on their husbands' estates. The mistress might grow herbs, blend medicines, plant corn, spin cloth, knit socks, sew clothes, slaughter pigs, pluck chickens, scour copper utensils, preserve vegetables, churn butter, dip candles, weave rugs, and work at numerous harsh and unromantic tasks to keep the plantation running. A man often left his wife alone on the estate to manage while he tended to business in town, held political office, or conducted military campaigns. While men were away, wives had to tackle the business of maintaining order and efficiency on the plantation. They dealt with slaves, negotiated with overseers (who were present on less than one quarter of even the larger estates), tended to merchants and creditors: all in all, their decisions substituted for the rule of the master. But these duties and decisions encumbered rather than exalted women: the female sphere expanded with little or no improvement in women's status within society.

Concurrently, while southern men enjoyed their machismo culture and slaves nurtured their own sense of community (a powerful subculture within the South), the plantation mistress stood alone. She was isolated and besieged on her husband's plantation. White women were immobilized, anchored to estates, severely hampered by stereotypes of frailty and femininity. Within southern society, ladies were expected to embody perfectionist ideals: chastity, piety, and purity. In order to keep white women from polluting contact with the outside world, southern masters literally confined females—to model behavior, enclosed by the boundaries of the estate, within the domestic circle. Southern patriarchs required absolute fealty from all their subjects: slaves, children, and white women. The hierarchical nature of southern society demanded loyal and unwavering devotion of all subordinates to "lords and masters," as planter-patriarchs designated themselves.

Slavery not only posed a threat to women's domestic sphere of the home and family but created an obstacle to women's advancement within the larger society. The system of holding people as property kept women's progress in check. Southern plantation mistresses seemed unable to link their inferior status with that of slaves. Northern females had much less trouble drawing a parallel between their oppression and that of slaves. Indeed, the feminist component provided a formidable force within the major reform crusade of the antebellum period—the antislavery campaign. And in turn this campaign would pave the way for women to identify their concerns as a group and intensify the struggle for improved status.

3
Ties That Bound

THE nineteenth century ushered in a social as well as an economic revolution for American women. The refinement of middle-class ideology profoundly affected females during the antebellum era. The majority of American women failed to realize the ideal represented by bourgeois values: the lady on a pedestal exalted by the cult of domesticity. The model woman was a cultural myth, bearing little resemblance to any woman's daily experience. Although few could embody her, most women were judged by this unattainable standard and thousands of women were socialized to this ideal through the widespread dissemination of periodical literature. Over one hundred magazines, specifically addressed to the quandaries and delights of "ladies," blossomed during this time, and none was more successful than Sarah Josepha Hale's *Godey's Lady Book*.

The creation of the cult of domesticity, the redefinition of the home as women's domain, was a delicate process designed to channel women's contributions into a proper course. Men of the post-Revolutionary generation wanted to bridle and guide women's energies. A few women initiated a feminist challenge almost immediately on the heels of the Revolution. As Judith Sargent Murray dared to write (although under the pseudonym of "Constantia") in 1790: "Should it still be vociferated 'Your domestic employments are sufficient'—I would calmly ask, is it reasonable, that a candidate for immortality, for the joys of heaven, an intelligent being, who is to spend an eternity in contemplating works of Deity, should at present be so degraded, as to be allowed no other ideas, than those which are suggested by the mechanics of a pudding, or the sewing of the seams of a garment?" Murray and other feminists obviously thought not.

Instead of liberty and equality, subordination and restriction were drummed into women, a refrain inherited from the colonial era. Women's only reward was lavish exaltation of their vital and unmatchable contributions to the civic state as mothers. This rejuvenated ethic was accompanied by a confinement to the domestic sphere. One antebellum author insisted: "Whenever she . . . goes out of this sphere to mingle in any of the greater public movements of the day, she is deserting the station which God and nature have assigned to her . . . Home is her appropriate and appointed sphere of action." Ideologues harped on theological and biological tenets to bolster claims of female inferiority: women were dependent domestic creatures destined to lead sheltered lives revolving around family responsibilities.

Once segregated from men by the confines of a new ideological order, women set about turning their liabilities into assets. Forbidden traditional pathways to success, post-Revolutionary women pursued other means of achieving esteem and influence within their society. These alternatives were pioneered by women who were in search of new influence but who refrained from invading the male domain—not for the sake of modesty, but rather as a strategy. Those women who were willing to forge their own networks, to stake their own claims within the culture, were considered by the male establishment as no serious threat to the existing order. Such women clearly accepted their status as a subculture, as a force operating within the limits prescribed by male authority. Their movement did not undermine patriarchal authority but demonstrated dissatisfaction with the extent of male dominance. Thus, certain women took their segregated status not as a badge of inferiority, but seized the opportunity to use their separate position as a base on which to build. These advocates of shifts and transformations within society's circumscribed female realms, it has been argued, were "domestic feminists."

Woman's domain was, despite confinement, expansive. She was charged with the moral, spiritual, and physical well-being of her entire family. Ironically, her reproductive role superseded all other cultural concerns at a time when the birth rate was declining. She was supervisor of the education of her children, tender of the hearth, and the symbol of the home. These indispensable functions, although primarily carried out within the home, were not restricted to it. Women perceived that they might extend female jurisdiction into the public and hitherto exclusively male realm by using their "domestic" role as a lever—wedging themselves into positions of power, however limited, through exploitation of their domesticity. In the early decades of the century, creative women took their rather circumscribed nooks and crannies, within the culture, and turned them into springboards. Women's talents and contributions were soon apparent within the larger social arena.

Religion played an important part in catapulting women into prominence. The Second Great Awakening (a term for the evangelical revival that swept across the republic during the first quarter of the nineteenth century, echoing the first large-scale movement of this sort, the Great Awakening of the 1740s) was a concerted effort on the part of ministers and the Christian devout to rekindle a spirit of enthusiasm among the people and to counter the disintegration of organized religions. Following the American Revolution, church attendance fell to an all-time low, the separation of church and state signaled a new era of declining influence for religious leaders, and the popularity of "deist" philosophers (such as Tom Paine and William Godwin) further weakened the impact of religion. The evangelical crusade attempted to counter this disintegration. Churches might have lost their following, but ministers were certain that the people hungered for religion. Preachers and divines headed for the countryside; itinerant ministers came to the people if the people would not come to them. With this spiritual dragnet stretched across the frontier to snag the sinful and world-weary, divines discovered that women, not men, would be their salvation.

As individuals, men might be concerned with spiritual welfare, but as a group they were less enthusiastic about the importance of the church in everyday life. But women, especially young females, were eager to accept male religious leadership. Faith was a more critical concern to the female members of a family, and thus perhaps preachers could have more impact on the home through women's influence. So, during the Second Great Awakening, which resulted in disproportionate participation by and conversion of young women, the ministers realized that their campaign was most successful when directed not at the patriarch, the head of the family, but at the women, the spiritual guardians of the household. A minister in 1828 described the format for female prayer meetings: "Each person was constrained to confess that she had not during that period had so lively an interest at the throne of grace—she had been involved more deeply in the cares of the world and had thought less of the condition of impenitent sinners." After tears and prayers, the pastor reported, many rededicated themselves to Christian work, and within a few months over sixty members were added to his church.

What drove women, in such significant numbers, into this revivalist frenzy? Some scholars suggest that the anticipation or realization of anxieties associated with socioeconomic changes (shifting markets, consumer growth, and other results of modernization) created a need in young people to shape their own destiny, affirm their own identity. Others have pointed out, however, that this desire would be harbored by men as well as women. Evidence suggests that men more often professed faith in the company of female kin (suggesting women's initiation of the process) but, more important, women often converted independent of their families. Records of revivals in the burnt-over district of western New York reveal the disproportionate "saving" of young women through grace: during a Baptist revival in Utica in 1838, when the population was only half female, 72 percent of the converts were women.

The fact is that women had fewer options than men to demonstrate autonomy. Choice of church, marital partner, and perhaps family limitation were the only decisions left to women. Evangelical revivals afforded women an opportunity to exercise control, to state a preference, to identify. It was young women in antebellum America, as the numbers indicate, who consciously seized and exploited this opportunity to their own ends.

During these years, it became apparent both to the shepherds and to the flock that religion was increasingly women's domain. By the middle of the century a silent partnership had been struck, in practical and ideological terms, between women enthusiasts and male ministers, resulting in what has been described as the "feminization of American religion."

Women were now accorded "essential roles" within the realm of religion. Females entered into the previously all-male domain of missionary work. Of course, women first made inroads as the wives of missionaries. During the early antebellum years, fewer and fewer ministers heeded the call without a female companion, and the parson's wife became an integral part of Christian mission on the frontier and abroad. One Presbyterian minister commented: "A lady with a missionary spirit can be quite as useful as her husband—often more so." By mid-century it was accepted that women could weather the ordeal of toiling among the heathen quite as well as men. Further, religious societies encouraged their emissaries to take a wife to prevent immoral mishaps. The American Board of Commissioners for Foreign Mission declared: "Wives are a protection among savages, and men cannot long there make a tolerable home without them. When well connected in respect to health, education, and piety, wives endure 'hardness' quite as well as their husbands and sometimes with more faith and patience." Slowly, women's capacity for religious influence not only matched that of men but, by the antebellum period, their talents clearly outshone those of men.

This foothold enabled women to expand in any number of previously prohibited directions, all in the name of Christian service. Females used their religiosity as a tool, a means of chiseling away at male authority. Just as Anne Hutchinson had challenged male domination in the seventeenth century, so her descendants inherited a similar intellectual conflict. But the transformation within the male power structure created a new set of rules for doctrinal battle. By the early nineteenth century, ministers were no longer the major political force in the culture; and subsequently women were able to play a larger role in the church.

During the early decades of the nineteenth century, women's concerns began to expand—in concentric circles—beyond the home. But when women began to step outside their immediate domain, they followed a path prescribed by domestic custom. Women performed services in the public arena which essentially they had learned within the family circle. Teaching and moral reform also became major avenues to female public influence.

Mothers were children's first teachers, as pioneering women educators often reminded statesmen. A minister in 1790 remarked: "What prudent mother will trust the commencement of the education of her child in the hands of a mercenary nurse?" The backbone of republican motherhood ideology was that mothers alone should minister to the needs of their children, avoiding the pernicious influence of careless nurses and incompetent governesses. But how could a mother accomplish these tasks unless she herself was educated?

After the turn of the century, parents in a position to educate their children sought to increase both the quality of female education and the opportunities for advanced schooling for women. Thus, 1800 marked the opening of the "age of the academy." Schools, single-sex as well as co-educational institutions, offering a rigorous curriculum (the classic English education: Latin, geography, history, mathematics, and composition), sprang up throughout the United States. There were no advanced educational opportunities for women until Emma Willard opened a seminary for females in Troy, New York, in 1821. In 1837 Mary Lyons set up a school in central Massachusetts, considered to be the oldest women's college in the United States (Mount Holyoke), and Oberlin College, the first co-educational institution, opened its doors to both men and women early in 1837. But Willard's role in female education is exemplary in that her institution became a training school for female educators throughout the country.

Willard herself was indefatigable. In 1846 she traveled nearly eight thousand miles conducting what we would today call workshops and lecturing on behalf of education. Willard's Troy students were stamped for life with a sense of women's equal ability and set on a course of intellectual achievement. Willard did not advocate anything other than "true womanhood" for her schoolgirls. But after being educated at the Troy academy, women were more likely to pursue careers, less likely to marry, and, if they did, were likely to have fewer children than women of their class with less education. Feminist Elizabeth Cady Stanton fondly remembered Willard's "profound self-respect," which doubtless made a favorable impression on her young pupil. But Willard's contribution was greater perhaps in the difference she made in the lives of the average rather than the outstanding among her graduates.

Willard graduates were known for high standards and capable talents. The school provided teachers for institutions throughout the country: Caroline Livy's academy in Rome, Georgia, trained over five thousand young women; Urania Sheldon went on to head the Utica Female Academy; Almira Lincoln Phelps founded the Patapsco Female Institute in Maryland. A survey of antebellum female education reveals that the "Troy ideal" was the model for over two hundred schools in nineteenth-century America. Willard played no small role in this improvement and expansion of women's education, both North and South.

Another major contributor to the female academy movement was a great promoter of domesticity: Catharine Beecher. This distinguished author and prominent reformer (sister of Harriet Beecher Stowe) also believed that teaching was a valuable means for women to wield greater influence within society. This remarkable woman spent most of her life outside the domestic circle demonstrating the ways and means for women to remain confined to this sphere. She wrote *Domestic Economy*, the housewife's bible for the antebellum period.

Beecher also established educational institutions throughout the country, especially in needy frontier areas. She was notably adept at coaxing funds from backwoods communities, making sure the money she raised was earmarked for the building of academies to be staffed by her protegées. Through teaching careers, young, unmarried, middle-class females could achieve some measure of independence and mold a new life for themselves as well as for future generations of women.

By 1870, more than half the two hundred thousand primary- and secondary-school teachers in America were women. At the beginning of the republic, teaching was not a common vocation for women, but by the end of the century women were the mainstay of the teaching profession—and they were moving up the ladder into administrative positions and serving on elected school boards. At first, women educators were resisted. Domestic feminists argued that teaching was a "natural extension" of women's maternal role. Further, some suggested that women were purer and more virtuous, less susceptible to the evils of the "outside world," and therefore better suited to work with young, impressionable minds. Once their educational options were increased, women developed greater expectations.

In antebellum America, the economy as well as the political culture had little room for autonomous women. In most cases, females of all classes were attached to households, dependent on males for status and wealth. Elite and middle-class women had limited opportunities to demonstrate their intellectual talents. But soon these restless and able women created means to express their gifts.

Because "true women" needed advice and refinement, an entire retinue of domesticity professionals (writers, educators, and lecturers) sprang up in response. Ironically, these women spent time and energy in pursuit of careers which were bound up with the celebration of home. The most popular manifestation of this movement was the explosion of periodical literature for women.

Magazines flourished throughout the country in the years before the Civil War. Many of these periodicals addressed questions of domestic economy as well as motherhood, treating the subject of health as well as recreation, morality and religion, reform, and indeed most subjects imaginable, with the notable exception of politics. The style and substance of these publications varied dramatically according to the interests of their editors. Some of the rather progressive guidance literature and the "anti-male" bias of many of the female writers have led present-day interpreters to view this as nascent feminism.

It is a very delicate business to transpose the values of one era to another. In this instance, in fact, articulate feminist journals also appeared, in stiff competition with the women's periodicals. However, it is evident that many of the advocates of domesticity developed attitudes antithetical to those promoted by men. The emphasis on female values and female culture posed a serious challenge to male hegemony. How commonly female culture fostered political feminism remains a subject of sore controversy.

Many women earned a living promoting women's dependency on men and a female's sole occupation as housewife. Since some of these single and widowed women authors were deprived of the comforts of a husband, their literary points of view appear even more puzzling. Were these women simply writing what the public wanted to read? Were they selecting themes which editors demanded? Was domesticity the only subject fit to print in antebellum women's literature? Or were these females "deprived" of the domestic circle romanticizing the road not taken, the comforts lost?

Modern readers of early nineteenth-century literature are not the first to discover the problem. Women writers themselves revealed deep and pervasive ambivalence on the question. A popular antebellum writer, Caroline Hentz, felt the necessity to disclaim her accomplishments in her novel, *Ernest Linwood*:

> Book! Am I writing a book? No indeed! This is only a record of my heart's life, written at random and carelessly thrown aside, sheet after sheet, sibylline leaves from the great book of fate. The wind may blow them away, a spark consume them. I may myself commit them to the flames. I am tempted to do so at this moment.

This is not a customary dose of literary humility. This carefully cultivated disclaimer of any real work was one that many women writers offered in order to appeal to the male publishing world. Women may have been the writers and they were overwhelmingly the readers of this literature, but the publishing purse strings were held tightly by men presumably unsympathetic to feminist concerns.

Most novelists whose works were published had proven their mettle in the ladies' magazines before turning to book-length fiction. Popular authors of the day, much like "romance writers" in modern America, published a series of volumes with rather hackneyed themes and plots. Some scholars have labeled these women "sentimentalists," dismissing their themes as womanly and disdaining their "saccharine" treatment of their subjects. Other readers have condemned this interpretation as a fundamental misunderstanding of nuance and vocabulary. Certainly, we must respect the views of the hardy scholars who have plowed through a hundred or more nineteenth-century domestic novels. Although both schools of thought conclude that most if not all of this fiction is not "great literature," opinion seems divided over the purposes and intent of the most prolific and popular women novelists: Mary Virginia Terhune (Marion Harland), Catharine Maria Sedgwick, E.D.E.N. Southworth, Lydia Sigourney, Caroline Gilman, Caroline Hentz, and Sarah Parton (Fanny Fern).

The contemporary press was caustic about the accomplishments of, as Nathaniel Hawthorne dubbed them, "scribbling women." Many critics deplored the "unfemininely bitter wrath" that many women displayed. If these women were simply fictionalizing the "true woman," then why should men have such strong objections to their work? (We can perhaps understand the complaints of a writer such as Hawthorne who shrewdly surmised that popular female novelists published more, outselling him and his male peers.) Further, those who maintained that such sentimental or sensational literature was harmful to women advocated more "serious" reading material.

This "great literature" was judged by male standards, which still dominate criticism, little altered by the influence of women on culture and society. The very label "domestic fiction" demonstrates the rigid and inflexible sexism which shapes such evaluations. Women wrote about the subjects they knew, but even more important, they described problems they faced in their everyday lives. In contrast to the fantasy and historical settings of modern popular women's fiction, antebellum women novelists tackled themes with which their readers could identify, with only occasional lapses into escapist adventure.

Since home was the author's primary concern, the household was the setting for the "domestic novels." But rather than merely celebrate this setting, some women provided sharp commentary. Mary Virginia Terhune attacked imprisonments of women in the home "which have racked and strained muscle and nerve, turned our daily bread into ashes, blunted our perceptions to all that was once beautiful to the sight, pleasant to the ear and stimulative to the intellect." Rather than portray idyllic conditions and characters, many women used their writing to illuminate the problems within families, homes, and marriages. Indeed, the "husband as villain" was a popular theme. The acerbic in women's fiction perhaps more than the sickly sweet led male readers to condemn popular women's novels as unworthy of such a large and faithful readership.

In any case, the debate over women's fiction continues. Some would argue these domestic writers invaded and conquered antebellum literature, driving underground the talented yet unpopular "great" writers. There is no denying the increasing popularity and apparent preeminence of women novelists in America. The impact of this "feminization" of the culture is another matter entirely. Whether it reveals a weakening of Calvinist tenets or the embracing of a humanist social approach remains a subject of debate. But we must continue to explore the conflict between ideology and practice among the leading exponents of domesticity, probing between the lines of their fascinating if somewhat polemical fiction.

The advantages of studying women writers and their abundant literary record are obvious. Female visual and decorative artists in nineteenth-century America also give us insights into the female experience. Because formal artists required training and cultivation, however, women were at a severe disadvantage.

Many successful American women artists were related to male artists, presumably profiting from their study with kin, since other forms of apprenticeship were denied them. Charles Wilson Peale's family included eight female artists—nieces, granddaughters, and even a daughter-in-law. The daughters of Gilbert Stuart and Thomas Sully, as well as Thomas Cole's sister, earned their livings as professional painters. Although we might think that their success was based on inherited talent, it is more likely that only women related by blood or marriage to established artists were afforded the necessary training.

Foreign study, an invaluable advantage for American artists, was rarely possible for women painters. Over half the professional women artists listed in the New-York Historical Society's *Dictionary of American Artists, 1564–1860* were single. Yet most remained financially dependent on male relations and undercompensated for their work. With the opening of the Philadelphia School of Design in 1851 and the women's branch of New York's Cooper Union Institute (the School of Design for Women) in 1852, women artists hoped lessening prejudices would make their advancement within the profession somewhat easier. Despite these "design schools" for women, female painters adamantly challenged the ban on women in life classes at most institutions. Female art students sought to overcome this handicap by attending anatomy lectures at medical schools or gaining admittance to hospitals, but many remained deprived.

Most antebellum women artists chose other subjects. They painted flowers and still lifes, and many earned their living as portrait artists. Evidence indicates that female painters specialized in miniatures well into the nineteenth century, and after male professionals' interest in this form had declined. Female lithographers, etchers, and engravers were rare.

Perhaps the most important gains were made by a small group of women sculptors during the 1850s. Their accomplishments are even more surprising when we consider that they achieved success in a field where both the expense and the necessary skill were almost prohibitive to amateurs, where study abroad and a working knowledge of anatomy were essential to success. It was also a field in which artists most heavily depended on public and private commissions. Most of these women gained fame internationally through exhibitions of their works in Europe and the United States.

The career of Harriet Hosmer is impressive and exemplary. The daughter of a doctor, she was able to wheedle her way into taking private lessons in anatomy. She then struck out for Rome (in 1852), where actress Charlotte Cushman held court, as well as the writer and impresario Fanny Kemble. But Hosmer had little time for salons. She studied with British sculptor John Gibson; Elizabeth Barrett Browning reported Hosmer's demanding routine: "She lives here all alone (at twenty-two), dines and breakfasts at the cafés precisely as a young man would; works from six o'clock in the morning till night, as a great artist must..." She was a pioneer whose success was due in large part to the generosity of male sponsors: first her father, then her instructor in Rome, and later a full-fledged patron. Indeed, Hosmer's unusual talent became a subject for scandal; in 1862, while her statue "Zenobia" was on display in London, journals credited her work to an Italian artist. Hosmer sued for libel, but detractors continued to plague her. A vitriolic critic carped: "As for Miss Hosmer, her want of modesty is enough to disgust a dog. She has casts for the entire *female model* made and exhibited in a shockingly indecent manner to all the young artists who called upon her."

Her pathbreaking spirit, rather than the quality of her artistry, was often at the root of attacks on her as well as other women's sculptures. Hosmer was soon joined by other celebrated women artists: Vinnie Ream, who secured commissions from the United States government for a memorial to Abraham Lincoln as well as a monument to Admiral Farragut; Emma Stebbins, who designed "Angel of the Waters" for New York's Central Park; and Edmonia Lewis, a half-black, half-Indian woman who arrived in Rome by way of Oberlin after leaving her Chippewa homeland in upstate New York. The drive and talent of these women was tremendous, especially in the face of indifference to women's artistic contributions.

Although schoolgirls were given art lessons in academies, few were encouraged to pursue professional careers. The lament of married artist Jane Swisshelm pinpoints the conflict between artistry and domesticity. She complained of the adage which held: "A man does not marry an artist but a housekeeper," which "fitted my case and my doom was sealed. I put away my brushes; resolutely crucified my divine gift, and while it hung writhing on the cross, spent my best years and powers cooking cabbage." Her bitter depiction of women's lot was not passed on to most American daughters. Rather, they were schooled to accept a way of life—artistic and otherwise—which would prepare them to fulfill their domestic functions.

Antebellum mothers taught their daughters, above all, to conform. Late-eighteenth- and early-nineteenth-century samplers testify to the success of maternal instruction. Each young girl of quality dutifully embroidered one of these wall hangings as testimony to her industry and readiness for domestic endeavors. One verse, taken from a post-Revolutionary sampler, sums up the art form: "With the close attention carefully inwrought,/ Fair education paints a pleasing thought,/ Inserts the curious line on proper ground,/ Completes the whole and scatters flowers round."

Prose and verse sentiments follow nearly identical patterns on each sampler, though the dates and names are different—the individual's only original contribution to her work. Scholars maintain that the creativity of sampler makers and, indeed, sampler styles was "inhibited." Socialization to conformity, restraint, and sentimentality created a predictable pattern. This was not the case with a particularly rich and expressive American folk art, quilting.

Quilting is especially interesting because it was an activity which a woman could pursue in solitude; but she almost always sought a collective contribution as well. After gathering the scraps and assembling her materials, the quiltmaker solicited her female family and friends to assist in the process. The quilting bee was a particularly popular American pastime, mainly staffed and attended by women. In the nineteenth century it provided company for those women who were isolated in their households. The use as well as pleasure of the object of her labor justified the lengthy interruption of a busy housekeeper's schedule. Quilts still follow set designs, but in many cases, in the nineteenth century, they told stories or portrayed events in their fabric canvas. A woman commonly inscribed a finished piece with her name and date. Quilts became precious heirlooms handed down from generation to generation, stored in hope chests or put on proud display, as symbols of the artist's impressive abilities.

In addition to the sampler of her youth and the quilt of her matronly years, an American housewife might also paint or embroider mourning portraits. These very stylized pieces often included classical or traditional symbols of death and everlasting life: the urn, the weeping willow in the background, a dove with a branch in its beak. Perhaps grieving family members might be depicted. In some cases an artist might leave a blank space for the date of death, to be filled in after her own death. These very common artifacts emphasize that women were constantly confronted with loss as well as drudgery in their domestic lives. The burdens of running a household and managing a family left most women little time for creativity and especially for activity that would reveal an inner self. Most women prided themselves on their accomplishments as homemakers and mastered domestic chores and family responsibilities. Some even managed with innovation and skill to provide us with evidence of their artistic achievements.

American female folk art demonstrates women's talents for triumphing over circumstance. Although only a handful were able to make art their life's work, the majority of women triumphed by having some of their creative artifacts endure. The accomplishments of women who were in fields which had traditionally been dominated by men must be examined in light of the hardships they faced. We must not view women's few achievements without exploring the standards which measure their contributions.

The clash of interpretations of the meaning and expressions of domesticity in antebellum America continues. Women who were formerly dismissed as sentimentalists are now championed as "domestic feminists." The lady in antebellum society was not merely a myth or a phantom but a powerful ideal. Increasingly, women pioneered by incorporating new interests into their realm: religion, literature, and art, to name a few. Most women may have been confined to domesticity, but the ways in which they challenged their imprisonment were diverse and fascinating. The interplay between ideal and reality must be examined closely to better comprehend women's roles and experiences, to piece together the puzzle of women's lives in the first half of the century.

4
Organization and Resistance

MANY roads led to feminism. It is perhaps futile to select and track any single contributing element. Investigation of the growth of an autonomous women's movement is of course more the study of a complex process than the compilation of a chronological list. But it is possible to pinpoint the major developments in the nineteenth century which stimulated women's determination to seek their own rights.

Female moral reformers and abolitionists were mainstays of the antebellum women's movement. Moral reformers (those who organized secular crusades to combat the sins of society) many times built their crusades on a contradiction-laden moral philosophy. Some alleged that women—ostensibly sheltered within the confines of hearth and pew—were purer and more spiritual than men. This religiosity supposedly gave women better insight and a stronger will to fight the evil in society. However, this battle often led women out of the house and literally into the street, all in the cause of reform. These campaigns exposed females to the outside world in a new way, and the reform organizations granted them an unprecedented semi-public status.

Women who championed the female sphere, the domestic realm which provided everything to which a woman should aspire, argued that this domain should be expanded. Female pioneers wished to extend their activities to become a potent public force.

Men—ministers, husbands, fathers, and brothers—were expected to uphold and enforce strict moral codes for American society. But women found both a moral laxity and a sexual double standard in effect. By joining the fray, women jeopardized their position; when they stepped off a pedestal and into battle, their actions spoke loudly indeed. But when they took to the platform, women had to learn to change their tone to please male supporters.

Women soft-pedaled the implications of their new positions. Female moral crusaders who took a vocal and active role in reform initially advocated conservative values. Despite their unorthodox methods, these women managed to project a traditional posture: they did not argue against the status quo, they merely insisted that Christian principles be obeyed. So women's shift into the limelight was accompanied by political compromise: they preached the superiority and suitability of motherhood, the importance of delicacy and purity for the female sex, and, indeed, that woman's place was in the home.

So, at its very center, moral reform carried seeds of self-destruction. The more women plunged into public campaigns, the less effective their plea for women to remain isolated in their domestic havens. The conflict of new realities with rhetorical roles blurred women's positions within the social spectrum. The philosophy of women reformers seemed at odds with their chosen paths.

Reform was an outgrowth of evangelical fervor. The first large-scale female organizations during the nineteenth century were formed to promote religion. Missionary zeal, the need to disseminate Christian knowledge, and other spiritual causes, stimulated females to band together against what they perceived as the weakening of religious fervor. Although benevolent institutions had been founded during the eighteenth century, social consciousness flourished in the early decades of the nineteenth century, during the Second Great Awakening. After the popularity of deistic thinkers during the American Revolution and following the "excesses" of the French, many post-Revolutionary leaders feared moral decline among "the people," and the instability of the "lower orders." Middle-class women in the new nation sought to shore up their faltering society by pouring time and energy into charitable activities. The city directory of Utica, New York, for example, included over forty voluntary associations in 1832; the aims of many of these groups testify to the interest in moral reform.

Originally many societies were organized as missions, simply to send preachers to the frontier. In 1800 the Boston Female Society for Missionary Purposes began to raise funds to finance ministers for "uncivilized areas." This was the first of many such organizations. Soon these groups began to focus on the needs within their own communities as well as those of frontier settlements, and "domestic missionary" societies became equally popular. From their humble beginnings, distributing Bibles and selling religious tracts, women's church auxiliaries moved into a wider range of philanthropic activity: the collection of food, clothing, and funds for the needy. And the needy were an expanding proportion of the urban population in the beginning of the century. Although later immigration created a more dramatic growth of American cities, the earlier spurt of population growth in towns woefully taxed inadequate social services.

So the emphasis of reformers shifted to encompass the indigent and ungodly of their own vicinity, as well as the heathen and fallen in faraway places. The most popular crusades were the "cent a week" campaigns. The middle ranks of society supposedly sacrificed their own needs to provide for the poor. These funds were funneled into programs to light the "path of true salvation" for the disadvantaged. Soon prayer meetings, charity schools, and even door-to-door visits to spread the gospel became part of the reformers' program. These widespread and ambitious undertakings were possible because middle-class women threw themselves into the business of reform. Benevolent societies anticipated modern programs of welfare with relief for the poor, assistance to widows and orphans, vocational education for the indigent, in addition to their primary mission of converting sinners.

It is important to recognize that although these organizations flourished in the larger seaboard cities, the spirit of reform was not just an urban phenomenon. We can trace the establishment of local branches of various benevolent and female reform associations in the antebellum era to Concord, New Hampshire, and Bedford, New York, to name but two rural communities which fostered female charitable societies. And in these smaller communities as well as in larger towns, a spirit of interdenominational cooperation prevailed. The bonds of female concern transcended those of religious sects, and women of various faiths banded together to combat the increasing ills of poverty, disease, and social displacement.

Many societies set impressive records. For example, the Boston Fragment Society, during its thirty years, aided over ten thousand families, giving away nearly forty thousand items of clothing and over $20,000 to charity cases. The New York Charity School during this same time grew in annual attendance to five hundred pupils. One group in Philadelphia, the Female Hospitable Society, organized by Quakers in 1808, progressively substituted paid work for charity. It provided needy women with temporary relief. Although this might be perceived as simply a referral organization for domestic help, it was a welcome service for the female poor as well as for the ladies who needed domestic workers. Although several of these charitable institutions supplied middle-class ladies with prospective servants, they at the same time provided assistance for those denied adequate resources from their own families. Charity and volunteerism, rather than paid work, were the rule for both reformer and reformed.

Many men, especially ministers, encouraged women in their volunteer work. Theories abounded that women, with tender hearts and sympathetic natures, were better suited to such pursuits. In addition, some slyly suggested that the idleness some middle-class women were starting to enjoy (allegedly the benefit of modernization) would be best replaced by a regimen of charitable activity. Instead of letting these ladies drift into fashionability and dissipation, why not let them labor for Christian goals? Some pious orators went so far as to suggest that women owed it to society to commit their lives to good works. A minister suggested: "Women appear to be under special obligation to embrace and promote Christianity, as our common original mother proved a tempter to her husband, and instigated him to the crime, which brought ruin on them both and on all the human race." Thus, women were cajoled, bribed, and threatened into roles as spiritual guardians of a diminishing American morality.

Women reformers working among the poor and oppressed were quick to recognize the social evils which contributed to ever-worsening conditions. Poverty, women recognized, was not a crime but a disease which flourished in a climate of ignorance and faithlessness. Women reasoned that, with education and a strong dose of Christianity, families could better survive their low station in life. Few middle-class matrons believed the needy could ever aspire to higher status—most simply desired an industrious poor instead of an indigent rabble. Closer contact with impoverished individuals led them to see the problems of the poor more clearly.

Many women learned that Christian missions alone could not solve the problem. Drink, debt, violence, and prostitution also threatened families. These ills were, of course, an outgrowth of "un-Christian licentiousness," but women recognized the need to define their immediate goals and refine their organizations into specialized task forces. Social evils were manifold, and women organized a profusion of reform crusades. Temperance was a top priority for Christian wives and mothers. Women of all classes suffered at the hands of drunken husbands. But among the working poor they were doubly burdened. Not only did inebriated men neglect or inflict violence on their families, but drunks deprived their homes of needed income. Wife beating and child abuse frequently resulted from family squabbles brought on by an alcoholic husband.

So throughout northern and middle-Atlantic communities women during the 1820s and 1830s formed leagues against drink (such as the popular Daughters of Temperance associations) or established women's auxiliaries of the Washingtonian Society (a self-sustained proletarian movement). Many female organizations ministered not only to alcoholics but to their spouses and children as well. The high level of liquor consumption in the early nineteenth century has led one historian to dub the country during these years as "the alcoholic republic." Males were the main offenders in early America. Taverns were primarily male domains: bars and pubs afforded men of all classes social relaxation as well as a place for political forums. During the Revolution, broadsides were tacked up in taverns to disseminate news to the community. Bars as "men only" preserves persisted well into modern times. But bars not only provided a climate of relaxation or a means of amicable communication; drink in taverns was often excessive.

Alcohol consumption cannot be reckoned precisely. Surveys vary, but the average annual alcoholic consumption per adult in America in 1810 has been estimated at six to seven gallons; it rose to seven to ten gallons by 1820. The present-day figure on adult liquor consumption is approximately two gallons. During the 1820s the crisis was met with resolve and moral indignation. In 1826 the American Society for the Promotion of Temperance was founded. By 1834 this "cold water army" was a million strong, with over five thousand local affiliates.

Violation of family sanctity was a direct threat to women as a group as well as to individual wives and mothers. Temperance was not merely a movement of prudish fanatics; the crusade against drink had a strong feminist component. Wives, trapped in the household and defined by their husband's status and income, took a justifiable interest in how much men drank. Most women perceived alcohol to be their special enemy and joined ranks to defeat the deadly foe. Many working-class men's organizations, including unions, volunteered for battle—recognizing that alcoholism was a weakness whereby the working man sacrificed the precious element of self-control.

Although women of all classes launched an attack on alcohol in the antebellum years, we can identify two distinct strains of this crusade: the reform from within, the campaign of working-class women; and the moral attack by middle-class matrons. The latter saw drink as one of the evils which afflicted society, although most were not threatened in their own homes. Drunkenness was contrary to social norms in most of the country, although a high tolerance of male alcohol consumption was prevalent in the South. Middle-class men were generally less physically abusive of women than working-class males were. Because of the distance between most middle-class women and the sordid effects of alcohol, the majority adopted a patronizing attitude toward the "unfortunate." The campaign was a good deal closer to home for women in the working class. Female temperance advocates who directly suffered the ills of alcoholism had more at stake, so they single-mindedly threw themselves into the cause, whereas middle-class women divided their interests among a variety of reforms.

Prostitution presented a particularly critical threat in the eyes of reform-minded women, since this evil required the participation of female as well as male sinners. Sexual transgressions became a subject of controversy for female activists. Unfortunately, we know more about the women who campaigned against prostitutes than we do about the prostitutes. What limited evidence we have draws on criminal records, which are quite obviously problematic. However, some basic patterns emerge. An 1858 survey of two thousand prostitutes who spent time in New York City jails provides some information. Almost 50 percent of the women arrested for sexual soliciting listed their occupation as servant, and 25 percent were seamstresses. Over 60 percent of the women were immigrants. Three out of four were under twenty-five, the majority teenagers. Half had children and half of these children were illegitimate. Seventy-five percent were single or widowed. Many of the married women arrested reported desertion or alcoholic husbands. A thousand (50 percent) of the women had syphilis. From these statistics, we can make some broad generalizations.

Obviously, women with the most limited employment opportunities sought money through selling themselves. The average prostitute was young, single, and many could not speak English. They suffered from venereal infection disproportionate to the female population. Despite drawbacks of low status and disease, prostitutes dramatically increased in number during the century. There were roughly six thousand prostitutes in New York City before the Civil War (approximately one per sixty-four adult males). By 1870 this number had grown to ten thousand. By 1890 the total had quadrupled to forty thousand. Sexual licentiousness was a prosperous business and of growing concern in postbellum America.

Although reformers agreed that true Christians should practice sexual purity before marriage and adopt a strict program of fidelity afterward, there were different proposals on how to deal with this issue. The major conflicts centered on the question of blame, methods of exposure, and the actual dimensions of the traffic in sex. But despite disagreements, most held that it was women's duty to guard against sin within their own families and to speak out against this evil in the larger society.

The size and scope of the crusade attacking sexual license varied from community to community. The major salvos were launched, as one might expect, in the larger metropolitan areas. In 1830 a young Presbyterian minister, the Reverend John McDowall, decried the scandals of Five Points, a red-light district in New York City. His tracts, *McDowall's Journal* and *Magdalen Facts*, chronicled the sin of the city. He claimed there were ten thousand fallen women roaming the streets. Reverend McDowall charged that women's moral failings were more dangerous than those of men: "A few of these courtesans suffice to corrupt whole cities, and there can be no doubt that some insinuating prostitutes have initiated more young men into these destructive ways, than the most abandoned rakes have debauched virgins during their whole lives." McDowall's charges alerted respectable women to the magnitude of the problem, but his sensationalist campaign garnered more criticism than support.

Women continued the crusade against prostitution, but on their own terms. They believed that laying the blame on one sex or the other was unproductive; they favored an equal distribution of guilt. In May 1834 an ardent group of reformers launched their own campaign:

> Resolved, That the licentious man is no less guilty than his victim and ought, therefore, to be excluded from all virtuous female society. Resolved, That it is the imperious duty of ladies everywhere and of every religious denomination, to co-operate in the great work of moral reform.

And thus the ladies organized the New York Female Reform Society. Within a year the group had established an impressive record. They published a journal to air their views and to denounce and publicly expose sin by publishing letters from their members. *The Advocate* became an effective and popular voice for women reformers. The society also hired Reverend McDowall and two assistant missionaries to minister to the fallen: in the city hospitals and jails, in the almshouses, and in the brothels themselves. On occasion, groups of women would join male emissaries, standing vigil outside the houses of ill repute that "polluted" their city. These "active visits" were a matter of great controversy, both within the organization and for those who questioned the propriety of respectable women meddling in such affairs. But the society found that the good accomplished by this tactic was worth any criticism such a strategy attracted. Large groups of observing and praying Christians outside brothels tended to discourage business. Women reformers also attempted to infiltrate the brothels: to gather information about runaway daughters, and to provide any women held hostage some means of escape.

The campaign to disrupt or even shut down the business of prostitution proved ineffective. However, women reformers gained strength and purpose through their organization. *The Advocate* continued to expose and expound well into the 1850s, with angry attacks on "the lascivious and predatory nature of the American male." Women throughout the country sent in their personal testimonies of men's crimes against women. The evangelical paper became one of the most widely read of the age, with over sixteen thousand subscribers. The publication also preached the need for a national union of women. This explicit feminist demand demonstrates that women reformers gained a consciousness about their own inequality and the need for collective identity through participation in these campaigns.

Crusades were launched in larger cities, but middle-class women in towns throughout the northern states also banded together in similar societies. In 1834, during a revival in Utica, the Reverend Samuel Aiken warned his female audience that their community was about to be overrun by "a whole tribe of libertines." He urged his Presbyterian congregation to organize "and become a terror to evil doers." It was three years before Utica women formed their own branch of the American Female Moral Reform Society, but two founders of the group were among those who had listened to Aiken's call. Slowly the spirit of moral outrage spread inland, so that by the 1840s and 1850s female reform associations were making headway in such relatively new cities as Cincinnati and Cleveland.

The decades which preceded the Civil War were enlivened by a plethora of groups dedicated to general and specific remedy of social ills. Most radical and all-embracing of these reformers were members of Utopian communities. Utopian groups varied in character and purpose: many stemmed from religious separatism, while others embodied far-reaching proposals for economic change. Most of these philosophical pioneers were involved with communal experiments which "failed," and then the members of the group dispersed to rejoin the larger society. But during their often brief tenure these visionaries had a vital impact on American life.

Brook Farm, to take one example, was an influential and significant enterprise. This 160-acre farm just outside Boston never attracted more than eighty members, but many of Emerson's Transcendentalist circle were drawn into it when it was founded in 1841. Margaret Fuller—the "belle of Transcendentalism"—was an enthusiast, but never a full member of this countrified communal experiment. She spent more of her life as a working woman: first as co-editor of *The Dial,* then as the first female reporter for the *New York Tribune.* Her career took her to Europe, where she threw herself into the cause of the Italian revolution. Fuller was an ardent advocate of women's equality who in 1845 wrote *Woman in the Nineteenth Century.* This book is striking not only because it so intelligently and convincingly argues for women's rights but because it is one of the literary triumphs of the antebellum age, a feminist tract by a self-supporting woman writer. Fuller was more of an observer than a participant in the activities at Brook Farm, but Hawthorne's literary portrait of Fuller in *The Blithedale Romance* firmly places her in the landscape of America's Utopian past. Brook Farm was the first of many movements fostered by American intellectuals attempting to divest themselves of materialist trappings in favor of a simple life of self-support. But the intelligentsia were not the only ones collectively to spurn society in favor of communities of their own making.

The countryside was sprinkled with other fledgling Utopias during the antebellum years: Fruitlands (also near Boston), Economy (Pennsylvania), Hopedale (Massachusetts), Pleasant Hill (Kentucky), New Harmony (Indiana), and Nauvoo (Illinois), among them. Some of these communities, most notably the Shakers, sought to rescue women from the burdens of childbearing by requiring celibacy. The Shakers and other religious communities (Rappites, Zoarites) recognized that conventional monogamy presented women with an undeniable handicap in the struggle for sexual equality, and many religious societies wished to relieve women of the pain and hardship associated with childbirth. Celibate societies sought to convert adults and to adopt children. Their avoidance of procreation was a means of keeping their flock spiritually pure, and, not surprisingly, more women than men converted to the crusade against sexual congress between men and women.

Perhaps one of the most unusual and advanced settlements of the times was founded in Oneida in upstate New York in 1847. Unlike other communities with irregular sexual practices, members of Oneida were not celibate. Instead, these visionaries rejected abstinence in favor of a more radical and modern attack on the status quo. This assault was led by the spiritual father and founder of this Utopia, John Humphrey Noyes.

Noyes fully developed his notions of "Male Continence and Complex Marriage" in 1846, arguing: "We are opposed to random procreation, which is unavoidable in the marriage system . . . We believe that good sense and benevolence will very soon sanction and enforce the rule that women shall bear children only when they choose." After Noyes's wife had given birth to five children within six years, four stillborn, he proposed that men and women freely cohabit (by mutual consent) within the community—to promote a more voluntary pattern of motherhood. Besides his bold attack on monogamy, Noyes encouraged his followers to practice *coitus reservatus*, a male method of self-control to prevent pregnancy—which could hastily be transformed into withdrawal for the less skilled practitioner.

These revolutionary concepts of social organization provided a dramatic—and many critics argued, dangerous—departure from American norms. Within Oneida, attachments were contracted by intervention of a third party: exclusive pair bonding was discouraged through the practice of "mutual criticism"—public ordeals whereby community members were subjected to evaluations in front of the entire settlement, requested to sit in silence while others spoke freely. These "criticisms" were meant to clear the air and promote good will among community members. Although the system seemed to prosper and served members well for over a generation, by 1879 Oneida was forced to abandon its complex marriage system due to public disapproval of their "strange" sexual practices. The community at Oneida was but one group persecuted for sexual experimentation. The "Modern Times" Utopian experiment in New York was equally attacked for its "free love" practices. And the Mormons were driven out of New York, Illinois, and finally into the Utah desert for their practice of polygamy. In some ways, antebellum America was more tolerant of movements which challenged the economic status quo than those which attempted to restructure fundamental relationships between men and women.

Utopian communities not only challenged the traditional institutions of marriage and family, but, equally important, many experiments attempted to restructure what one critic called "that eternal prison house for the wife," the home. During these years, prescriptive literature and popular ideology, as we have seen, celebrated women's exalted role in the home, declaring the hearthside as her "throne." Many Utopian radicals wished to attack this new movement, to liberate women from their oppressive role. The Friendly Association for Mutual Interests, a group settled near Valley Forge, Pennsylvania, during the 1820s, advocated not only equal rights for women but domestic work for men. They adopted these views from those of the English radical, John Gray, who published his tenets in London in 1825. In the same year William Thompson made a similar attack in a tract with a self-explanatory title: *Appeal to one half of the Human Race, against the pretensions of the other Half, Men, to retrain them in Civil and Domestic Slavery.* He believed that women were entitled to a better life through financial support during pregnancy, communal child care, and an opportunity for paid work outside the home. These changes would lead to female economic independence and a more perfect society. Gray, Thompson, and other English radicals were following the lead of a revolutionary Utopian idealist, Robert Owen, who had put many of his theories into practice at his textile mill in New Lanark, Scotland, from 1800 to 1824.

Owen, a pioneering nonsectarian socialist, included plans for community kitchens, cooperative nurseries, and day care for working mothers in his design for an ideal Utopian community. Unfortunately, his dream community was never built, but his philosophy inspired a dozen or more cooperative communities in the United States during the 1820s. Perhaps the most famous of these experiments was the settlement at New Harmony, Indiana, where in 1826 Robert Dale Owen (Owen's son) migrated to put into practice his father's ideals. Although disharmony disrupted this community and the main settlement disbanded in 1827, Owen had found his vocation as an activist and reform author. He edited the *New Harmony Gazette*, and advocated free public education and the formation of workingmen's political parties. Owen wrote a book which attracted extreme and negative attention because of its radical views on the forbidden subject of sex, *Moral Physiology* (1830), the first birth-control tract published in America. Owen argued in favor of fewer children and better education and maintained that decisions concerning birth control should rightly be within women's domain. He further endorsed economic and political parity for females, stressing that "to emancipate women from political degradation, and to place them in a situation to speak their thoughts and regulate their actions freely is of all means the most effectual to aid the great cause of human improvement." Owen served as a congressman from Indiana during the 1840s, and was involved in both the antislavery and the spiritualist movements. But he is perhaps best remembered for his early association with radical causes, especially his collaboration with Fanny Wright.

Wright and Owen had common experiences in that they both traveled to America from Europe to found revolutionary and innovative communes, which quickly failed. Both devoted themselves to promoting their ideals throughout the country following the collapse of their neophyte communities. Their partnership was one of the most productive in antebellum reform.

Frances Wright, an heiress, was a widely traveled and published author. She emigrated from Scotland to America and decided to found an ideal community in 1825. Wright bought a plantation near Nashoba, Tennessee, and hoped to put into practice her abolitionist ideals by managing a prospering estate with free rather than slave labor. When the task overwhelmed her and she fell ill, Fanny Wright recuperated at New Harmony, where she met Owen. The failure of New Harmony in 1827 was followed by the disintegration of Nashoba in 1828. Wright and Owen abandoned their rural operations and moved to New York City, where they jointly edited *The Free Enquirer* and became political organizers. Their campaign was one of committed involvement in workingmen's politics. They organized lobbying groups (nicknamed "Fanny Wright Societies") to persuade state legislatures to adopt universal free education. Wright and Owen pressed for a political voice for workers, which resulted in the founding of the New York Workingmen's Party (which achieved no small victory in the election of 1829).

Wright established a formidable reputation as a public speaker. A rousing oration in Indiana during the Fourth of July celebration near New Harmony in 1828 distinguished her—the first woman destined for a career as a lecturer. She embarked on a tour of the Midwest (Cincinnati, Louisville) before moving East to continue her crusade. The very fact of her public lectures as well as the subjects she discussed openly (national education, communitarian economic enterprises, and, most pointedly, rights for women) stimulated interest and controversy. Her appearance (a short hairstyle and a loose tunic over bloomers) startled her audience. She discontinued her speaking career in 1830, by which time her effectiveness was considerably undermined by her notoriety: the popular press had labeled her "the Whore of Babylon."

Wright's radical views included unorthodox attitudes toward sex and marriage. She advocated birth control, divorce reform, protection of women's property rights, and a spectrum of libertarian ideals which came under the heading of "free love." Although monogamous commitment was the rule for Wright, Owen, and their followers (traditional marriage ceremonies were performed with the omission of vows of obedience), the public misconstrued these advanced theories. Though Wright had merely declared "the proper basis of the sexual intercourse to be the unconstrained and unrestrained choice of both parties," critics attacked her as a promoter of lewd and promiscuous behavior—indeed, a participant in decadent and immoral communal arrangements. Defeated by public disapprobation, Wright married in 1831 and moved to Paris. She resettled in the United States in 1844 to resume her writing and lecture career. When she divorced her husband, she was unable to regain control of her own inheritance—a victim of the very laws she attempted to reform. But her career is testimony to the vitality and variety of the debate over women's role in antebellum America.

Like most women reformers of her day, Wright was concerned with the growth and influence of slavery. Although she opposed slavery for economic and political reasons, most of the American females who joined the crusade against slavery did so to signify moral and Christian duty.

During the early years of the republic, women's fervor and spiritual enthusiasm were the mainstay of American religion. Missionary zeal led many women into moral opposition to slavery. In the North, this energy was directed into evangelical channels. In the South, elite males tried to prevent women from participating in reform campaigns. They expected women to devote themselves to caring for slaves on the plantation rather than to the cause of antislavery. But by the third decade of the century, antislavery in the North had escalated from a spiritual concern into a full-fledged political crusade. Females were indispensable to the antislavery network. Their tireless efforts resulted in heightening consciousness among millions of Americans, and women gathered thousands of signatures on behalf of abolition. Angelina Grimké advocated: "The right of petition is the only political right that women have." Women waged campaigns on the local and state levels. The contents of these documents varied, but one Massachusetts petition included the familiar refrain: "We also respectfully announce our intention to present this same petition next year before your honorable body, that it may at least be 'a memorial of us' that in the cause of human freedom 'we have done what we could.'" When women escalated their efforts into a national campaign, the defenders of slavery dramatically responded. One observer reported that when the former President, Congressman John Quincy Adams, submitted a petition to the House of Representatives signed by 148 Massachusetts women, Virginians "raved incoherently . . . pounded the table with their fists . . . cursed Massachusetts and . . . wished that the women of the state . . . might swing . . . from a lamp-post." The southern members of the House of Representatives introduced the gag rule to stem the tide of female protests against slavery, attempting to derail the female crusade by denying them a public arena. Women countered with prayer groups, fairs, and traditional volunteer work, while stepping up their political movement, judging the ban on petitions as a sign of their impending victory. They developed a taste for more militant activity.

From the gradualism of antislavery, many females shifted into the immediacy of abolitionism. Instead of believing that good Christians should bide their time, waiting for slave owners to see the light and emancipate blacks, many women argued in favor of activism. Although their vocal and public stance appeared out of character to some, many of women's protests stemmed from concerns affecting the domestic, private sphere. Females had been assigned their roles as spiritual guardians, so they zealously went about the business of eliminating evil. Women had a vital and electrifying effect on the movement.

First and foremost, women's evangelical fervor drew invaluable attention. Their participation bolstered prospects for success of this "fringe group." Females who worked ceaselessly during their lifetimes and created generations of reformers spawned an antislavery tradition—moral individuals would challenge and indeed eventually defeat the slave power, despite southerners' opposition.

Antislavery gained followers through women's efforts to recruit and convert men to "the Cause"—as abolitionists styled their movement. Wendell Phillips, who became one of the outstanding orators of the movement, was drawn to it when the woman he was courting, Ann Green, asked him to dedicate himself to this worthy vocation, as she, a woman and a chronic invalid, could not. William H. Seward was similarly converted. More often than not, however, determined women established independent abolitionist careers.

In the beginning, females were forced into parallel organizations within the antislavery movement. They formed their own organizations after men established the American Antislavery Society in Philadelphia in 1833. It is ironic that there were often separate groups for blacks and whites, as well as for men and women. Many New England towns supported four separate antislavery societies: a local antislavery society, a female antislavery society, a colored antislavery society, and a colored female antislavery society. Despite this organizational breakdown, women did not play gender-restricted roles within the movement.

Antislavery nurtured an outstanding generation of women leaders: Maria Weston Chapman, Abby Kelley Foster, Sojourner Truth, Lucretia Mott, Sallie Holley, Lydia Maria Child, and the Grimké sisters. Angelina and Sarah Grimké were brought up on a South Carolina plantation. Their father, a wealthy judge and slave owner, raised his daughters to embody the southern female ideal of submissiveness. But the sisters had other goals in mind. They exiled themselves to the North, became Quakers, and repudiated their culture and inheritance by joining the abolitionists. When the two became agents of the American Antislavery Society, and Angelina lectured throughout the North, espousing immediate emancipation, she became especially famous not only for her radical views (a former southerner, therefore an "eyewitness"), but as an oddity—a woman addressing "promiscuous" (mixed male and female) audiences. The Grimkés collected over twenty thousand signatures on an antislavery petition for submission to the Massachusetts legislature. When Angelina offered the group her petition and offered her views, she was the first woman to testify before a government committee. The Grimké sisters continued their campaign, despite their being assailed for unladylike behavior–not the last of the abolitionist women to face open hostility on account of their sex.

When faced with men who refused to work with female comrades, Maria Weston Chapman countered: "Women, whose efforts for the cause could not be hindered by men, were more valuable auxiliaries than the men whose dignity forbade them to be fellow laborers with women." She was one of the founding members of the Boston Female Antislavery Society in 1832. Although some called her the Lady Macbeth of the movement, she was accorded considerable respect by most Boston colleagues, and won admiration as William Lloyd Garrison's "right hand." She began her career by editing *The Liberty Bell*, a book promoting the Cause, and running antislavery fairs which raised thousands of dollars for support of political activities, and indeed underwrote the movement for many years. She gathered the support of important literary figures such as Longfellow, Lowell, Margaret Fuller, and Harriet Martineau.

In addition, Chapman was a dynamo within the abolitionist organizations, serving on local, state, and national executive committees for nearly thirty years. She co-edited the *National Anti-Slavery Standard* from 1844 to 1848, taking over from fellow abolitionist Lydia Maria Child. In 1847 she complained to a friend: "I have been all summer driven hither and thither with matters pertaining to death and shall probably be all winter driven still more furiously by affairs of life. So that it seems to be a matter of life and death with me all the time . . . with the mortifying reflection that if I were only on a level with a cat and had nine lives, I could carry on the work with geometrically proportional results."

Chapman's counterpart in Philadephia was the indomitable Lucretia Mott—mother of six, and a minister in her Quaker congregation. She founded the Philadelphia Female Antislavery Society in 1833 and was its president for over a quarter of a century. Mott was one of the delegates who went with Garrison to the World Antislavery Convention in London in the summer of 1840. The American Antislavery Society had been seriously split over the question of women's status within the organization earlier in the year. When a woman was elected to the National Committee, many males took the opportunity to oppose female participation, to put a stop to equal status for women once and for all. The group split: half the movement endorsed the equal participation of women (Garrison's wing), and the others favored women's exclusion from decision-making within the organization.

Many early suffrage leaders like Elizabeth Cady Stanton and Susan B. Anthony had their first crusading experiences in the abolitionist cause: they garnered invaluable experience fighting slavery. Schooled in the basics of political organization and reform strategies, women abolitionists were formidable opponents in the moral war against slavery. Indeed, historian James B. Stewart has called these abolitionists "holy warriors." It is easy to understand how women turned these egalitarian sentiments for blacks into the basis for a "holy war" for themselves. Elizabeth Cady Stanton argued the case at an American Antislavery Society anniversary meeting in 1860:

> Herein is woman more fully identified with the slave than man can possibly be, for she can take the subjective view. She early learns the misfortune of being born an heir to the crown of thorns, to martyrdom, to womanhood. For while the man is born to do whatever he can, for the woman and the negro there is no such privilege. There is a Procrustean bedstead ever ready for them, body and soul, and all mankind stands on alert to restrain their impulses, check their aspirations, fetter their limbs, lest, in their freedom and strength, in their full development, they should take an even platform with the proud man himself.

Ideologues and tacticians were not the only ones who won admiration for women. The antislavery campaign was equally strengthened by the thousands of women who held weekly prayer vigils against slavery, who poured petitions of protest into Washington, who staged annual events to fund antislavery organizations, who subscribed to abolitionist periodicals, who, in effect, participated without reward or recognition—and who held steadfast in the face of hostility after 1840–41, when many men blamed women for the split within the movement, rather than blaming the men who precipitated the rift. The abolitionist crusade was one of the most successful grass-roots movements of the century and one of the most impressive in American history.

Despite the lesser role women have been assigned in the history of this movement, female participation was not only substantial but essential to bringing the slavery issue to the forefront of sectional politics. Once antislavery found a foothold, southern fire-eaters raged over meddling Yankees. The battle over slavery emerged as the "great divide" of the nineteenth century. And, in the bargain, the fight to free slaves propelled women into an equally long, rigorous fight for their own liberation.

5
Battling Women

IT WAS a logical step from women denouncing slavery and championing the cause of blacks to standing up for their own rights, but this step represented a dramatic advance. By the 1840s women were mobilized on their own behalf to campaign for numerous goals, ranging from suffrage to dress reform, from property rights to higher education. The women who led the rebellion against male domination had been trained in other reform movements. Many advocates of women's rights were also outspoken abolitionists. Indeed, most feminists acquired public-speaking skills in the antislavery forum. After activist Lucy Stone earned her undergraduate degree from Oberlin in 1847, she embarked on a tour as an agent of the American Antislavery Society. Her purpose was twofold: "I expect to plead not for the slave only, but for suffering humanity everywhere. *Especially do I mean to labor for the elevation of my sex.*"

Women who pursued public careers were outraged by the legal handicaps society imposed on them. It was an indignity to women who were able to lead relatively self-supporting and independent lives that they should be denied legal rights because of their sex. Married women lost all control over their property and earnings (except that which was protected by trust or prenuptial contract, in which case a woman's father or brother would maintain control). Many women who published and lectured on behalf of moral reform and antislavery were frustrated by sexual discrimination. Lydia Maria Child recorded her fury at needing her husband's signature on her will: "I was indignant for womankind made chattels personal from the beginning of time, perpetually insulted by literature and law and custom. The very phrases used with regard to us are abominable. 'Dead in the law.' 'Femme couverte.' How I detest such language."

Despite the doctrine of marital unity, American jurisprudence granted women advantages not shared by women of other Western societies. As early as 1796, in the Connecticut case *Nickols v. Giles,* a mother was awarded custody of her child. Although the father claimed his legal prerogative, the court exercised "judicial discretion," an option which protected the child's best interests. The fact that the law clearly favored a father's rights (in this and many cases to follow) did not prevent the court from ruling in favor of maternal custody. A father's claims might be outweighed by other factors. Although evidence indicates it was not common even for a propertied and pious mother to win custody of children in court battles, neither was it impossible for her to keep her children. The age and gender of the offspring involved, as well as the father's character, were crucial to the decision, and courts could and did weigh "the child's best interests" and, in some cases, hold that a mother's care was preferable.

Some judges refused to separate children from fathers regardless of circumstances, however. One New York Chief Justice argued in 1837: "In this country the hopes of the child in respect to its education and future advancement is mainly dependent on the father." The judge went on to suggest that if children were remanded to their mother's care they could "hardly expect to inherit" from their father. So the courts might well rule in favor of common law, despite the doctrine of judicial discretion. Without legislative remedy, the female parent had an inferior status before the bench in child-custody cases.

When legal reforms in the 1830s merged common law and equity, as a measure "to provide one form of civil action," feminists called for codification of women's rights, especially those which had already been recognized under equity jurisdiction: to hold and maintain property, to contract, to sue, to testify in court. Feminists fought to transform these previously observed equity principles into statutes, to guarantee women their rights.

Such reform campaigns signaled a move toward a full-scale women's movement. Scattered across the country, involved in dozens of voluntary associations, the reformers combined to launch a feminist crusade. Most historians mark the start of the political campaign on behalf of women's rights by the Seneca Falls convention in 1848. This conference was the first public political meeting solely dedicated to women's issues, and one which set feminists apart from the wide range of women reformers.

The impetus behind the convention was the resolve of two women who befriended one another at the World Antislavery Conference in London in 1840. When Lucretia Mott, the Philadelphia Quaker abolitionist, was denied her seat on the floor of the British convention (despite being a duly elected member of the assembly), she was forced to observe the meeting from the gallery. Although William Lloyd Garrison joined his female comrade in the balcony as a show of solidarity, Mott realized that the "woman problem" was as significant as the slavery issue and would require its own political discussion and public campaign. She had long and earnest talks with Elizabeth Cady Stanton, the wife of another delegate to the conference. Stanton and Mott agreed that women's grievances were well worth a campaign back in their native United States.

When they returned home, however, they were caught up in the cause of antislavery: Mott sailed back to Philadelphia, and the Stantons settled in Boston. When Stanton removed to Waterloo, New York, very much isolated from her reform network and saddled with the drudgery imposed by her family of six, she was faced with the alienation which confronted many other women. Her memoirs reflect her discontent, anxiety, and sense of oppression. Stanton was determined to agitate on behalf of women's rights. When Lucretia Mott and her husband vacationed in upstate New York early in the summer of 1848, Elizabeth Cady Stanton convened an informal caucus of women. A group of five (Stanton, Mott, Mott's sister Martha Wright, Mary Ann McClintock, and Jane Hunt) endorsed a proposal to call a convention of women. They put a notice in the paper, drew up an agenda, with Stanton alone insisting on a demand for women's suffrage. Stanton's husband was so displeased by his wife's role in this new movement that he left town during the historic meeting, July 19–20, 1848.

It is remarkable that these five women met, determined a course of action, put a notice in the local paper, drafted a "Womanifesto" (based upon the Declaration of Independence), and secured a chapel for the conference—all within one week. (Four of the five women were Quakers and perhaps more accustomed to active roles.) Although plans for this official two-day meeting might appear hasty, the protest movement was many years in the making. Despite relatively little publicity, the conference was well attended and a great success. The organizers had planned on excluding males from the meeting, but when over forty men turned up on the first day (in addition to two hundred women), the organizers lifted the ban.

Despite their fears that mobilization might be met with a lukewarm response, the call for a discussion of "the social, civil and religious rights of women" was enthusiastically welcomed: women's protests struck a chord in mid-nineteenth-century America. Stanton must be heralded as the heroine of the occasion, and indeed as one of the most dedicated feminists of her day. With her husband absent in protest, with her co-proposers (even Mott) opposed to demanding the vote, she must have approached the platform with great trepidation. But her words were clearly inspired by the occasion: "I should feel exceedingly diffident to appear before you at this time, having never before spoken in public, were I not nerved by a sense of right and duty, did I not feel that the time had come for the question of women's wrongs to be laid before the public, did I not believe that woman herself must do this work." The Declaration of Principles included demands for granting women equal education, equal opportunity for employment, equality before the law, an equal right to public platform, and the vote. Stanton had launched on a fifty-year feminist career, and her efforts fostered a movement which was soon to involve hundreds of thousands of women throughout the country.

The overwhelming and positive response to this protest meeting, on the part of men as well as women, demonstrated the need for a strong and articulate movement specifically seeking rights for women. Other groups had laid the groundwork for the feminist crusade, and women were making headway prior to the Seneca Falls convention. New York passed a law in 1848 providing for women's separate estates of real and personal property while married. (Although Mississippi had passed a Married Women's Property Act nearly a decade before, in 1839, this legislation was not inspired by feminist demands but was enacted following the disastrous panic of 1837 clearly to assist bankrupt husbands who wished to hold on to assets in their wives' names. Alabama passed a similar act in 1848.)

In the North, women activists had lobbied long and hard against the legal invisibility which condemned married women to an inferior status before the bench. Susan B. Anthony was outraged that the law failed to recognize women's progress, maintaining: "The real character and position of woman has entirely changed, from the thoughtless ignorant toy or drudge of the past, to the enlightened, dignified moral being of today." Feminist efforts were rewarded by a steady but slow change. By 1860 fourteen states had reformed their laws dealing with married women's property. Some have argued that this legislative remedy bore little relation to feminist demands, and the evidence from southern states bears this out. In addition, the guarantee of property was the bourgeois concern of a female elite. Regardless of the reasons for granting women this limited legislative remedy, antebellum women exploited these concessions for their own ends. And feminist organizations fought for and won the right of women to keep their own wages, beginning with a New York statute in the 1860s. This and other campaigns demonstrated that broad-based feminist concerns as well as elitist issues were promoted by mid-century.

Women radicals publicized their concerns in a series of women's conventions. The first, modeled on the Seneca Falls one, was organized in Rochester within a fortnight. The next followed a year later, in Salem, Ohio. By 1850 women activists had organized an intrastate movement. At this first "national" convention, many of the most famous feminist leaders gathered in Worcester, Massachusetts. These delegates included not only converts from the abolitionist crusade such as Stanton, Mott, Sojourner Truth, Angelina Grimké, Abby Kelley Foster, Paulina Wright Davis, and Ernestine Rose, but also Antoinette Brown (the first woman in America ordained as a minister), Harriot Hunt (a pioneer in medicine), and Elizabeth Oakes Smith (a lyceum lecturer who took an interest in the feminist crusade only after contact with women through the convention network). For the next decade, the annual convention became a focus for these feminists who were widening their sphere of influence throughout the nation. At the 1851 conference women explicitly stated their claims: "We deny the right of any portion of the species to decide for another portion . . . what is and what is not their 'proper sphere': that the proper sphere for all human beings is the largest and highest to which they are able to attain."

Thus, women began to challenge the very notion of a separate sphere. The 1850s were enlivened by varied feminist campaigns to secure women's rights. Some women, inspired by lecturers and literature, refused to pay taxes, in protest. Many others attacked institutions which denied access to women, such as the 1858 campaign headed by Sarah Burger against the University of Michigan, which did not admit women until 1869. Reformers like Amelia Bloomer and Paulina Wright Davis edited journals. Bloomer is best remembered for advocating more practical fashions: she wore loose-fitting harem pants—Turkish trousers—with a tunic blouse, which became known as the "Bloomer costume." In her feminist publication *The Lily*, Bloomer attacked "senseless restrictions" such as corsets and stays. The issues explored in these feminist tracts also reflected other significant concerns: liberalization of divorce laws, protection of women's earnings from seizure by husbands, custody of children, health reform, as well as temperance, antislavery, and "purity" (moral reform).

The open discussion of these issues fascinated women. Some "ladies' magazines" which had traditionally championed separate spheres and feminine moral superiority began to broaden their scope to include a rational rather than a romantic view of women. And further, women's alleged moral superiority allowed them to denounce laws which fostered victimization at the hands of men. This double assault on the status quo led to lively debate over women's changing role. All across the New England, middle Atlantic, and even midwestern states, women were joining what might be called the forerunners of "consciousness-raising" groups. Feminist leaders of the 1850s disdained a central committee to run their movement, preferring to concentrate on grass-roots organization. They did organize concerted efforts in target areas, such as the 1853–54 New York campaign for reform legislation led by Susan B. Anthony.

Anthony joined the feminist crusade after the groundwork had been laid. Reared in an abolitionist family, she began her political activities as a champion of temperance: she revealed a sensitivity to women's plight when she commented: "As public sentiment and the laws now are, the vilest wretch of a husband knows that his wife will submit to live on in his companionship, rather than forsake him, and by so doing subject herself to the world's cold charity, and be robbed of her home and her children." When in 1852 Anthony was prohibited from taking the floor at a temperance convention—it would be "unseemly"—she abandoned male comrades and, with Stanton, organized the New York State Women's Temperance Society. She became a tireless campaigner who cultivated and refined strategies for the women's movement. Indeed, Anthony, who never married, pursued feminist goals with an intensity which would at times surpass that of Stanton; she had occasion to criticize women with husbands and children who divided their energies between family and feminism. Stanton and Anthony were a compatible and formidable team; their comradeship lasted the rest of the century.

With Stanton's support, Anthony branched out into a multifaceted feminist crusade. In the autumn of 1854 the two strategists sought to inundate the New York legislature with women's petitions listing three demands: suffrage, control of earnings, and custody of children in divorce cases. Stanton and Anthony appointed "captains" in each New York county to canvas for support and secured six thousand signatures. Next, Anthony devoted several winter months to the statewide lecture circuit. The two women planned to stage a women's rights convention in Albany. Their valiant efforts were rewarded when Elizabeth Cady Stanton was invited to appear before the state legislature.

Once again, Stanton incurred family disapproval by her willingness to speak out for women's rights. She spent weeks consulting with legal scholars and fellow feminists to perfect her presentation to the Albany legislators. Her speech on February 14, 1854, cogently outlined the legal reforms sought by the women's rights movement. She lambasted the current laws:

> We demand the full recognition of all our rights as citizens of the Empire State . . . We have every qualification required by the Constitution, necessary to the legal voter, but the one of sex. We are moral, virtuous, and intelligent, and in all respects equal to the proud white man himself, and yet by your laws we are classed with idiots, lunatics and negroes . . . Can it be that here, where we acknowledge no royal blood, no apostolic descent, that you, who have declared that all men were created equal—that governments derive their just power from the consent of the governed, would willingly build up an aristocracy that places the ignorant and vulgar above the educated and refined . . . an aristocracy that would raise the sons above the mothers that bore them?

Her speech was a powerful indictment, full of wit as well as wisdom. Mott and others praised her text, although Sarah Grimké volunteered a chiding criticism: "It was too caustic."

While Stanton was most often tied to her home, saddled with enormous family responsibilities, Anthony was able to spend much if not most of her time traveling on behalf of women's rights. She labored in the backwoods—enduring exhaustion, frostbite, and recurring physical ailments—to convert women. Anthony believed that she could bring her message even to women who were "ignorant" of their own oppression. Her mission represented the "personal politics" of the feminist movement.

Anthony and her "captains" did not falter after their failure to convince the New York legislature to change the laws in 1854. Rather, feminists were heartened that their campaigns had reached so many and that their members were improving their publicity and organizational skills. The hardening of opposition often strengthened women's resolve. Their growing strength contributed to a more militant campaign. And in New York, where Stanton and Anthony focused their energies, hard work finally paid off. Reform laws passed in 1860 were some of the most advanced in the nation if not the world: women gained the right to sue, to keep their own wages, and to exercise greater control over a husband's property at his death.

The recalcitrance of legislators was only one of a myriad of obstacles to feminist reform. As in the campaign in New Jersey at the turn of the century (where state legislators battled against women's political participation with jeers and sarcasm before they banned them from the polls), antebellum males employed ridicule to undermine the movement. Although women reformers pushed for sensible legislative remedy, politicians and editors lampooned feminists and harped on the most marginal of women's issues. Cartoons repeatedly satirized the dress-reform campaign, and statesmen lamented "husbands in petticoats"—the "emasculation" of men who gave women their due. This campaign had its effect. By the middle of the nineteenth century, snide male antagonists were secondary to the problem of females who were antifeminist.

A sizable sector of American women had expanded its influence with the promise of upholding "traditional" values. Society was willing to accept women's superior status in the domestic and spiritual realm in exchange for female deference on all other, especially political, public concerns. Women who argued that they were merely trying to secure more just laws so that females could exercise their moral judgments (i.e., custody of children for a divorced woman) failed to convince advocates of the status quo that their dominant interests would be protected. Feminists made direct and bold attacks on the law and the men who upheld such tyrannical rule. Some women believed that they made greater strides with a slow and cooperative system of social change, and objected to the "damage" militant campaigns did to their good work. Many of the means and ends of feminist reform were deplored by advocates of domesticity. A "purse of one's own" was anathema to many females who built their worlds around dependency on husbands. In addition, many feared that the limited gains they made (in education, reform, and religion) might be denied their daughters as retribution against "uppity women."

Men did not need to enlist female support of the antifeminist campaign: a vocal minority of women vigorously attacked feminism. Elite women had little interest in the agitation for a woman's right to keep her own wages. Many middle-class women prized their exalted role as mothers and homemakers, with few ambitions beyond the household. Lower-class women for the most part concentrated on the harsh realities of survival. Their preoccupation with economic hardship left them little time to contemplate purity, religiosity, and other "feminine" issues. Poor women were concerned about clothing their family, not dress reform. When working-class females were politicized in nineteenth-century America, they most often worked on behalf of labor parties and unions. Political feminism failed to attract women, for a variety of reasons.

In mid-century as in modern America, being a feminist (or an advocate of women's rights, as they were known in the nineteenth century) was not defined by any single issue. As female agitation grew during the post-Civil War years, more and more women were identified as supporters of women's rights only in terms of their political position on the vote. Women's rights organizations concentrated on women's suffrage as the campaign wore on. Political feminists believed that if they secured this precious right, they could elect representatives who would press for the various reforms for which it seemed they labored in vain.

Because of the momentum women were gaining in their various crusades, it is difficult to understand why winning the suffrage campaign took several generations. A national suffrage measure (in 1920, with the Nineteenth Amendment) became law only after half a century of concerted effort. The impetus gained by women's apprenticeship in the antislavery, temperance, and purity movements was no match for the tumult of the Civil War. The war brought changes of staggering proportion. Most were changes in degree: public arenas in which women had only token representation before the war were brimming with women during wartime. At the same time, the temporary shortage of manpower created new opportunities for women. War was a great catalyst for change among men, and it brought enormous transformations for female activities as well.

Women mobilized on behalf of the war effort in the South as well as in the North. Ladies' societies directed their energies to the care, feeding, and nursing of the army. When war broke out, it was easy for the government to draw on middle-class women's talent and experience on behalf of war relief. In April 1861, over three thousand New Yorkers turned out at Cooper Union to rally to the northern cause. Out of this massive response, the New York Central Association of Relief was founded, with twelve women on the twenty-five-member board. This group, in addition to collecting and distributing supplies, trained nurses for work in hospitals and on the battlefields. The New York group was but one of seven thousand local societies which constituted the Sanitary Commission, the most effective and important institution developed by women during the war. Supplies worth millions of dollars were doled out to needy soldiers, widows, and orphans. Women used many of the innovations developed during the antislavery days, such as the sponsoring of fairs and bazaars, to raise funds. In 1863 the northwest branch of the Sanitary Commission sponsored a two-week fund-raising fair in Chicago, which netted over $100,000. Boston, St. Louis, New York, and other cities followed suit. Southern women were less successful in their fund-raising efforts, but no less enthusiastic on behalf of their cause.

Both Union and Confederate governments recognized the important contributions women were making. In some cases, Lincoln and Davis accorded women official rank. In June 1861, Dorothea Dix was appointed Superintendent of Nurses for the Union Army. She set up strict regulations for the training of women, establishing a minimum age of thirty for her corps. Her stipulation that nurses be "plain in appearance" drew considerable criticism from pretty applicants and male patients. Dix and other women pioneers in medicine were aware of the prejudice many men harbored against unmarried women participating in immodest activities. She wanted to insure that her nurses would be above reproach. But as the war wore on, the forty cents per day (plus subsistence and transport) appealed to many more than just widows or married women with husbands away at war. Many women did not merely want to make themselves useful but also needed the extra income. Younger women, deprived of social activities as well as beaux, wanted to serve patriotic and personal needs by nursing. Many wartime romances blossomed in hospital wards, with consequent marriages often crossing the political boundaries—Confederate prisoners returning home with northern brides, and wounded Yankee captives marrying their southern nurses.

Confederates seemed even more concerned with the "impropriety" of having ladies ministering to "ruffians." Some accused the Confederates of launching a "rich man's war and a poor man's fight." Most of the enlisted men, and the majority of Confederate wounded, were from the lower classes in the South. Despite conservative male opposition, southern women mobilized on behalf of all southern soldiers. Sally Tompkins, who headed a small infirmary in Richmond, began her campaign modestly, borrowing the house of a friend for a twenty-two-bed clinic. President Jefferson Davis accorded her the rank of captain in the Confederate Army, and the energetic spinster's one-woman enterprise mushroomed. By war's end, "Cap'n Sally" had treated almost thirteen hundred men, with only seventy-three deaths. Tompkins was not alone in her lack of concern for public opinion and her dedication to the war effort. Another spirited southern woman argued: "A woman's respectability must be at low ebb if it can be endangered by going into a hospital." Some southern ladies even brought their slaves with them into hospitals, both as assistants and as protection.

Women not only cared for soldiers in hospital wards, but many earned praise for their tours of the battlefields. Mary Ann Bickerdyke, an accomplished nurse, spent much of her time at the Union's military hospital in Cairo, Illinois. But "Mother Bickerdyke," as she was affectionately known to the troops, also tended to wounded on nineteen battle sites. The efficient Quaker woman was a welcome sight to the fallen soldier in the field. Clara Barton was another outstanding nurse. She worked independently of the army, in the state of Massachusetts. Through her personal appeals, thousands of dollars were raised for food and medicine for Union soldiers. The South was less well organized than the Union. Women in the Confederate nursing corps were hard pressed to earn a living, with inflation eating away at their poor pay (in Confederate scrip, which grew worthless as the war wore on). Over three thousand women became army nurses during the Civil War, the majority in the North.

Although women had broken into the medical profession as doctors before 1861, women doctors made little headway during the war. Despite the desperate need for physicians, when war broke out no women were commissioned as doctors by either the Union or the Confederate medical departments. Elizabeth Blackwell earned her medical degree (the first for a woman) from Geneva Medical College in 1849. After completing her studies in Europe, she returned to the United States in 1851 and settled in New York. Blackwell found the medical establishment firmly opposed to her entry into the profession. In 1857 she formed the New York Infirmary for Women with other women denied a medical practice, her sister Emily and Dr. Maria Zakrzewska, who later taught at the New England Medical College for Women. Prejudice against women doctors crippled women's progress. The one woman doctor to receive recognition from the Union government, Mary Walker, applied for a post when the war broke out in 1861. The Union refused to grant her a commission until 1864. Her application approved, she was sent to the front at Chattanooga, Tennessee. Shortly thereafter she became a prisoner of war and was quite a curiosity to her captors. After being exchanged for a Confederate physician, Walker went on to supervise the Female Military Prison in Louisville. She was honorably discharged and awarded a medal by President Andrew Johnson. Her talent and willingness to serve were not extraordinary, but the recognition she received proved exceptional.

In the South, women doctors were even rarer. Little is known of the southern pioneer Louisa Shepard, who completed her training in 1861 at the Graefenberg Medical Institute in Dadeville, Alabama. Physician Elizabeth Cohen of New Orleans limited her practice to "ladies only." Women doctors were a threat to the image of southern ladyhood and the Confederate medical establishment. Many if not most southern women were trained by necessity to minister to patients isolated on farms and plantations in the rural South. These medical practices were strictly informal and widely praised. It was only when women attempted to professionalize their standing or obtain institutional affiliation that men discouraged women's cultivation of medical skills.

Many women who started with the army as nurses were soon employed as scouts and spies. Dr. Mary Walker was captured while on an intelligence mission. The famed Belle Boyd joined the Confederate Army as a nurse while still a teenager in her home of Martinsburg, Virginia. Her prowess on horseback and her courage soon brought her more challenging work. She was a celebrated heroine for her exploits in the valley of Virginia. Boyd once rode thirty miles in a single night to reveal vital plans of secret attack to a Confederate officer. She was betrayed and arrested in July 1862. The northern press painted her as a "village courtesan," implying that information could not be elicited without resorting to immoral sexual conduct. It is far more likely that, especially in the early phases of the war, overconfident soldiers on both sides were careless with military information. Since women were viewed as passive observers, they were more easily able to obtain and pass on military secrets. Mary Chesnut, writing behind Confederate lines near Richmond, confided to her diary: "Women from Washington come riding into our camp, beautiful women. They bring letters in their back hair, or in their garments."

Southern society hostess Rose O'Neal Greenhow was placed under house arrest in Washington, D.C., in August 1861. Confederates claimed the widow and her eight-year-old daughter were subjected to undue humiliation. During the first week of her confinement, she was forced to sleep with her door open while sentinels kept watch over her. The lack of privacy was but one indignity. Greenhow and other suspects held at her home (which became known as Fort Greenhow) were kept from all but their immediate families, had their mail censored, and were denied newspapers. Released from imprisonment in 1863, she ran the blockade to travel to Europe. After placing her daughter in a French convent and making diplomatic visits on behalf of the Confederacy, she sailed home to the South in October 1864 with gold and documents in her diplomatic pouch. Sighting Union patrols outside of Wilmington, she feared seizure of her ship. She and her party boarded a rowboat to reach shore, but the boat capsized and she was drowned. Greenhow became a martyr to the Confederate cause.

The Union had equally colorful heroines, including actress Pauline Cushman. Born in the South, she was a popular performer in her native New Orleans. She gained notoriety as an outspoken Rebel supporter, vowing her loyalty privately and in front of the footlights. Despite her Confederate origins, she secretly passed information to Union officers while on theatrical tours of the border states. In 1864 she was caught with plans she had stolen from a Confederate engineer. She escaped to freedom, but when recaptured was sentenced to death. She was rescued by federal troops in Tennessee. Following her return to the North, she resumed her acting career.

Not all such patriotism was so lauded. Many more women served at thankless tasks for the Union and Confederacy. Army camps were not exclusively male domains. Officers were occasionally allowed to have families visit them, at the discretion of individual commanders. Women cooks and laundresses were employed by both sides. In addition to performing familiar domestic chores in camps, many women served as soldiers—disguised as men.

During the war, over four hundred women were discovered posing as soldiers. Their reasons for cross-dressing were varied. Ellen Goodridge wanted to accompany her Union fiancé to the front. Sarah Edmonds changed her name to Franklin Thompson to serve as a male nurse with the Second Michigan Cavalry. In 1865 she published an account of her exploits as a nurse, spy, mail courier, and soldier. In 1884 the government awarded her a pension of $12 per month in recognition of her service to her country. Franny Wilson of New Jersey fought with Union troops for eighteen months before her ruse was discovered after she was wounded at Vicksburg. Indeed, most of the female imposters were "found out" when they were wounded and admitted to hospitals. Northern women were not the only male impersonators during the war. Far less frequently, southern women also disguised themselves as men to join the army—most often to accompany their husbands. Amy Clark continued to serve as a soldier after she was widowed at Shiloh. She was discovered only after her capture by the Union.

Only the wives of a few officers were permitted to accompany their husbands to war. Female cooks and nurses traveled with the army, but the soldiers promoted the myth that the camps were a man's world and women found nearby were "camp followers," or prostitutes. It was true that large numbers of women, out of financial necessity or choice, supported themselves as prostitutes during the Civil War. Many prostitutes saw the roving masses of soldiers as a boom to business. Although some did "follow the camp," many simply remained behind when one side moved out of an area, and greeted the invading soldiers with little or no fear. Commanders had scant concern for the dangers posed by prostitutes, with the single and major exception of disease.

Officers were concerned more about infection than about immorality. In July 1863, while stationed in Nashville, General William Rosecrans ordered the deportation of "all prostitutes found in the city or known to be here," due to "the prevalence of venereal disease." Rosecrans ordered his provost marshal to ship the women to Louisville. This proved no simple task. The Union officer commandeered a new pleasure cruiser, the *Idaho*, rounded up 111 women (approximately one-third of the prostitutes in the town), boarded the women, and sent them on their way with a crew of three men and a very disgruntled shipowner. When the ship docked at Louisville, the women were denied permission to debark. The *Idaho* passengers were also refused permission to land at their next stop, Cincinnati. A few days later, when the ship finally returned to Nashville (minus several women, who had stolen ashore during the journey), the owner pointed out to Rosecrans that the women had wrecked his ship and his reputation. The incident was celebrated as that of the "Floating Whorehouse" and it was three years before the boat owner could recuperate his $5,000 loss. Both the Union and the Confederacy were unsuccessful in their campaigns to wipe out prostitution. Army officials, wisely, were more preoccupied with winning the war.

Battles were fought mainly in the border states. Virginia, Tennessee, Missouri, and Pennsylvania suffered multiple and protracted invasions. These prolonged campaigns took their tolls on civilians as well as enlisted men. Sherman's March to the Sea, the occupation of New Orleans, and other Union campaigns imposed tremendous burdens on southern women. Farm wives as well as those left behind in village and town were expected to continue raising food and providing clothing, not only for themselves but for the enlisted men as well.

The women of the South had to cope with terrible shortages. In Vicksburg there were only rats to cook by the end of the several months' siege. Women were threatened by scarcity, inflation, and, by the winter of '64, impending starvation. Women were the instigators and participants in many food riots and the looting of government supply warehouses, especially for the precious commodity of salt. The lack of opportunity for female employment and the presence of fewer charitable agencies contributed to southern women's growing desperation.

In addition, southern women were portrayed in the northern press as particularly vituperative toward Yankees, as "rebel spitfires." General Ben Butler, the Union officer in charge of occupied New Orleans, wanted to put a stop to Confederate women's contemptuous behavior toward his troops. He issued a statement that any woman who voiced disrespect for Union officers or soldiers (including blacks in uniform) was to be "regarded and held liable to be treated as a woman of the town, plying her vocation." The chivalrous South was deeply offended by this Yankee outrage.

Confederate women were especially hard hit by the occupation. They were forced to witness the burning and looting of their homes. Often, females were forced to be serving maids and cooks, and perform every wifely duty short of sexual companionship, for their Union conquerors. When the soldiers in blue moved away, the women were left with no livestock, grain, or other supplies to feed their families. By war's end, Union troops resorted to a "scorched earth" policy, and when the soldiers in gray came through, although the Confederate women willingly aided these troops, the southern soldiers cleaned out the plantation households as thoroughly as the enemy troops did. In addition, women in both North and South faced the fact that, whether their cause was winning or losing, the hardships of war remained.

The North lost 360,000 soldiers and the South lost 260,000 during the war. An entire generation of young men were wiped out by this prolonged battle. Brides were widowed, children were orphaned, wives and mothers were overwhelmed by the problems of coping with the dangers of war without men. And after the war a generation of women would be forced to continue without male companionship.

There were, of course, meaningful and positive gains made by one group of southern women, the slaves. Emancipation offered them unprecedented gains. They could own property, marry, move about more freely, and at long last were accorded the privileges of freedom. Unfortunately, only males were granted the primary right of citizenship, the vote. Black women, like their white sisters, were saddled with second-rate status. Black women remained at the bottom of the ladder. Sojourner Truth was outspoken on this issue as she was on so many important questions. She commented in 1867: "There is a great stir about colored men getting their rights, but not a word about the colored women; and if colored men get their rights, and not colored women theirs, you see the colored men will be masters over the women, and it will be just as bad as it was before." But Sojourner Truth was in the minority. Sarah Parker Remond and other black women abolitionists pushed to secure black suffrage—even if only for men.

Several outstanding black women distinguished themselves during the war. Susie King Taylor served as a laundress to the Union's first black regiment: she became a nurse and later a teacher. Harriet Tubman continued her fight against slavery. Born a slave in Maryland, she escaped before the war to live as a free woman in Philadelphia. She soon became a conductor, shepherding slaves to safety, on the Underground Railroad. Before the war, she was instrumental in rescuing from fifty to three hundred slaves. With her notoriety and success, southerners put a steep price on her head: $10,000. She was forced to move to Canada, but with the outbreak of war, she volunteered to work in occupied areas of South Carolina, under the protection of the Union Army. She ostensibly served as a nurse for freedmen, but also contributed valuable work as a Union spy. After the war, Secretary of State Seward sought to give her compensation for her important government work; but she did not receive a pension until 1897.

During the war, northern women also were drafted to serve in the South, to fill positions with the newly established Freedmen's Bureau. This government agency was set up as a temporary network to assist freed blacks, to find food and shelter, and to deal with the issue of land administration (of confiscated Confederate estates). Josephine Griffin spurred Lincoln into funding this effort, and she marshaled volunteers to work for the bureau. By 1869 there were nine thousand teachers for ex-slaves in the South, and nearly half were women. Many years later W.E.B. Du Bois heralded the accomplishments of these women who struggled against prejudice and considerable handicaps, calling them the "tenth crusade."

Charlotte Forten, a well-educated middle-class black woman, left her comfortable circumstances in the North to teach free people sheltered on the Union-occupied South Carolina Sea Islands. Forten lived and worked at Port Royal for two years and recorded her experiences in a detailed diary of her wartime service. She reported after only a few months in South Carolina: "Talked to the children a little while to-day about the noble Toussaint L'Ouverture. They listened very attentively. It is well that they sh'ld know what one of their own color c'ld do for his race. I long to inspire them with courage and ambition (of a noble sort), and high purpose." Despite the ridicule and even violence that these women encountered, many remained in the South even after the federal troops withdrew in 1877.

Black women were in a particularly difficult position in the post-bellum South. Despite emancipation, they shared with black men the evils of racism and with white women the debilitating effects of sexism. Freedom held vastly different meanings for the two sexes, and for the two races, in the postbellum age.

Ex-slave women forced former masters to understand that they interpreted freedom as the right to privileges accorded to white women: free women adopted tenets of domesticity as their own. Plantation owners throughout the South faced a reluctant work force: black men preferred to work their own land or, if possible, abandon agriculture for employment in the city, while black women were even less willing to serve as workers in the field. Henry Watson, an Alabama planter, complained in 1865: "The women say that they never mean to do any more outdoor work, that white men support their wives and they mean that their husbands shall support them." Many white planters deplored this development. However, with the introduction of sharecropping and tenant farming, many if not most southern black women were reintroduced to field work, as recently emancipated families attempted to maintain a decent household income. Nevertheless, the black family, rather than the white overseer, determined women's participation in cotton production after the war.

White women in the South felt especially oppressed by postwar hardships. They were subjected to lengthy travails for a war which, as one woman put it to a female friend, "you and I are not responsible for." Women had shouldered burdens throughout the war, but with the defeat of the Rebel government and the restoration of Union rule, Confederate women rightly perceived that their futures would be filled with disinheritance, relative impoverishment, and prolonged deprivation. Men filled their heads with talk of the Lost Cause and former glory, but women faced the reality of keeping the household running, the family healthy, and trying to make life more than endurance.

Not only did the Confederate Army lose one in four soldiers, but the economic and political devastation that followed the war was pronounced in the South—for white as well as black. The North actually gained in population during the war. European immigrants poured into eastern cities throughout the 1860s. In the South, however, besides a decline in population, a sexual imbalance (with women outnumbering men) persisted until the 1880s. Young men often left their native South, hoping for a fresh start elsewhere. Many moved onto the southwestern frontier, some migrated North, and a few hardy souls headed for Central and South America. This exodus of marriageable men increased the surplus of females after the war. Alabama alone had eighty thousand widows seeking relief, and thousands more southern women needed financial aid from bankrupt southern governments. The Panic of 1873 hit hardest in the rural South.

These were very real setbacks for white women in the South, while women in the North made considerable gains in employment, especially in male-dominated occupations. In 1860 there were 270,000 females working in northern factories—mainly in the textile, shoe, clothing, and printing industries. This is in stark contrast to only twelve thousand in southern factories. The war created one hundred thousand new jobs in northern industry. At the same time, women pioneered posts with the Union government. Most administrators viewed these "government girls" as temporary employees. However, many women were able to remain white-collar workers after the war. Although women were paid half or less what male co-workers earned, women eagerly continued to seek these positions.

Before the war a handful of women, despite male protests, had secured posts as clerks in the patent office. With the appointment of Frances Spinner as Treasurer of the United States in 1861, women began to enter government service in larger numbers. There were nearly five hundred employed in Washington by 1865, over one hundred in Spinner's office alone. Despite the high cost of living in the capital, women were able to maintain a decent standard of living on their government salaries. The women of the Treasury office were paid handsomely under Spinner's supervision: $600 per year (raised to $720 by war's end). Women in other government divisions, notably in the Post Office Department (they were first hired by this all-male preserve to work in the Dead Letter Office), were paid less than male co-workers.

Women workers in government set commendable records. Most often, male colleagues were surprised at their proficiency. However, at war's end, "government girls" were the victims of severe backlash. Many government officials insisted that jobs held by women be relinquished to returning veterans. Others argued that it was unseemly for men and women to work in the same office. This argument was put forth several years after harmonious integration of white-collar workers had taken place.

Conservatives charged that co-mingling led to misconduct, and proceeded to investigate such alleged wrongdoings. In 1864 Congressman James Brooks of New York launched an investigation of the Treasury Department. Brooks was goaded into his inquiry by Lafayette Baker of the War Department, who led a virtual vendetta against a Treasury official named Spencer Clark. Baker convinced Brooks that Clark was seducing young girls, preying on them in his office. In the course of the investigation, federal agents broke into the boardinghouse of three young women who worked with Clark, read their diaries, and interrogated the women when they returned home. Unable to uncover any incriminating evidence, investigators threatened the three women that they would publish their suspicions of debauchery in the newspapers unless the trio signed confessions condemning Clark, which the vulnerable women did.

One week before the congressional hearings, one of the women, Laura Duvall, died. Baker accused the dead girl of having had an abortion, which allegedly led to her death. When he ordered an autopsy without family permission or without consulting other authorities, even the headline-grabbing Baker had gone too far. Laura Duvall, the doctors found, had died of complications stemming from pneumonia. Although the three co-workers were found innocent of the charges (one posthumously), many in Washington were content to trust the adage "Where there's smoke, there's fire," and to think the women guilty once their names were smeared in the headlines.

Wartime technology, the postwar rise of the robber barons, and the influx of millions of immigrants in the later part of the century fostered the growth and expansion of corporations. Women clerks were relatively rare until the end of the century. However, the opportunity for office work provided by the Civil War proved a significant step for women, and they later came to dominate the field. Although women represented only 3.3 percent of office workers in 1870, this figure had doubled by 1880, the proportion tripled by 1890, and in 1900 over 75 percent of the office work force (both private and government) was female. By 1900 two-thirds of stenographers and typists were young women (between the ages of fifteen and twenty-five). The majority, still single, lived with parents. These women who went to work in offices in the 1880s and 1890s were the counterpart of the antebellum influx of Yankee daughters into New England factories. Women who worked in offices and stores (salesladies, as they were called) were considered more "genteel" than those who went into domestic service or held factory jobs.

During the Civil War, women quickly replaced men as store clerks. Sales work meant long hours, sometimes in excess of one hundred hours per week, and poor pay (as little as $5 per week). Yet rural daughters were drawn to urban centers to work in the 1870s, just as their grandmothers had been attracted to the mills in the 1820s. There are ironic parallels. During the 1830s women at the mills complained of living by the bells imposed by the factory system; in the 1880s women who worked in stores were prisoners of the time clock. Department stores imposed stiff fines for lateness and allowed only brief breaks for meals (cut even shorter during holiday seasons). Saleswomen risked having their pay docked if they did not remain on their feet while on duty. Militant workers mounted campaigns for store owners to provide stools for clerks; they were, of course, available for customers. An even more exploited class of employees were the stock girls, who spent equally long hours running change to and from central cashiers, fetching stock for clerks, and sweeping up after closing. Even so, the tedious and tiring work in stores compared favorably with factory labor.

Industrial workers endangered their health and safety in many factories. By the latter half of the nineteenth century, factory work was back-breaking, unsanitary, and often dangerous. Those who bore most of this burden were immigrants with no other employment options. The more "genteel" pursuits were reserved for daughters of the native-born. Some stores and offices refused applications from the daughters of foreign-born parents, forcing women to change their names and conceal their origins to secure sales or office work.

Transformations in the postwar work force (integration of women more fully into white-collar industry, the temporary withdrawal of black women from "production," and the virtual explosion of industries staffed by immigrants, many of them women) wrought important changes in American society. At the outset of the war, women, in the main, sought to define their goals as active members of society. The war gave many unparalleled opportunities to explore new fields and to pioneer on behalf of their sex. Important inroads were made during this brief period. Wartime modernization propelled women into greater prominence and afforded access to jobs which they were denied in peacetime. These dazzling gains were not without a price.

Recent study has shown that the feminist movement suffered bitter defeat after the war. Some historians have depicted black and abolitionist defection from the crusade for women's suffrage as betrayal. Certainly many women abolitionists were bitter; as one woman complained: "They always unifed the words 'without regard to sex, race, or color.' Who hears of sex now from any of these champions of freedom?" The Equal Rights Association—a coalition of abolitionists and women's suffrage supporters founded in 1866—pushed for both blacks' and women's rights.

Female abolitionists were divided over the Fourteenth Amendment. One and all could support the Thirteenth Amendment, which provided for emancipation, but the wording of the Fourteenth Amendment alarmed feminists. This amendment specifically referred to "male citizens," the first such mention of gender in the federal Constitution, and a major threat to the advocates of the vote for women. It was clear the Radicals and blacks wished to disassociate themselves from any commitment to women's suffrage. Stanton was appalled at this desertion, complaining: "Abolitionists have demanded suffrage for women for the last ten years, and why do they ignore the question now?" With the passage of the Fourteenth Amendment and its offensive inclusion of "male," feminists were forced to reconsider their coalitions.

Unfortunately, opportunism divided allies, weakening the effort. After Emancipation, almost all male and some female members of the antislavery movement suspended their campaign for women's suffrage to concentrate on winning the vote for black men. They believed the compromise was necessary during the chaotic early years of Reconstruction. At the same time, many other feminists (notably Stanton and Anthony) were willing to join forces with any group which advocated women's suffrage, even if some of these were openly racist. Both sides argued that they supported black rights and women's rights in theory but that political campaigns created the need for pragmatic priorities. The vehement and varied positions taken in this battle created bitter division, especially the "Kansas campaign" of 1867, where separate referendums on the vote for women and the vote for black men were introduced. One Democratic wag put his sentiments into verse: "Women votes the black to save/The black he votes to make the woman slave/ Hence when blacks and 'Rads' unite to enslave the whites/'Tis time the Democrats championed women's rights." The women lost, despite their alliance with Democrats in local campaigns in Kansas and New

York. Even alliances with labor groups and Stanton's formation of the short-lived Working Women's Association did little to advance the cause of women's suffrage. These setbacks forced women to form their own independent organizations, associations which were dedicated solely to women's rights.

Even with the development of a single purpose, the women's suffrage movement remained split. The American Women's Suffrage Association (AWSA) attempted to secure women their rights on a state-by-state basis. Julia Ward Howe, Lucy Stone, and Henry Blackwell, among others, broke with Anthony during her crusade in Kansas due to differences of opinion as well as opposing methodologies. Stanton and Anthony broke away from this group, advocating a national amendment. The fight for women's suffrage might appear to have been weakened by this division; however, the establishment of parallel organizations provided a broader base of support, offering women a choice of conservative as well as radical feminism.

Radical feminism was given a great boost in 1868 when Stanton and Anthony launched a renewed and independent crusade, heralded by the publication of *The Revolution*. Their journal's motto was: "Men their rights and nothing more; women their rights and nothing less." The next year they established the National Women's Suffrage Association (NWSA). Although Stanton and Anthony's militance was undeniable, the pair was assuredly surpassed by the outstanding radical of her day, Victoria Woodhull.

Woodhull was born in Ohio in 1838, one of ten children. She had an impoverished and vagabond childhood. As a young girl, Woodhull became enamored of spiritualism. She married at the age of fifteen, but continued to travel, pursuing a career as a clairvoyant. During ten years as a professional medium, she divorced and remarried. When she met Cornelius Vanderbilt, she convinced the millionaire to back her financially, so she might establish a New York brokerage company. She brought her sister Tennessee into the firm and they became known as the "Lady Brokers of Wall Street." In 1870 these enterprising sisters wheedled funding from Stephen Pearl Andrews, a socialist, to publish a paper to air their radical political and feminist views. *Woodhull and Clafin's Weekly* not only advocated equal rights for women, but the editors preached a doctrine of "free love." They argued that a single standard of morality should be enforced for both sexes, that sexual hypocrisy should be abolished. Woodhull became famous and, some would say, notorious. Because of her radical sexual views, she was labeled in the popular press as "Mrs. Satan" and the "Queen of Prostitutes." However, she was also the first woman nominated for President, the candidate put forth (with Frederick Douglass as Vice President) by the People's Party in 1872. Woodhull was not only the most controversial feminist of her day but perhaps the most charismatic.

Stanton and Anthony had considerably mixed responses to Woodhull's politics. However, when Woodhull appeared before the United States Congress in 1871, the first woman ever to address this body on the subject of women's suffrage, the NWSA leaders were won over. Woodhull believed that the Fourteenth and Fifteenth Amendments guaranteed rights to all persons born or naturalized in the United States. As suffrage was a right of citizenship, Woodhull held, women were already entitled to the vote. She argued that a mere congressional act would endorse this view and enfranchise women. The bold simplicity of this position attracted women supporters; hundreds went to the polls in 1871 and 1872 to pledge their support.

Susan B. Anthony staged a "vote-in" in her hometown of Rochester during the 1872 federal election. She expected to be denied her right and planned to sue. To her surprise, women were not turned back at the polls. However, two weeks later a federal marshal came to Anthony's home to arrest her on charges of "illegal voting." Although she lost in the courts, Anthony used this case to publicize and promote her cause. In 1875, in *Minor v. Happersett*, the U.S. Supreme Court ruled that suffrage was not a "right" conferred on national citizens but a privilege granted by individual states. After this defeat, NWSA feminists were resigned to pressing for a national amendment to secure women's suffrage.

Most feminist concerns were considerably overshadowed by the problems posed for women by the Civil War, despite the dynamic developments in the middle of the century. During Reconstruction, much as it had been following the Revolution, females were expected to return to pre-war status. Women's spectacular contributions as "surrogates" for males in business and industry, agriculture and enterprise, were heralded, but men were eager to restore male supremacy as well as exclusivity in the economic and political realm.

Part of the return to "normal" included realignment of sex roles.

Yet, due to the extreme sexual imbalance in many communities, fathers often were happy to have daughters earn wages when there were no suitable husbands available. Men still saw wage earning by females as temporary. Until very recently, unmarried women dominated female wage earning, and spinsters, divorcées, and widows have been a small proportion of the adult female population. Only when married women entered the work force in large numbers could society tolerate the transformation of deeply entrenched cultural mores.

At the end of the Civil War, the political women's movement was divided over their battle to put the vote for women on the Radicals' agenda. In 1865 most Republicans were overwhelmed with the issue of the newly freed people of the South and did not wish to use their energies to promote women's suffrage. Feminists believed they were entitled to enlarged spheres of power and legal guarantee of their political privileges, not only by natural right but in appreciation of their important contributions to the war effort. These women were not defeated by their failure to secure feminist reforms during Reconstruction. Rather, this temporary setback strengthened women's resolve to organize and canvas for feminist issues with not one but several independent women's organizations. Nineteenth-century feminists defined the women's movement as a fight for suffrage, a privilege which they believed would lead to many other changes. By concentrating on a single issue, these reformers provided a goal on which they might fasten their hopes and a campaign which would focus their energies. Suffrage advocates established more permanent networks and organizations which drew in thousands of women throughout the country. This expanded and in a sense deepened the commitment to feminism in late-nineteenth-century America.

6
Natives and Immigrants

AFTER the Civil War, the country worked at healing its social and political divisions. Despite the South's fear and loathing of the North after the war, the "New South" power brokers wanted to rejuvenate their flagging economy. Although the chasm between northern industrial advancement and southern stagnation widened rather than narrowed during the postwar decades, most of the country expanded and many prospered at an unprecedented rate. The expansion and national extension was fueled by two important mass migrations: the movement of hundreds of thousands into the trans-Mississippi West, and the immigration of millions of foreigners to American shores. Women's roles in these two migrations are the stuff of folklore, and have been celebrated until recently more in works of fiction than in fact.

The westward migration had its greatest impact on the people whose lands were being invaded. Despite the Northwest Ordinance's (1787) pledge that "the utmost good faith shall always be observed toward the Indians; their land and property shall never be taken from them without their consent," from Washington onward, Indians suffered at the hands of American Presidents. Although in 1832 Supreme Court Justice John Marshall sought to protect Indian rights—defining the native people as having "dependent nation status"—the Chief Executive, Andrew Jackson, was one of the main instigators of hostile policy toward tribes blocking frontier settlement. Forced removals and bloody massacres increased in the nineteenth century. Indians wars were a feature of American domestic policy.

Homesteaders began a steady march westward, especially after the defeat of the Confederacy. Many nineteenth-century Americans satisfied their curiosities about Indian lore by poring over captivity narratives, the tales of those "stolen" from their homes and later restored to white culture. Unfortunately, most of these accounts were sentimental rather than informative, pandering to a popular audience. In addition, most captives complained about their "barbarous treatment," bitterly describing the primitive conditions of Indian life. Rachel Plummer, held by Comanches after their attack on a Texan fort, lamented her twenty-one-month ordeal. In her 1839 narrative, she revealed her prejudices by confiding that the Comanches' "habits are so ridiculous that this would be of little interest to any." Plummer continued her biased portrait: "The women do all the work, except killing the meat. They herd the horses, saddle and pack them, build the houses, dress the skins, meat, &c. The men dance every night, during which, the women wait on them with water. No woman is admitted into any of their Councils; nor is she allowed to enquire what their councils have been. When they move, the women do not know where they are going. They are no more than servants, and are looked upon and treated as such."

We get a more favorable view of female culture in native tribes from testimony taken from travelers and other observers. Most nineteenth-century accounts emphasize the persistence of traditions within a given Indian tribe. Indian women may have been saddled with physical labor and endured exclusion from spheres of power (like women in white culture). Yet most native American females had some measure of control over their lives denied "civilized" women. A Moravian minister described in his account of life among northeastern tribes, primarily the Delawares: "Marriages among the Indians are not, as with us, contracted for life; it is understood on both sides that the parties are not to live together any longer than they shall be pleased with each other. The husband may put away [divorce] his wife whenever he pleases, and the woman may in like manner abandon her husband." An observer among the Cherokee similarly commented on liberal Indian views on adultery, "They have been a considerable while under a petticoat-government, and allow their women full liberty to plant their brows with horns as oft as they please, without fear of punishment."

A woman who spent her life among several tribes of Midwest Indians during the latter part of the century provided a wealth of insights in her autobiography, collected and transcribed by a government ethnologist in 1918. This member of the Fox tribe not only affords us an interior view of Indian life but illuminates the critical importance of gender in her culture. Generally, labor was rigidly sex-differentiated. The idea that native women were the slaves of Indian men stems partly from this rigid gender-differentiation of work. The labor which native women most often undertook revolved around agricultural production and farming. When whites saw women performing labor which was associated with male sex roles in European society, they condemned native culture for its harsh treatment of women.

In her youth, this Fox woman, like most Indian girls, led a life apart from males and was trained to adult responsibilities wholly by her mother. However, her account also emphasizes the compatibility of sex roles in the community, the divided responsibilities, and the equal consideration for males and females in family matters. Indians promoted attitudes toward love and marriage which differed radically from those of white settlers. Unhappy with her first husband, who was lazy and abusive, the Fox woman decided to live alone. When she agreed to remarry, her suitor said: "Well, at last it is the time you set for your consent. To-night at night do not latch your door firmly. I shall come to you." The Fox woman lived happily with her second mate, but was childless and alone after his death. She determined to marry a third and final time in order to have children.

During her second marriage, frequent miscarriages caused her to seek medical remedy. She wanted to prevent conception, despite an active sex life, and was administered a potion. She never became pregnant. When the Fox woman remarried and wished to have children, she once again sought the aid of an older woman in the tribe: "Is there perhaps a medicine whereby one might be able to have a child if one drank it?" She consumed another medicinal concoction and became pregnant, and in fact she had a number of children during her life. These highlights from an Indian memoir and testimony from other sympathetic observers (as opposed to the accounts of prisoners of war or military foes) show how some native women were able to exercise some measure of choice in their lives, in very vital and sensitive matters.

During the post-bellum years, Indians were confined to reservations, decimated by armed conflict, disease, and famine. General Philip Sheridan summed up the military policy: "The only good Indians I ever saw were dead." For those Indians who survived, the American government imposed assimilation. Indians schools separated children from their "savage" parents to "Americanize" them. At one such institution, the Carlisle Academy in Pennsylvania, founder Richard Pratt promoted his goal: "To kill the Indian and save the man." The Dawes Act of 1887 sabotaged the Indian custom of all tribe members holding land in common. Under the new law, western tribes were forced to adopt the white man's concept of private property. And with the admission of Oklahoma into the Union in 1906, the Indian Territory ceased to exist. Indians became hostages in a country that had once been theirs.

Indian-white interaction throughout the American past remains a relatively unexplored part of American social history, and knowledge of native American women remains shockingly scarce. At present our historical appreciation of native culture is so limited that we lump together as "Indians" over one hundred tribes with diverse language groups and economic and political structures, from across the continent. Anthropologists and historians have done much in the past few decades to remedy this situation. Some of the more valuable recent historical literature on native-white relations has come from socio-economic analyses of the fur trade.

Recent surveys of "mountain men" of the Far West reveal that the majority of these men were married, and many (almost 40 percent) had Indian wives. The marital records for this era and region are scanty, and tracking the course of these marriages is difficult. However, there are numerous indications that the fur trappers readily adjusted to the customs of the indigenous people. For example, few couples, when they wished to separate, instituted formal "divorce" proceedings—rather, they parted by mutual consent, as was the Indian custom. In addition, some men were polygamous, adopting the practice of their in-laws. There is indication that many men contracted these marriages to gain status or land. We can also observe that the farther north and west a trapper ventured, the more likely he was to marry an Indian woman. Traders in the Southwest often married the daughters of Spanish-speaking settlers, to obtain land as well as "to live happily ever after."

The nomadic and harsh life of western hunters was unattractive to most women migrants from the East. White women often refused to marry men whose work would take them away from home for weeks, months, even seasons; and, unlike whaling wives, who collected in seaport communities, white women in the West lacked a female network because they were scattered in isolated locations on the mountain frontier. In addition, the West had a reputation for being rowdy and dangerous well into the twentieth century. Many writers sentimentalized the trappers as seeking an almost heroic solitude, as loners and misfits who could not or would not fit into civilization. Civilization most emphatically included women. Many mountain communities (such as Hardscrabble and Greenhorn along the Arkansas River in southern Colorado) suffered a conspicuous absence of white women, much like the mining camps of the region.

When James Marshall made his legendary discovery of gold at Sutter's mill in a California stream in 1849, over one hundred thousand struck out to make it rich in the West. Only half the residents of the ramshackle towns which sprang up from Colorado to California were miners: the camps also supported a wide range of service industries. Merchants, cooks, gamblers, and prostitutes were among the more prominent contributors to the colorful life on the mining frontier. Many attributed the lawlessness and bloodshed of these communities to the "want of respectable female society." Saloons and brothels were more common than churches and schools. The steady stream of fortune hunters created a boom-and-bust settlement pattern. Although San Francisco and Denver mushroomed into large cities in a relatively short period (San Francisco's population grew from one thousand in 1848 to a quarter of a million by 1870), more often than not, as the century wore on, the population of mining towns dwindled. Within a few decades, the West was littered with ghost towns.

We have little data on the demographics of these settlements. One observer relates that women's clothing was put on display with a price for viewing—being such a rare sight for the isolated male miner. We can conclude that women were in short supply and the "respectable" variety was exotic to the region. However, some enterprising females did venture onto this rough-and-tumble terrain. Western folklore overflows with portraits of sensational female characters. When Mrs. E. J. Guerin was left widowed and penniless, she abandoned domesticity, donned male attire, and assumed a new identity as "Mountain Charley." Mountain Charley was a popular trail guide who led settlers across the plains and deserts to California. When Mrs. Guerin, aka Mountain Charley, led her first expedition in 1857, it was the beginning of a successful thirteen-year career as a wagon-train driver. Female sharpshooters and cowgirls were equally celebrated pioneers.

Many women in frontier towns arrived unmarried and were soon employed in service industries, working in dance halls, saloons, brothels, and other non-"respectable" trades. Sometimes, in fact, and almost always in the popular imagination, in the frontier town the roles of dancing girl, barmaid, and prostitute were blurred into a single symbol of female disrepute. It remains a matter of speculation whether the earliest single female inhabitants of western towns were full or part-time prostitutes—or whether they were victims of stereotype. Part of the problem lies in the fact that most of these females married and some became pillars of the community. Few wanted to be reminded of less than spotless pasts once they had "arrived" in local society.

Some of these women had a substantial impact on the towns in which they lived. We are able to reconstruct some careers from legend and legal records. One notorious businesswoman, Montana entrepreneur Mary Josephine Welch—who came to be known as Chicago Joe—was the archetypal frontier businesswoman. Born in Ireland, Welch migrated to the United States in her teens. At the age of twenty-three, the still-single Welch left her hometown of Chicago for the mining frontier. She settled in Helena, near the Last Chance Gulch strike, in 1867. Her Red Light Saloon cashed in on the lack of females; Chicago Joe imported women from Chicago, signing them up as dollar-a-dance companions for patrons of her saloon. These "hurdy-gurdy girls," as they were nicknamed after the popular stringed instrument found in most frontier bars, collected up to $50 an evening, splitting the proceeds with their employer. A newspaper account described her Valentine's Day ball: "Frail coquettes in silken tights and decolletted bodices, their symmetrical limbs and snow white arms revealed to public gaze, glided to the enchanting numbers of melodic music over the glassy floor, forming a picture pleasing to behold." But moralists were not so pleased, as the reporter also confided: "Orgies were the order of the evening."

In 1873 the Montana legislature—in a bid to clean up the "substratums of society" which Joe and others represented—declared dance halls illegal. Montana, like other western states, grew hostile to the interests of transient opportunists and wanted to attract a larger, more stable population. Although Chicago Joe and others engineered elaborate methods to exploit loopholes, many accepted the inevitable. They were victims of the changing mores of those on the Rockies frontier.

By the end of the century, most of the West had undergone a considerable face-lift. Gold miners and trappers were outnumbered by ranchers, merchants, and homesteaders. Families as well as bachelor fortune-seekers settled the West. One frontiersman complained of this transformation in his 1890 memoir: "The whole country has thrown off its wildness . . . Pleasure parties roam about over the mountains and instead of being loaded down with firearms and ammunition as we used to be when we ventured into the same localities, they carry lunch baskets and amateur photographing outfits." Most credited women with the transformation. Calling females "gentle tamers" of the West is only a half-truth, however. Recent explorations of the role of women in the settling of the frontier would lead us to believe these women were more tough than gentle after their journeys on the overland trail.

Over 350,000 men and women made the trek by land to California and Oregon (and many more settled on the way West). Most of these migrants were families seeking homesteads. The trans-Mississippi migration, unlike the gold rush, included almost as many women as men and has been the source of popular fiction and numerous stereotypes, with an iconography particular to women: Madonnas of the Prairie, Saints in Sunbonnets, and Pioneer Mothers. Hamlin Garland's recollections of the Midwest as well as Willa Cather's early novels promoted romantic images of women. Fictional portraits of a later time are almost as deceiving as the rosy pictures painted by contemporary guide literature, intended to lure families to the frontier with fantastic tales and promises of riches.

The motivations, experiences, and impact of women on the westward movement remain subject to conflicting interpretations. On the one hand, some have argued quite persuasively that women were "victimized" by the migration experience. Life on the frontier was drudgery for most women, with few opportunities to improve or advance. Others have countered that the West offered women new and important challenges, which most met with energy and resolve. By fulfilling these new roles, women achieved a higher status in frontier communities. Historians of women in the West will most likely continue to wrangle: Did the advantages of successful migration outweigh the disadvantages of transplantation for women? Did the temporary assumption of male roles allow permanent gains for women on the frontier? Did the scarcity of females in the West contribute to their gaining women's rights at an earlier stage than in the East?

It is not surprising that most women moved West with their husbands or fathers, and they had little voice in the matter. Waves of European immigrants during the 1840s led to a glutted labor market and overpopulated cities on the eastern seaboard. With the advent of trailblazing and the discovery of gold, the trans-Mississippi West no longer presented such forbidding danger to migrants. The twenty years before the Civil War witnessed only the beginning of an enormous westward exodus.

During the antebellum years, prescriptive literature, as we have seen, celebrated women's domestic and spiritual talents, which were best enshrined in the home. Home, of course, could be on a desolate frontier as well as a snug, metropolitan domicile. It was a woman's duty to nurture domesticity. The literature and tenets of this ideology fostered a "woman's culture." Historians argue that westward migration during this era had a traumatizing effect on women. Migrant women felt exiled from and deprived of the domestic comforts to which they had been born. They could never fulfill the genteel ideal in a region so disruptive as the western frontier. And the challenge broke the spirit of many women.

The women who traveled the overland trail were, for the most part, the wives of farmers. The very wealthy hardly needed to gamble to have a comfortable life, and the poor had no funds to undertake the expense of relocation. The lengthy and expensive journey West became the trademark of middle-class families seeking upward mobility. Travel overland took from five to seven months and required extensive supplies as well as transport. Outfitting a family of four for the trek West cost an estimated $600, a considerable sum in the nineteenth century. Although the sale of an ox team and wagon at the end of the journey could offset the initial outlay of cash, migrants had to have financial resources to make such an investment. Wagons traveled fifteen to twenty miles a day, along the Platte River valley on the north-central plains, across the Rockies into Wyoming, during the summer season. Besides the tedium of travel, pioneers encountered hostile Indians, adverse weather conditions, and numerous other obstacles. The resources and stamina required were formidable.

Although women were also interested in westward expansion, many were daunted by the prospect of the overland journey. Most were naturally apprehensive about the trip and the wilderness which awaited them at the end of the trail. Almost all were distraught at the thought of abandoning family and friends for the unknown, ostensibly, forever.

Elizabeth Goltra, a Kansan on her way to Oregon, confided sad thoughts to her diary in 1853:

> I am leaving my home, my early friends and associates never to see them again, exchanging the disinterested solicitude of fond friends for the cold and unsympathetic friendship of strangers. Shall we all reach the "El Dorado" of our hopes or shall one of our number be left and our graves be in the dreary wilderness, our bodies uncoffined and unknown remain there in solitude? Hard indeed that heart be that does not drop a tear as these thoughts roll across the mind.

Many if not most women undertook the trip with just such fears. However, another perspective on this transition is shown in the journal of a new bride in 1852: "We had nothing to lose and we might gain a fortune."

On wagon trains, women still had to contend with the daily chores of household labor: cooking, mending and laundering, child care, and doctoring for the family. Complaints varied, but almost all women on the trail repeatedly lamented the toil associated with feeding families while in transit. One woman reported: "From the time we get up in the morning until we are on the road, it is hurry scurry to get breakfast and put away the things that necessarily had to be pulled out last night... and at night all the cooking utensils and provisions are to be gotten about the camp fire and cooking enough to last until the next night." After the evening meal, while the men relaxed around the fires, the women were still at work cleaning up, washing, and settling in their children before they could rest.

Not only was this routine taxing, but under the circumstances, the chores were particularly difficult. Most cooks cursed the necessity of gathering dry buffalo dung to use as fuel. A popular folksong of the era mocked the syndrome: "The ladies have the hardest time, that emigrate by land, / For when they cook with buffalo wood, they often burn a hand; / And then they jaw their husbands round, get mad and spill the tea, / And wish the Lord, they'd be taken down with a turn of the di-a-ree." Although this song reflects the truth, the lyricist was of course joking about a woman welcoming diarrhea. The harassed wife and mother might wish for an illness to indulge herself in a rest, but diarrhea was a deadly disease at this time.

Another debilitating event for women in transit was giving birth on the wagon train. Conestogas were uncomfortable enough without the added burden of pregnancy. Caravans kept to tight schedules to push through mountain passes before weather made the crossing impossible. Wagons were able to pause for only a brief respite during a woman's confinement. One woman recalled her sister's ordeal: "It all seems like a jumble of jolting wagon, crying baby, dust, sagebrush, and the never ceasing pain." Quite clearly, the trail pushed these daughters of domesticity to their physical and emotional limits.

Despite the drawbacks of the journey, women acquired not only skills but greater confidence in their abilities. Historians have shown that many men expected wives to serve as full partners on the trail. This partnership often included women's assumption of roles previously restricted to males. During the course of the trip many women might learn "unladylike" habits. A young girl reported the thrill of learning to drive a wagon: "How my heart bounded a few days later when I chanced to hear father say to mother, 'Do you know that Mary Ellen is beginning to crack the whip . . .' I felt a secret joy in being able to have a power that set things going." Mary Ellen Todd went on to report she was somewhat "shamed" by her pride in masculine pursuits; she and others like her were burdened with both the hardship of new responsibilities and an outmoded set of values to measure their accomplishments.

Obstacles to domestic contentment did not disappear at the end of the trail. Some women found the frontier itself a new problem. A Nebraska pioneer woman commented: "These unbounded prairies have such an air of desolation—and the stillness is very oppressive." The terrain and population varied from region to region. The frontier was—by its very name—sparsely settled, rough country. Families lived miles apart. The typical farmhouse of a plains homesteader was a one-room cabin (usually 16 × 20 feet) built of available wood. Cracks were filled in with rags and mud. Closets were pegs on the wall, and furniture was carted by wagon or hand-hewn. These abodes were hardly dream houses.

Even more crudely constructed were the sod dwellings, carved out of the land on the midwestern plains. One woman balked at such a primitive residence upon reaching her new home, a sod dugout. She cried for months, complaining she "never knew when to stop dusting." Another plains dweller remembered that when her mother went to visit a neighbor, she disapproved of the sloppy housekeeping, commenting that the neighbor "had grass growing under her bed."

Most women homesteaders found their chores almost as demanding as on the trail. A pioneer described his mother making biscuits (only one of a dozen daily duties associated with food preparation): "Stoke the stove, get out the flour sack, stoke the stove, wash your hands, mix the dough, stoke the stove, wash your hands, cut out the biscuits with the top of a baking powder can, stoke the stove, wash your hands, put the pan of biscuits in the oven, keep on stoking the stove until the biscuits are done. Mother had to go through this tedious routine three times a day . . ." He also commented on the disagreeableness of collecting dung for fuel. The sign of seasoning on the prairie was said to be when a woman found herself too busy to wear gloves at this task.

Sod houses and wood cabins alike were plagued by leaky roofs. Most cooks had to remember to keep lids on skillets, so mud, rain, and other muck from the ceiling would not make its way into the evening meal. In addition to the grueling pace of daily household duties, women labored in the barnyard and dairy. Gardens were also women's domain. Mothers not only supplied the family with food, but butter and egg money from household enterprises often supplemented the family income. These small sums offered women some measure of economic autonomy. Despite a woman's needs, home improvements were last on the list of farm priorities. One historian concludes: "There was a tendency for the new homesteader to buy new machinery to till broad acres and build new barns to house more stock and grains, while his wife went about the drudgery of household life in the old way in a little drab dwelling overshadowed by the splendour of machine farming." Despite the fact that women made major contributions to homesteads, wives had marginal influence over financial decisions on the farm.

Many women who had been promised rewards in the golden West were severely disillusioned. One woman recounted that her father had gone through four wives in the process of homesteading on the Nebraskan frontier: he left one bride behind when he went off to stake his claim, a second wife "went mad" on the claim; a third, a mail-order bride, deserted her husband after a fortnight. Finally this hapless homesteader imported yet another bride from Europe, and she was forced to remain with him after becoming pregnant almost immediately. She was unhappy with her lot, and her daughter's memoir reveals a bitter past. One lonely woman driven mad had to walk five miles to find a tree tall enough on which to hang herself. The folklore of the West is filled with tales of women's sacrifice and stoic endurance.

As the frontier began to fill up, town life provided women with some small diversion. In addition, the proximity of neighbors allowed women a community to promote female interests: sewing circles, quilting bees, benevolent societies. With increasing numbers of families settling the wilderness, the countryside was transformed. The expanded rail network—especially with completion of the transcontinental railroad in 1867—contributed enormously to the settlement of the open spaces between the oceans. Decade by decade, after the Civil War, homesteaders expanded westward to make the continent a country.

The Civil War congress encouraged this migration with passage of the Homestead Act in 1862. Anyone who was twenty-one years old or the head of a household could stake a claim of 160 acres for a mere fee of $14. After five years of continuous residence and proof of improvement on the land, final title would be awarded to the homesteader. Because this law enabled women to make their own claims, a small but significant number of frontier females did just that. A mother of nine, Mary O'Kieffe, was plagued by her errant husband. After O'Kieffe's series of disappearances, his wife decided to pull up stakes from their farm on the Missouri River to lay claim to land in Nebraska. She and her children hitched the horses, loaded the cultivator, strapped a cage of poultry to the wagon-top, and made a fifty-one-day, 500-mile trek. The family worked on their sod house and the O'Kieffes succeeded on the frontier. When Rosie Ise's husband died in 1873 after they had resettled in Kansas, she reared eleven of their twelve children. Mrs. Ise, "remembering regretfully her own half day in school, sent nine of them through college." She was able to accomplish this thanks to the Morrill Land Grant Act, which provided for agricultural colleges throughout the nation. This provision was especially important in newly organized western states.

It is almost impossible to ascertain the marital status of most women who filed claims. Many married couples filed claims on adjoining lands in separate names to enlarge family holdings. Often brothers and sisters would file claims adjacent to their parents' land. So the evasion of prohibitions and homesteaders' complex subterfuges complicate our understanding of the demographics of the land rush. Nevertheless, there is evidence that single women were welcomed, along with others. Clarissa Griswold migrated from her Iowa home to Nebraska in 1885 after she visited a friend's ranch: "I have always been accustomed to the hills and woods near the Mississippi River and did not find the prairie attractive; but youth likes change and I found the people cordial and friendly . . . I went to Valentine, the nearest land office, and filed." Because these women were filling men's roles on the prairies, many were treated at times to the privileges such a status afforded, and almost always to the punishments associated with such responsibility. Some women were hanged for misdeeds on the range.

First and foremost, women filled male roles in almost all employment, although certainly in token numbers, except in homesteading. This accomplishment by enterprising females coincided with the early granting of citizenship rights to women in the West. In the early postbellum years, suffrage was a ploy of western legislators which had very little to do with commitment to women's rights. In the case of Wyoming, where the first women's suffrage provision was passed in 1869, the bill was a pet project of a flamboyant lawyer named Edward M. Lee. Lee hoped that women's suffrage would attract women to Wyoming, which had at the time a ratio of six men for every woman. Thus, women gained both the vote and the right to hold office at a remarkably early stage. Unfortunately, the suffrage issue failed to bring the hoped-for stampede of women. But the state provided an example for women suffrage leaders for several decades. When statesmen in the East suggested that women who wanted the vote should migrate West, female suffrage supporters were understandably outraged. They responded with renewed campaigns in their home states.

The case of Utah is even more complicated. The followers of Joseph Smith (who established the Church of the Latter-Day Saints) trekked from upstate New York to Illinois. When Smith was slain in 1844, Brigham Young led the brethren into the promised land, to settle and cultivate the great salt flats of Utah. Women were a vital part of this colonization. Smith and his successor Young supported women's activities: "If the ladies would get up societies by which they could promote the home labor of their sex, they would do what was pleasing in the sight of heaven." The Mormon migrants had devised another strategy for women "pleasing to heaven" which was not so pleasing to the majority of Americans (especially New England promoters of women's influence and domesticity): polygamy.

Taking plural wives, which came into practice during the 1830s, created a furor among the Mormons' neighbors. The doctrine was announced in 1852, but not before rumor and the practice were rife. The Mormons were reviled for their unacceptable marital patterns. It has been speculated that this doctrine developed in response to demographics: the number of older single and widowed women who converted to Mormonism. The unmarried females would have been unlikely to marry—and in turn to reproduce more Mormons—unless the church modified its policy. Although most Mormons were monogamous, instances of multiple wives—especially common among church leaders—horrified outsiders.

Many women champions of female suffrage argued that Utah's women needed the vote so they could outlaw polygamy. Ironically, when women were granted the vote in Utah in 1870, female Mormons did not abolish polygamy, or in any way oppose official church policy. The church patriarchs influenced Utah legislators to bar women from public office, although they were granted the vote. Thus, the female Mormon vote became an instrument by which church fathers were able to maintain control of the state, and prevent inroads by non-Mormon settlers. Women's suffrage was no "immigration gimmick" in Utah, where the sex ratio was balanced. Instead, it insured the election of Mormons as state officials.

After the Civil War, we discover feminist activism in other western states. Abigail Scott Duniway was a pioneering champion of women's rights. She arrived in the Oregon territory in 1852 at the age of seventeen. Forced to support her family of six children when her husband was disabled by an accident, Duniway was radicalized to the importance of women's rights in the social, political, and economic realms. Her efforts in Oregon were not as successful as campaigns in other states. Although the Oregon Equal Suffrage Association was founded (by Duniway) in 1873, the state legislature repeatedly failed to pass a women's suffrage bill; the measure was not adopted until 1912. Meanwhile, Duniway was instrumental in securing suffrage measures in Washington territory in 1883 and in Idaho in 1896. She was frequently at odds with national suffrage leadership, especially over the connection of suffrage with temperance. Duniway rightly argued that liquor interests—with considerable power and influence in western state capitals—would effectively block the vote for women if temperance and suffrage were linked. But Duniway and her movement show that the West nurtured a viable feminist campaign which—along with expedient nonfeminist motives—contributed to gaining the vote for women in western states.

Transformations of the western frontier caused by homesteaders matched changes wrought in eastern cities by waves of immigrants. Approximately five million immigrants poured into the country between 1815 and 1865: two million Irish, one and one half million Germans, a half million Scandinavians, and another million of other nationalities. Almost 80 percent of the immigrants settled in the Northeast in heavily industrializing states. A number of Germans struck out for the West, hoping to parlay their considerable farming abilities into building a New Germany. Colonies of German immigrants settled Missouri in the 1830s, Texas in the 1840s, and Wisconsin in the 1850s, where German influence can be found even today in such disparate urban centers as San Antonio, St. Louis, and Milwaukee. Generally, the land-hungry Scandinavians also ventured directly west in large numbers, with many Swedes migrating to the upper Midwest to establish farms. Many immigrants served as the labor force on canals and railroads, working their way inland from the eastern seaboard. A large proportion of workers who migrated were young unmarried men who left families behind in eastern cities.

In the families left behind, young unmarried women worked to bring income into the household. Surveys of immigrant women indicate that wage earning was common among young, single females. Most retired from work outside the home when they married. Almost 60 percent of teenage Irish women joined the labor force. To a lesser extent, German women and other foreign females followed similar employment patterns. Despite strict patriarchal dictates in certain ethnic groups, men allowed women to work outside the home as a temporary measure to boost household income. In Italian families, many daughters brought home their pay envelopes unopened, turning over their entire earnings to support the family. In some Italian families, daughters rather than sons were sent out to work, while male offspring furthered their education. In Jewish families, it was even common for wives to work, so that their husbands could continue "holding the book," as study of the Torah was so revered. No higher status could be achieved by men than that of rabbi, and all family members contributed to this effort. Immigrant women served family interests and patriarchal priorities before seeking personal fulfillment by wage earning.

Following the Civil War, economic conditions in the United States continued to attract millions of Europeans. Between 1880 and 1930, when immigration restrictions were imposed, over twenty-seven million immigrants landed in America—mainly from southern and eastern Europe. The peak year for this influx in the nineteenth century was 1882, when almost eight hundred thousand entered the country.

Poverty and political persecution brought many immigrants. The drastic worsening of conditions in Italy compelled three million Italians to migrate to the United States between 1880 and 1910. Pogroms in the 1880s and 1890s forced Eastern European Jews out of the Old World. Of the two million Jews who fled (almost three-quarters from Russia), over 90 percent settled in America. Poles, Czechs, Slovaks, and other Baltic peoples migrated to America in the millions as well. Smaller numbers of Greeks, Portuguese, Armenians, Syrians, and others also relocated in America at the turn of the century.

Although folklore paints the average immigrant to America as "peasant," most immigrants left from towns and villages, or even more likely cities. Some of the most successful brought their skills to the New World: mechanics, jewelers, clockmakers, butchers, bakers, and other artisans. For example, almost 70 percent of the adult Jewish male immigrants were classified as skilled workers. The first members of an immigrant family to make the transatlantic journey were almost always males migrating alone. After a brief time, many were able to save to buy passage for the rest of the family. It is estimated that as many as 70 percent of the immigrants in the late nineteenth and early twentieth century had prepaid tickets bought by relatives and friends already in the United States.

Steamship lines fought to transport these migrants; by the 1880s nearly fifty companies were vying for the trade. Travel in steerage was both filthy and crowded. A ship's surgeon deplored the conditions on shipboard: immigrants traveled with animals, fought for food, and, he recalled, "the torments of hell might in some degree resemble [their] suffering." The transatlantic passage gradually improved. The time was cut from fourteen days during the 1860s to fewer than six days by the end of the century. Despite the hardship of the journey, most immigrants welcomed the chance to live in America. Whereas a farmhand in Sweden could earn a little over $30 a year (plus room and board) in the 1870s, in America the same worker could earn an annual salary of $200. If he chose to work in the Pennsylvania mines, he might make as much as $40 a month. Railroad workers were paid $1–$2 per day. A male immigrant could easily earn the passage money ($12 to $15 from England, and $30 out of Copenhagen) necessary to bring his family to America. The prospects seemed unparalleled.

Of course, tenement life in the cities, as well as brutal conditions in the Pennsylvania coal fields or on an Illinois construction gang, proved disappointing to the immigrants who had hoped to find American streets "paved with gold." Nevertheless, the possibilities for upward mobility were high. Immigrant households had collective strategies to further the family interests. Most often, the wishes of women were sacrificed to male priorities. Recent studies of immigrant women indicate that some preferred Americanization. Adoption of the dominant culture would allow for women to be educated, to remain within the household, and even to improve their status within the family. Research on wife beating shows that many immigrant wives looked to the laws and customs of their new country for protection. The process of assimilation and its impact on both sexes within an ethnic family is an important unwritten chapter of late-nineteenth-century history.

By 1900, although 55 percent of the total white female population were native-born, this group constituted only 35 percent of wage-earning women in America. Fifty percent of the working women in the United States were foreign-born. Immigrant women had a disproportionate role in the female work force, and their slow and steady monopolization of certain trades was accelerated by the Civil War. Whereas in 1850 only 37 percent of the female spinners and 18 percent of the women weavers in the cotton mills were Irish, by 1865 their proportion grew to 76 percent and 66 percent, respectively. In Cohoes, New York, four of five women between the ages of fifteen and nineteen worked in the cotton mills. Most of these were immigrants or the daughters of immigrants.

This shift in the cotton industry created social conflict. An observer in Chicopee, Massachusetts, commented in 1852:

> Foreign girls have been employed in such numbers that what American girls are employed they experience considerable difficulty in finding society among their workmates congenial to their tastes and feelings.

There was a practical aspect to this conflict: the influx of immigrants in the mills coincided with a decrease in wages, a decline in the value of their labor. Women were used to earning less than men. Females traditionally took home from two-thirds to one half the pay of men. But physical conditions in the workplace deteriorated as well.

Northern women moved into the cities during the Civil War after the cotton mills declined for lack of raw material. Many former millworkers began to work in the needle trades. Seamstressing was revolutionized during the war. Large-scale garment manufacture boomed, including the introduction of clothing sizes. The number of sewing machines in operation doubled during the war. Sewing a man's shirt, which had taken up to fourteen hours by hand, required only an hour's labor on a machine.

After the war, northern mills multiplied and textile factories expanded into the South. When Irish immigrants moved out of the New England textile towns, they were soon replaced by French Canadians. Cotton met a ready market with the rapidly expanding garment industry. Conditions for seamstresses steadily worsened during the century, and sweatshops sprang up in most urban centers.

The clothing industry fostered low wages, unsanitary conditions, and unhealthy workers. Middlemen contractors provided workrooms in tenement flats. A New York State factory inspector commented: "It is not unusual when the weather permits to see the balconies of fire escapes occupied by from two to four busy workmen. The halls and roofs are also utilized for workshop purposes very frequently." These spaces were perhaps preferable to the stifling, crowded, dimly lit factories. Workers labored fifteen to sixteen hours a day, and during the busy season some worked even longer—sleeping on bundles in the workroom to save rent as well as time. The very best men in the shop earned only $10 per week, while hardworking women were paid $3–$6 for equal hours.

Many foreign women, hampered by a lack of marketable skills and the language barrier, found few alternatives to the sweatshop. Most families were unable to support a girl until she could gain an education that would permit escape from this occupational ghetto. Although teaching was the most desirable profession to which a Jewish woman aspired, few achieved that goal. The labor force in the needle trades was predominantly women. Sixty-five percent of the seamstresses in New York City were young, unmarried, and Jewish in 1900. Pay was so poor that many were forced to supplement their incomes with part-time prostitution. The "genteel trades," staffed by native-born whites and closed to the daughters of foreigners, were equally poor-paying (a salesgirl might earn $5 a week, and librarians $3). But in addition to conferring a higher status, these occupations were less physically debilitating and less dangerous.

Many immigrant women who involved themselves in labor agitation saw their roles as a natural outgrowth of the oppressive conditions fostered by American industry. Between 1873 and 1877 three million workers were jobless. The cities witnessed bread riots, and deserted infants were found on doorsteps and starving children in the streets. Depressions, continued indifference to worker safety, and other abuses contributed to labor militancy. Rose Schneiderman, a leading labor organizer at the turn of the century, described her awakening to women's exploitation:

> The hours were from 8 AM to 6 PM, and we made all sorts of linings... It was piece work, and we received from 3 to 10 cents a dozen, according to the different grades. By working hard we could make an average of about $5 a week. We would have made more but we had to provide our own machines which cost us $45... We paid $5 down and $1 a month after that... when the factory burned down, destroying all our machines—150 of them, this was very hard on the girls who had paid for their machines. It was not so bad for me, as I had only paid a little of what I owed. The bosses got $500,000 insurance, so I heard, but they never gave the girls a cent to help them bear their losses... After I had been working as a cap maker for three years it began to dawn on me that we girls needed an organization.

The organization of workers was not new. One of the earliest unions was in Troy, New York. In 1864 the collar laundresses (who specialized in detachable collars and cuffs for men's shirts) organized to improve conditions. They earned $2–$3 per week for twelve- to fourteen-hour days. They labored in rooms filled with furnaces and tubs of hot water, in temperatures that often reached one hundred degrees. Their work was back-breaking and prolonged: washing, blueing, dying, rinsing. The Troy laundresses were supported in their efforts to form a union by the men of the town, many of whom were puddlers and boilers in the iron industry, and union members themselves. The Troy Collar Union grew to four hundred members during its peak; in 1866 it donated $500 for striking bricklayers in New York City and $1,000 for iron molders on strike in Troy. When the women staged a similar action of their own in 1869, union men repaid their support with $500 a week and promised "to continue the same for weeks to come rather than see such a brave set of wenches crushed under the iron heel of these laundry nabobs." But paper collars and company resistance broke the union of collar laundresses.

Although women were encouraged to form a union, male labor leaders were split on the desirability of women working. Some feared that the inclusion of women in industry would lower the men's pay. In 1856 a proposal of the Boston Typographical Union to "discountenance any member working in an office that employs female compositors" had been defeated. But women had a long tradition of participation in the printing industry. When this group admitted women in 1868, they were the second male union to do so, as the National Union of Cigar Makers had opened itself to blacks and women in 1867.

By 1880 immigrant workers were associated with labor agitation, and eventually "un-Americanism." It is ironic that this phrase was coined and championed by Edwin L. Godkin, editor of *The Nation* and himself an Anglo-Irish immigrant. One of the most famous victims of this "un-Americanist" hysteria was an immigrant activist, Emma Goldman. She was not only a voice for labor but a feminist-anarchist and an outstanding revolutionary. Goldman emigrated from Russia at the age of seventeen. Unhappy with her economic and intellectual impoverishment as a seamstress in Rochester, New York, she relocated in New York City. She became involved with Alexander Berkman; the lover-comrades plotted to assassinate industrial magnate Henry Clay Frick in July 1892. Goldman remained free, while Berkman was sentenced to twenty-two years in prison, and she continued the struggle without him. She was jailed three times—charged once with inciting a riot, once with disseminating birth-control literature, and once with obstructing the draft—during her career as an orator, midwife, editor (*Mother Earth*), and advocate of feminism and revolution. In 1919 she was deported during the infamous "Red Scare," but her work had tremendous impact on the American Left.

The 1880s and 1890s were years of virulent xenophobia that witnessed a rebirth of the nativist movement of the 1840s and 1850s. During the first large antebellum migration of Europeans, "native whites" had organized political parties which championed their cause at the expense of the rights of immigrants: the Know-Nothing Party. A similar, mainly anti-Catholic movement sprang up in the last decades of the century. In 1887 the American Protective Association was founded (with a membership which reached 2.5 million) to support public schools, immigration restriction, and stricter naturalization laws.

Anti-Semitism increased as well in post-Civil War America. Ironically, the first victims of this vicious prejudice were those who were most assimilated. During the 1870s clubs and resorts enforced a new "Gentiles only" policy. The German Jews who had migrated long before the Civil War, not the masses of Soviet Jewry who poured in following pogroms, were the first casualties. But social slights were only the beginning of the discrimination: housing and employment prohibitions followed. Also, in 1891, government officials at Ellis Island and other detention centers enforced antipauper laws. Immigrants had to find sponsors or demonstrate that they had enough money to support themselves in the United States. This measure was introduced at a time when millions of Jews were being driven out of Eastern Europe, their valuables confiscated and their lives threatened.

Some of the most virulent hostility and the toughest restrictions were directed not at Catholics or Jews who flooded into eastern cities but at an even more exploited immigrant minority: the Chinese in the western states. Thousands of unmarried men were imported from China to work on the railroad during the Civil War. After completion of the Central Pacific line, many stayed to work as miners, farm laborers, and cannery workers. Lower-class whites in the West were violently anti-Chinese because this "yellow labor" drove down wages. Yet company owners were happy to exploit the cheap foreign labor.

Most of the Chinese women brought into this country between 1840 and 1880 were imported as prostitutes. The China trade in women was a profitable business. Most women did not migrate on their own, or even of their own free will. Often families sold daughters into servitude, and female offspring honored parental will. The economics of prostitution are sordid and exploitative. Some families survived in China on the money their daughters sent home. Further, this practice was condoned by many American capitalists who neither paid Chinese workers enough to maintain families nor wanted to encourage permanent settlement. By the 1850s Chinese organizations regularly supplied West

Coast brothels with women. These Chinese prostitutes catered mainly to Chinese men, although some wealthy whites "bought" Oriental concubines. The Hip-Yee Tong, a Chinese secret society, imported six thousand women (mostly young girls) from 1852 to 1873. Although California prohibited the importation of "lewd or debauched" women, during the 1870s the American consul in Hong Kong received kickbacks and blithely granted importers clearance, netting $10 for every woman shipped to the United States.

The lives of these women were miserable. The young, imported Chinese prostitute aged fast, and many died before escaping the trade. Some were falsely promised they would be released from their contract at the end of a fixed term. Many were forcibly addicted to opium. This exploitation so aroused public opinion that California legislators held hearings in 1876 to investigate prostitution. A minister from San Francisco provided testimony:

> The women, as a general thing, are held as slaves. They are bought or stolen in China and brought here. They have a sort of agreement to cover up the slavery business, but it is all a sham... after the term of prostitution service is up, the owners so manage as to have the women in debt more than ever, so that their slavery becomes life-long. There is no release from it... Sometimes women take opium to kill themselves. They do not know they have any rights, but think they must keep their contracts and believe themselves under obligations to serve in prostitution... They have come to the asylum all bruises. They are beaten and punished cruelly if they fail to make any money. When they become worn out and unable to make any more money, they are turned out to die.

This trade prevented assimilation and miscegenation, but even so, many Californians were shamed and horrified. In addition, mounting labor tensions created waves of anti-Chinese feelings in the West. An 1871 disturbance, the Sandlot Riot in Los Angeles, fueled prejudice against these immigrants.

Racism, fears of "the yellow peril," and hard times nurtured western xenophobia. This resulted in America's first immigration restriction: in 1882 the United States passed a Chinese Exclusion Act which effectively banned importations as well as migration. Although Chinese brothel owners continued to prosper (and many took to kidnapping within California), this measure virtually eliminated the importation of females from China. Many whites in the West hoped as well that this restriction would send many Chinese men back to the Orient, since they could no longer import "picture brides" from their homeland. Although many Chinese did return to China, many more remained. Anti-Chinese sentiment in the West exploded in 1885 with three major riots in Tacoma, Seattle, and Wyoming. Although xenophobic hysteria would reach new heights with deportations during the 1920s, the anti-Chinese campaign of the 1880s displayed some of the most virulent anti-immigrant sentiment in nineteenth-century America.

While Americans were divided or undecided on the question of quotas for immigrants, most agreed that the material conditions for immigrants in America were deplorable. Millions of foreigners were crowded into city ghettos with few social services for the poor. Most urban apartment dwellings had no running water or toilets. Fleas, bedbugs, and lice plagued immigrants in their homes. Pneumonia and tuberculosis were common. Women aged rapidly with repeated pregnancies. Diet deficiencies contributed to a staggering rate of infant mortality. Many upper- and middle-class whites were content to dismiss this misery as "racial inferiority" or an indifference to cleanliness and order. Others argued that, despite their origins, the problems of the city would not go away. Some reckoned these social ills would only increase in the years to come.

Immigrant women's lives often were consumed by the struggle to survive and assimilate. America afforded them numerous opportunities, but the challenges were staggering. Women from rigidly hierarchical, patriarchal cultures found American social mores a rude shock. They saw women in positions of relative independence and authority, with social and geographical mobility unparalleled in their own countries. Indeed, the very social workers whose careers were dedicated to assisting immigrant families often offended and scandalized the women whom they were trying to help. Women's new role after leaving the Old World often became a bone of contention within the immigrant family, a barometer of cross-cultural conflict. With the challenges of survival and assimilation facing them, few immigrant women had the time or energy to reflect on the improvements middle-class reformers attempted to institute.

During mid-century a flood of women settled the West, trying to impose order on the hostile frontiers of the trans-Mississippi plains. An equally hardy group of women settled in the New World, braving much more than a trans-oceanic passage in seeking a place in America. Both groups of migrants were, each in its own way, pioneers. In the West and in the cities, natives, migrants, and immigrants contributed to women's progress in the nineteenth century.

7

Pathbreaking and Backlash

FOLLOWING the Civil War, in an era of social realignment and accelerated economic development, education became perhaps the paramount factor in improving women's status, especially for middle-class females. The lack of marriageable men after the war forced many young women to pursue careers who would otherwise have chosen domesticity. Temporary changes often had permanent impact: some young women preferred the independence of wage earning to marriage. This generation of determined and independent women pioneered in medicine, the law, and academe.

Most of these career women were nurtured by the feminist crusade. Indeed, feminism primarily appealed to educated and middle-class women, rather than black and working-class women. A cornerstone of the movement was a demand for higher learning. Feminists and their sympathizers crusaded for the establishment of separate colleges and the admission of women to elite academic institutions.

The increasing number of educated women created a steady flow of women teachers for grammar schools and shaped role models for young women coming of age in the 1870s. School attendance continued to rise throughout the nineteenth century. New England maintained the highest rates—although the influx of immigrants accounted for a slight decline in the percentages during the two decades before the Civil War. In addition, the Northeast was a pioneering region in educational innovation and reform. In 1839 Massachusetts became the first state to establish a "normal school," or teachers' college, Lexington Academy. Other states, primarily in the North, followed Massachusetts's lead before the war; then reform spread southward after the war. The professionalization of teaching through training schools eased women into a male-dominated profession. When Catharine Beecher established the Board of National Popular Education in 1840 to certify women teachers before sending them westward, she was legitimating as well as encouraging women's entry into the field.

Many young women who pursued teaching careers were adventurous spirits, not the demure stereotypes associated with the "schoolmarm." Ellen P. Lee left her home in Princeton, Massachusetts, to take over a school in Hamilton County, Indiana, in 1852. She wrote home: "When I came here there was a prejudice against female teachers; they had always employed men, and had never had a school six weeks without trouble, and they thought of course if a man could not govern their boys, a woman could not; but I was allowed to take my own course, and I gave them only one rule, that was—Do right." Ellen Lee was a success in her Indiana community, but she did confess: "I sometimes sigh and long for Christian sympathy." Most unmarried women schoolteachers were "boarded round" with parents during the antebellum years. But by the latter part of the century, women could live alone or in spinster pairs as long as they maintained a devotion to the schoolmistress ethic of self-sacrifice, the legacy of self-denial that was the teacher's own. As the heroine of an 1856 fictional story confessed, she possessed "that readiness with which a true woman assumes burdens that a stalwart man would find intolerable."

There were drawbacks to a teaching career, especially the lack of social esteem and political influence within the community. But by the turn of the century the many thousands of women who pursued careers as schoolteachers were able to establish important roles for themselves as "molders of the young." In addition, the change in the social climate allowed many to take pride in their status rather than to be pitied as unmarried career women. In an 1892 fictional portrait of a schoolteacher, the heroine "had never been so happy in her life as she was the day on which she stepped upon the platform at school and assumed the responsibilities of 'schoolmarm.' [She] loved to teach and she loved also to rule... [She] revelled in her independence; and if she thought of matrimony in connection with herself, it was as a state of bondage to be avoided at any cost."

The republican mothers and domestic feminists who held that women's noblest duty was to educate the young championed the role of mothers, not women teachers. But many young, single women used this ideology to pioneer women's entrance into the teaching profession. Scholars estimate that one of every five women in Massachusetts taught school at least once in her life by the middle of the century. Teaching careers afforded women a taste of independence before they married and settled into domestic and dependent routines. Although this interim was not always a pleasant one (loneliness, transplantation, and exhaustion were frequent complaints), many women were happy to escape the monotony and drudgery of farm labor. Patience and endurance, preceptors came to believe, qualified women to serve in the classroom (as well as in the household and the mills).

Most women prized their careers, although, in reality, society afforded them few other opportunities for employment or advancement. Wages for women teachers were always less than the salaries paid to men: women earned, at best, only 60 percent of what their male counterparts were paid. And in fact, "feminization" caused a decline in the status and pay of teachers. Women dominated grammar-school teaching by mid-century, but females were slow to be hired in secondary schools and institutions of higher learning, and they were excluded from supervisory posts.

Education had a special meaning for women, despite these economic handicaps. It was their privilege as citizens in the new republic. For a number of ambitious women, education was a means to an end, the first step up the ladder. By the middle of the century, education was a largely female domain, and a feminine mission.

Following the Civil War, women educators faced three major challenges. Immediately after the war, the South required a special campaign to combat widespread illiteracy. Even white literacy was considerably lower in the South than in the North. Women argued that education was an important tool in the effort to make the nation whole again, to improve conditions in the backward states of the former Confederacy. Later, an even greater challenge were the waves of immigrants who poured into America. And finally, women confronted the inadequacy of their own education in light of their increasing commitments to educational service and with an eye toward enlarging their sphere of influence. Although the three educational crusades were independent, they created a cadre of women educators who fostered a new generation of educational pioneers and advocates of feminism.

Northern teachers who moved South during and after the Civil War had a tremendous impact on the freed people and the patterns of change in the rural South. These women, both black and white, journeyed to a new and hostile environment and became true heroines. Recruited in northern rural and urban communities, they and their male colleagues were the forerunners of the modern civil-rights movement. This was the first large migration South by northern liberals to support the aspirations of blacks for equality in education and economic opportunity. Many of these "missionaries"—ambassadors of northern culture—failed in their paternalistic hopes to cultivate "Black Brahmins": ebony replicas of the New England middle class. However, their struggles improved the status of freed people in the South.

Some Yankee teachers, such as Mary Ames and Emily Bliss of Boston, ventured South despite their family's disapproval. These young women settled in South Carolina, spending almost two years on Edisto Island, where they tutored almost one hundred and fifty students, both adults and children. The majority of the four thousand women who set up schools for the Freedmen's Bureau had returned North by the 1870s. However, some remained to spend a lifetime dedicated to the cause of black education. Laura Towne, a Philadelphia abolitionist, established the Penn School in September 1862 on St. Helena, an island off the coast of South Carolina. Many others who were part of this Port Royal Experiment (the attempt to transform southern society through black education and free labor) abandoned hope, especially with the withdrawal of federal troops in 1877. Yet Towne and her lifelong companion, Ellen Murray, continued their efforts throughout the century. Towne attached a normal school (a training institute for other teachers) to the original Penn School. She devoted herself to public health, temperance, and the Penn School programs for nearly forty years, until her death in 1901. The school attracted northern philanthropy and provided an important network of support for black education. Laura Towne was but one of a score of women reformers who had a permanent impact on southern education.

Dozens of women returned North to spread the gospel of the Reconstruction campaign. Many published sentimental memoirs of their years in the South. Sheltered women discovered that prejudice was almost as great a problem as ignorance: their problems with whites were quite as considerable as the challenge presented by freedmen and women.

Some of these women carried out their work in a climate of bitter opposition and threatened by violence; as one woman reported in 1865: "The sight of a 'nigger schoolhouse' was more than the chivalry could bear. It had not been occupied many weeks in quietness, before three ruffians, calling themselves 'Confederate soldiers,' but really guerillas, appeared in the night time, set the house on fire, set the schoolhouse on fire, rudely summoned Mrs. Croome from her house adjoining it, and bade her hasten away before that also should be given to the flames..." But Mrs. Croome, having lost her husband to violence during the war, held her ground. The school was rebuilt, and blacks armed themselves to guard their school and their teacher.

Many of the schoolteachers who stayed on in the South, who witnessed firsthand the virulence of racism, became involved in political activism. This was a result of their careers as educators. Women agitated for an increase of state funding for black schools in the South, and this led women to press for black land claims, black suffrage, and other radical issues. Women educators found themselves drawn into the concerns of southern blacks, not just in the schoolroom, but in society at large. Thus, educators became educated as well.

This process had its painful and frustrating aspects—for both parties. Some white teachers were frustrated by black indifference to the Puritan ethics they were attempting to impart. Even black northern women commented that ex-slaves stubbornly refused to adapt to new mores foreign to rural, southern life.

This handful of schoolteachers did not revolutionize black education in the South, despite their enormous sacrifice and important contributions. The 1870 census revealed that although whites had an illiteracy rate of only 12 percent (with a disproportionately higher number of white illiterates in the South), black illiteracy was nearly 80 percent. Schools for freed people made some headway during Reconstruction, but progress slackened with the end of federal rule in 1877. Despite the loss of momentum, educators provided an important beginning for the first free generation of black children, eager for knowledge. Black southerners cherished this legacy of learning as they struggled in the last quarter of the century to build their own schools. The partnership between southern blacks and northern philanthropy blossomed as a result of the strong bonds forged by these women of "the tenth crusade."

By the 1870s many northern women launched campaigns in their own back yards rather than move South to find a cause. Indeed, the thousands of immigrants filling city tenements alarmed middle-class matrons concerned about deteriorating urban conditions. These families were poor, undereducated, underfed, and overworked. Disease and despair abounded in the city ghettoes where immigrants were forced to live in burgeoning slums. Women tackled the larger problems which created these deplorable circumstances, and many hoped to better conditions for the children of these laboring poor through "Americanization" within public school systems.

Educators and statesmen alike saluted this noble purpose. The law required school attendance, and women reformers were active in campaigns against exploitation of child labor. Public schools were praised as "melting pots" where immigrant urchins might be disciplined and tutored, homogenized into respectable American citizens. The assimilation of these "foreign hordes" was a paramount goal of American education. Julia Richman, herself an immigrant, had risen to the post of school administrator by 1900. She reminded an audience of teachers gathered for a National Education Association meeting: "Between the alien of today and the citizen of tomorrow stands the school, and upon the influence exerted by the school depends the kind of citizen the immigrant will become."

This was no small task for underpaid teachers in overflowing urban classrooms. In New York City, for example, schools absorbed fifty thousand new students every year in the last decade of the century. Almost two-thirds of the students could not speak English, and as many as thirty different languages might be spoken in the homes of pupils in a single classroom. The challenge was formidable. Many of the teachers were immigrants themselves or the daughters of immigrants. Most were not trained in normal schools, and had a level of education not much above their pupils. At the end of the century, school posts were prizes handed out to the daughters of loyal political bosses, favors for ward heelers in the urban jungle. Understaffed and overburdened, schools had a difficult time fulfilling their goals. Many teachers were content to instill obedience and respect for authority, tenets which they were themselves forced to learn within the bureaucracy.

In the generation following the Civil War, daughters of the native-born dominated schoolteaching. By the turn of the century, immigrant women were making great strides in the teaching profession. When ethnic women began to teach, Anglo-Saxon Protestant women moved into supervisory positions, although their number was negligible until well into the twentieth century. However, pioneers earned these administrative posts as early as 1872. The first woman superintendent of schools was elected in Kansas in that year: five were elected in Massachusetts in 1874, and ten in Iowa in 1876. Then, after 1880, the number of female supervisors declined until the turn of the century.

This reversal had several origins. Educators wanted a malleable, compliant work force: young, single women fit this image. The exploitive pay scale for women teachers (much like the low wages for women in the textile mills) met with little challenge as long as teachers had only a temporary commitment to the profession. This docility was insured further by the relative lack of economic alternatives for women. Yet once females could find employment in other sectors, schoolmistresses began to chafe at the long hours and depressed wages to which they were subjected. When women attempted to keep their jobs and acquire husbands, educational administrators balked.

The move against women's progress in education took a new direction in the 1880s when schools began to dismiss women teachers who married. This policy was instituted in Washington, D.C., and moved westward. An indignant editorial writer in Cincinnati condemned those who proclaimed: "Husbands are an ornament not to be allowed to women who work." A married schoolteacher signaled a permanent commitment to the profession, and many argued the impropriety of the policy. Radical departure from traditional views of womanhood met with stern disapproval. Although working-class and black married women might earn wages at back-breaking labor, ladies were forbidden to work for pay if they also served as homemakers. Married women were expected to bear children. The specter of a pregnant schoolteacher was more than Victorian America could accept. Within the sexual ideology of the culture, childbearing and a career simply did not mix.

But married schoolteachers were not the only women who were criticized. Females were welcomed into the profession during the antebellum years, when male and female teachers were equal in number. But by the 1880s two-thirds of the public-school teachers were women. By 1892 this proportion rose to five-sixths. Women's increasing dominance of the profession created waves of resentment. Whereas statesmen during the antebellum era argued how well fitted women were to the educational profession, this changed when females overwhelmingly outnumbered their male colleagues (even if men continued to dominate educational administration). Many male educators railed, warning that women were weak role models for the boys they were teaching. By the turn of the century a full-scale campaign was underway against the predominance of women schoolteachers.

Nonetheless, women poured into normal schools and carved out careers for themselves. In addition, many women who faced the choice of forsaking a teaching position in favor of a husband abandoned the prospect of marriage. Thus, a dedicated generation of women educators—more numerous and more committed than ever before—resisted the constraints culture attempted to impose. They struggled to make an independent, autonomous contribution to society.

Women in late-nineteenth-century America had made great progress, yet they faced strong resistance to the expansion of opportunities in education. When educated women began to push for improved institutions and access to graduate study, when they insisted on practical application of their education, society responded with alarm and denunciation. What was the genesis of this revolution? How did this demanding generation of educated women blossom in post-bellum America?

By 1879 nearly half the colleges in the United States were co-educational. Oberlin pioneered in 1833, followed by Antioch (1852), the University of Iowa (1856), and Swarthmore (1864). There were many more in the West, where women seemed better able to find equal opportunities. In 1890 both the University of Chicago and Stanford were founded, open to both sexes. Although the South boasted many "semi-colleges" for women, it lagged behind New England, the Middle Atlantic, and the Midwest. The University of Mississippi admitted women in 1882, the first southern state institution to do so.

The new land-grant colleges (funded through the Morrill Act of 1862) were co-educational and provided students of both sexes with unprecedented educational opportunity. Despite the equal-admissions policy, women were often at a disadvantage. These state universities apparently maintained "gender differentiated" curricula. For example, in 1865 at the University of Wisconsin, forty-one male students were enrolled in traditional college courses, with no women registered in them. At the same time, sixty-six women were students of the "normal school," with no men enrolled in this program.

These public institutions fostered a dual system of education that resulted in less than satisfactory conditions for women. Clara Colby, one of the first women to challenge the restrictions at the University of Wisconsin, requested that she be admitted into previously all-male courses in Latin and philosophy. She was able to enroll, despite the objections of the college president. In 1869 she was elected to Phi Beta Kappa and was class valedictorian. Even with the example of Clara Colby, the college discouraged women from pursuit of equal educations. And even after 1872, when the University of Wisconsin women were at long last granted full access to the college curriculum, female students were barred from registering in a course if men had already filled it. The university required men and women to use the library on different days. These regulations and restrictions made women second-class citizens, even in public institutions.

Private institutions were also slow to integrate. Assaults on elite male colleges created strong resentment in post-bellum America. The initial male university to tackle the problem of women's education was the nation's first college: Harvard. In 1874 Radcliffe was organized as an annex to Harvard. Despite its separate identity, Radcliffe women were instructed by Harvard faculty. Columbia University welcomed a similar arrangement with the founding of Barnard in 1889. Although Barnard maintained its own faculty, women shared the library and other facilities with the parent university. In 1887 Sophie Newcomb became the female branch of Tulane University, and in 1891 Pembroke became the women's college of Brown University.

Women's entrance into these elite colleges was contested. In 1871, when women challenged female exclusion at Amherst, a student claimed in the school paper: "Amherst College was never intended for the education of females . . . Widely different educational means and methods ought to be employed in fitting men and women for totally different spheres of duty and usefulness." A student in favor of women's admission replied: "For the sake of the thoughtless many who constantly need restraint, we ask for the presence of women in our midst. We believe it is not only possible but certain that her presence would effect a complete reformation in many of those immoralities which now disgrace our college."

Male supporters of the integration of women into all-male colleges championed the cause with financial as well as moral support. In 1872 James Freeman Clarke advocated co-education at Harvard, which would "increase the means of the University and its power of usefulness." The following year, in a paper given before the Social Sciences Convention, T. W. Higginson stated an equally compelling case:

> Harvard College belongs to the public. Its wealth comes from the State of Massachusetts; it does not come from individuals. Even that share of it that comes from individuals was given so long ago—half a dozen generations have intervened—that we have the right to consider it public property... If Harvard College wants to draw back within the line of certain theories and her own conceptions, let her disgorge the contributions of the State...

The transformation into a co-educational institution was not smooth. In fact, women's affiliation with all-male institutions was achieved in the midst of one of the most hotly debated issues of late-nineteenth-century feminism: the intellectual capacity of women. Academics and scientists brought to bear sociological, biological, and neurological arguments to demonstrate the physiological inferiority of women. The physical evidence, they suggested, indicated the mental inferiority of women as well. A leading authority in 1873, Alexander Bain, reported that the average European brain weighed 49 grams whereas the average female brain weighed only 44 grams. This sort of "proof" gave credence to the popular claim that women were intellectually incapable of competing with men. Further, many educators were concerned that a woman would damage her health with rigorous pursuit of a baccalaureate degree.

Massachusetts reformer Edward Clarke was one of the leading proponents of the theory that a woman's capacity to contribute to society was limited by her unique physiognomy. As women were the physical instruments for reproduction, they must necessarily temper their behavior to fulfill their biological destiny, motherhood. In his controversial and best-selling *Sex in Education* (1873), Clarke drew on the work of Darwin and Spencer to bolster his claims. He argued a biological basis for antifeminism: "The problem of woman's sphere, to use the modern phrase, is not to be solved by applying to it abstract principles of right and wrong. Its solution must be obtained from physiology, not from ethics or metaphysics..." His learning led him to warn of the dangers of excessive education for young women. He argued that "identical education of the two sexes is a crime before God and humanity that physiology protests against and that experience weeps over." Clarke used case studies of college women (from Vassar) to demonstrate that "dysmenorrhea, chronic and acute ovaritis, prolapsus uteri, hysteria, neuralgia and the like" resulted from college training for women.

Clarke firmly believed that women's reproductive systems would be destroyed through mental overexertion. Interestingly, many of these educational experts compiled statistics comparing the death rate of male and female college graduates. Even an unsophisticated quantifier might wonder why these experts did not measure the death rates of females who earned degrees and those who did not attend college. They might have discovered what President Andrew White of Cornell asserted in his report of 1872 in favor of women attending the university (women were admitted that year): "The health of the young woman is quite as good in college as out of it."

The specter of race suicide would haunt feminists for years. A bellicose educator proclaimed in 1915: "The farmer that uses his land for golf-links and deer preserves instead of for crops has but one agricultural fate; the civilization that uses its women for stenographers, clerks and school-teachers instead of mothers has but one racial fate." Theodore Roosevelt took up the battle cry during his Presidency, and the Supreme Court in its decision *Muller v. Oregon* (1908) ruled in favor of protective legislation for women, citing medical evidence: since society reproduced itself by means of females, women's bodies must be protected by the state.

During this prolonged ideological battle, women not only were trying to break down barriers by integrating men's colleges; women established their own separate institutions of higher learning. The founding of women's colleges, of course, predates the Civil War. But the nurture and support provided by feminists during and after the middle of the century fostered the development of exclusively female institutions. Women educators contrasted the merits of separatist and integrationist education, but the nineteenth-century debates seem less heated than twentieth-century discussions. Most who pressed for exclusive female institutions did so because male institutions refused to admit women.

The all-female colleges, by century's end, achieved reputations competitive with those of the elite male colleges women sought to integrate. Although Mount Holyoke was opened in 1836, it did not offer college instruction or institute collegiate standards until many years later. Vassar in 1865 was the first bona fide women's college. But not until Smith and Wellesley opened in 1875 were women's colleges able to claim that their qualifications for admission as well as their curriculum matched those of male institutions. Another elite college for women, Bryn Mawr, opened in 1885. Colleges for women flourished, too, because of the feminist desire for female communities as well as for academic excellence.

The exclusively female colleges (Radcliffe, Wellesley, Smith, Mount Holyoke, Vassar, Bryn Mawr, and Barnard, called the "Seven Sisters") maintained their own faculties (with the exception of Radcliffe) and set independent standards for admitting and training undergraduates. This network of women's colleges became a powerful counterpart to the "Ivy League." Despite the fact that Cornell (in 1872) and the University of Pennsylvania (in 1876) were co-educational and Harvard boasted a female annex, these Ivy institutions were symbolic male bastions. Even more important than providing a female counterpart for male exclusivity, the female colleges provided employment as well for intellectual women.

Despite the varied origins of the women's colleges (Radcliffe, a convenience for Harvard faculty daughters; Vassar, the philanthropic gesture of a beer manufacturer; and Smith, founded by disappointed advocates of co-education for Amherst), by the end of the century these institutions had made an indelible impact on American society. Although these women struggled for reforms, as historian Rosalind Rosenberg describes it, "in the shadow of Dr. Clarke," their efforts met with no small measure of success by the turn of the century.

The new institutions were not the realm of the pampered upper class: the graduates of women's colleges were essentially middle-class. College provided a tremendous boost up the ladder for an ambitious young woman, and this first generation perpetuated the doctrine of female intellectual equality. Although institutions such as Cornell opened their doors (and their coffers) to receive women undergraduates, the faculty remained all male. By contrast, two-thirds of the Smith faculty were women. The women's-college educators shaped the future of women's advanced education in the United States.

The career of Alice Freeman Palmer illuminates the times. She was an early graduate of the University of Michigan, where she studied history before pursuing a professional teaching career. When Alice Freeman became the president of Wellesley College (having been appointed acting president at the age of twenty-six), she maintained that intellectual attainment would afford women richer domestic lives. She raised the academic standards of the school during her tenure (1881–87), and she considered herself the head of a large family, referring to the students as "my girls." Her emphasis on domestic values reflected her personal as well as political tenets that "the duties of motherhood and the making of a home are the most sacred work of women, and the dearest to them, of every class." After six spectacular years, during which she was able to abolish the "preparatory department" and strengthen the curriculum, Freeman gave up her career to marry George Herbert Palmer, professor of philosophy at Harvard.

Freeman had been strongly committed to her role at Wellesley, yet after meeting Palmer in 1884, she felt duty-bound to abandon her career for marriage. Palmer urged Freeman to resign from Wellesley; he argued that keeping her professional ties to Wellesley, continuing to work, would be "suicide." She was obviously ambivalent about his offer and struggled with conflicting emotions. When she finally left Wellesley to marry Palmer in December 1887, she expressed her feelings in a poem entitled "Surrender":

Great love has triumphed. At a crisis hour
Of strength and struggle on the heights of life
He came, and bidding me abandon power
Called me to take the quiet name of wife.

Despite her commitment to academic excellence, she argued that marriage and a family were a woman's preeminent obligation. This was the doctrine she preached to her students, and the majority of Wellesley students (57 percent) did marry. However, this was lower than the national average. But it was significantly higher than the percentage of graduates of another outstanding women's college, Bryn Mawr.

It is instructive to contrast Alice Freeman Palmer's career with that of feminist educator and Bryn Mawr president, M. Carey Thomas. She had strong family ties to the college she later headed: her father and uncle were founders of the school. Thomas was a student at Johns

Hopkins during the 1870s, but she encountered bitter opposition when she tried to complete a graduate degree in English. She went to Europe, where her chances of success were much greater. She finally earned her doctorate from the University of Zurich—graduating summa cum laude in 1882. Thomas returned to the United States determined to battle the handicaps that hampered women's academic careers.

She was appointed professor of English at Bryn Mawr and was soon named Dean of Faculties. When the president died in 1895, Thomas assumed the post. Although at Bryn Mawr, as in other women's colleges, undergraduates were required to reside in dormitories on campus, Bryn Mawr, unlike Smith and Wellesley, did not emphasize "domestic values" for women. Bryn Mawr fostered a "sisterhood" rather than an atmosphere of preparation for maternity. Thomas turned Bryn Mawr away from the rather traditional interpretation of women's education, the notion that this training prepared women to be the intellectual equals of their husbands, a doctrine her rival six sisters were promoting. Unlike Alice Freeman Palmer, she did not believe education was valuable in and of itself only or as preparation for marriage. Thomas believed that women must take their place alongside men in the world, both in the workplace and in the professions.

Thomas was a vociferous champion of women's causes, active in the Association of Collegiate Alumnae (ACA), founded in the 1880s to assist young women in the pursuit of undergraduate degrees and to promote opportunities for these graduates. In 1899, when Harvard President Charles Eliot applied Darwinian theory to uphold the segregation of men and women (in education, the professions, and other fields), Thomas denounced this prominent spokesman. She publicly ridiculed Eliot, saying he was suffering from "sun spots on his brain." Her outspoken challenge of the male opponents of women's education boosted the morale of her Bryn Mawr students.

Evidence indicates that Bryn Mawr graduates eagerly fulfilled their college president's feminist ideals. A survey of Bryn Mawr alumnae who graduated between 1889 and 1908 shows that 62 percent went on to get advanced degrees and 90 percent were wage earners at some time in their lives. Thomas urged her graduates to pursue college teaching, and over 10 percent of Bryn Mawr women went into college teaching (as opposed to 2 percent of Wellesley alumnae). In addition, though the 1910 census indicated that 88 percent of American women married, only 45 percent of Bryn Mawr graduates did. And of those who were married, over one-third remained childless.

This last factor created great concern at the turn of the century. The increasing fears concerning the declining birth rate of upper- and middle-class women continued to plague feminists. One leading theorist questioned: "Is the women's college as now conducted a force which acts against the survival of the race which patronizes it?" Educational experts conducted studies to determine the effects of education on women's rates of marriage and family size. A 1908 study of the women graduates of the University of Wisconsin indicated that 100 percent of the 1869 alumnae were married, while only 54 percent of the women graduates in 1900 were, and only 41 percent in the class of 1906. As nearly two-thirds of these women pursued teaching careers after graduation, the study concluded that perhaps many of the graduates of more recent classes would eventually marry. But the study reflected a pattern of declining rates of marriage and childbearing.

A study of eastern colleges conducted in 1915 reached similar conclusions. Only 53 percent of the Vassar graduates (classes of 1867–92) had married by that year. A similar sampling of Wellesley alumnae (1875–89) revealed only half were married by 1915. Research the following year indicated women graduates of the University of California had a slightly higher marital rate: 60 percent of those in the class of 1900 were married by 1916. This study of a western college gave credence to the argument that women undergraduates of co-educational institutions were more likely to marry. In this and other cases, female graduates of co-ed colleges by a large proportion married men who had taken degrees at the same alma mater.

By the second decade of the twentieth century, statisticians showed two trends which alarmed the public and put many feminists on the defensive: college-educated women had a lower rate of marriage and those who did marry had fewer children (most likely because they married later). Although studies also indicated that these better-educated women had lower infant mortality rates, this seemed a negligible factor to those who lectured against "race suicide." This alarm was not directed solely at the relatively small number of women with college degrees (only seventy-three thousand women had college degrees by 1910)—but their achievements challenged the premise that women's role in American society should be restricted.

The ideologues who railed against women's education claimed that this pathway to equality would seriously undermine women's health. At the same time thousands of immigrant women toiled in sweatshops, thousands of black women labored in southern fields, and even native-born white women spent ten to twelve hours a day six days a week as underpaid, exploited salesgirls. Surely back-breaking physical labor would be more debilitating to women's reproductive capabilities than mental exertion? But male opponents also argued that women were mentally inferior, incapable of pursuing an advanced degree. Again and again, women pioneers disproved these prejudices. Yet women with degrees would very likely meet with stiffer opposition once they attempted to put their degrees to practical use. The debate was clouded with confusion between the actual and the articulated rationale against women's equal access and opportunity.

Even the domestic feminist Alice Freeman Palmer abandoned her home and husband in 1890 to serve as Dean of Women at the newly founded University of Chicago. When the university's new president, William Rainey Harper, was unable to recruit George Herbert Palmer to head the philosophy department, he doubly despaired. Harper knew there were only a few women in American academe qualified to meet his high standards, and Palmer's wife was one of them. Despite her husband's severe reservations, Alice Freeman Palmer agreed to take the new position at the University of Chicago (as assistant professor of history and Dean of Women). She accepted her post provided Harper agreed to hire her friend Marion Talbot (founder of the Association of Collegiate Alumnae after her graduation from Boston University in 1881) as assistant professor of sociology and as assistant dean. She further stipulated that she would accept the post only if she might spend only twelve weeks a year in residence—leaving her duties during the remainder of the academic year in Talbot's able hands. Harper was delighted with the arrangement. After three years of marriage, Alice Palmer in essence abandoned her husband (if only periodically) to resume her career. Although she was an exceptional woman, her career shows the lengths to which women would go to maintain professional status.

More commonly, women with careers, especially educators, resolved the conflict between marriage and career by remaining single. Only 40 percent of women with careers in education were married, and only 25 percent of them had children. In fact, many women educators openly scorned marriage, applying the radical feminist critique that marriage was "legalized prostitution" whereby a woman abandoned her rights, her individualism, and any chance for spiritual fulfillment. Most of these women lived independent lives—yet few were alone. Some paired off into spinster couples ("Boston marriages"), with or without sexual components. Even if an unmarried woman lived alone, she might be sustained by a community of peers, a network of women who provided mutual comfort and support. This sisterly spirit braced women against the social alienation many spinsters suffered. These women who defied social norms needed a cause to promote their special interests. Most chose feminism.

Since many if not most of these women were defined as "misfits"—old maids incapable of finding husbands—they had to develop a new social ethic to match their status and to win them social respectability. Ostensibly, these women led lives of dedication and self-sacrifice, but they also needed recognition and some reward, despite their rejection of traditional female roles. Professional careers (in academe, law, medicine, and eventually reform and social work) afforded this feminist vanguard avenues for major contributions to late-nineteenth-century American society.

Female colleges paved the way for women to achieve academic status. These institutions provided women with unparalleled opportunities for achievement. Maria Mitchell, born in 1818, learned astronomy from her father, an enthusiastic amateur who taught her how to calculate celestial positions and other lore. Mitchell studied while serving as librarian at the Nantucket Athenaeum. In 1847 she discovered a comet, which brought her international fame. She finally attained an academic position when Vassar opened in 1865. During the next several decades, Mitchell carved out an impressive career, boosting the prospect for success for future generations.

It was unusual for professors in late-nineteenth-century America to earn Ph.D.s, and nearly impossible for women. The first American women to obtain doctorates did so abroad, following the example of M. Carey Thomas. Helen Webster attended the University of Zurich and earned a degree in comparative philology in 1889 before teaching at Wellesley. Margaret Maltby, the first American woman to do original work in physics, attended Göttingen University and received her doctorate in 1895. She returned to the United States in 1899 to teach physics at Barnard. Following graduation from Vassar in 1868, Mary Watson Whitney, a student of Maria Mitchell's, was allowed to study at Harvard for a year, at the behest of her mentor. In 1872 she earned a Master's Degree from Vassar, following her tenure at the Dearborn Observatory in Chicago. But despite her ability and talent, she was forced to go to the University of Zurich to complete her graduate study in celestial mechanics and mathematics. On her return to the United States, she was able to find work only as a high-school teacher. Mitchell hired her former pupil as a private assistant, and upon Mitchell's retirement in 1888, Whitney took over Mitchell's post at Vassar as director of the observatory and professor of astronomy. It is clear that without the support of female networks and the establishment of separate women's institutions, women would have remained far longer outside the groves of academe.

Although Helen White earned her doctorate in Greek in 1877, she was a rare exception. Florence Bascom wheedled her Ph.D. from Johns Hopkins University in 1893, after earning a B.A. and an M.A. from the same school. This "special dispensation" was quite a victory, following less than a decade after M. Carey Thomas had been forced to go abroad by the same university. Bascom's case—despite her advantages as the daughter of the president of the University of Wisconsin—represented a breakthrough in the battle for doctoral degrees. However, Johns Hopkins did not officially admit women into its graduate programs until 1907. Bascom went on to teach geology at Ohio State, before joining the faculty at Bryn Mawr, where she was appointed a professor in 1906.

The founding and success of the University of Chicago had a tremendous impact upon women's progress in earning advanced degrees. For twenty years following the granting of doctorates in 1892, the University of Chicago trained the greatest number of women Ph.D.s in the country. The university's record in the sciences is outstanding: of the 319 women who held doctorates in science before 1920, sixty-three held Chicago Ph.Ds. This progress accelerated elsewhere during the 1890s, although elite male institutions continued to discriminate against women. As late as 1895, Harvard refused Mary Whiton Calkins a doctorate in psychology, although she had completed the required work.

The legal profession effectively barred women from practice until the post-bellum era. A hardy group of women began to challenge these barriers in the late 1860s. Arabella Mansfield was the first woman in

America licensed to practice law, attaining this honor with a petition to the Iowa bar in 1869. Surprisingly, Mansfield met with little opposition. For at the same time Myra Bradwell, an abolitionist who had served on the U.S. Sanitary Commission during the war, was involved in considerable controversy with her crusade to reform the law in her home state of Illinois. Bradwell was a respected leader in Chicago: an organizer of the local branch of the American Women's Suffrage Association, the wife of a Cook County judge, and editor of *Chicago Legal News*, a weekly paper founded in 1868.

In 1869 Bradwell launched an even more radical campaign: single-handedly she set out to break down discrimination in the legal profession and in the Illinois statutes. When Bradwell petitioned the Illinois Bar Association for admission in 1869, they refused. In 1870 a lower court upheld the Bar Association's right of refusal. Bradwell appealed and brought her case to the highest court in the land. In 1873 the Supreme Court denied that women had any claim to protection under the Fourteenth Amendment. The Court declared that individual states might interpret the rights of its citizens, and found for the State of Illinois bar. However, by 1872 the Illinois legislature, under pressure from Bradwell supporters, passed a bill providing women with equal access to the bar. In this same year Bradwell was made an honorary member of the state bar. She also agitated on behalf of married women's right to retain their earnings (which passed the state legislature in 1869) and for women's right to become notary publics (granted in 1875).

Law schools refused to admit women students in significant numbers until the 1890s. Most women who did seek admission were married to lawyers. Most women who were finally admitted to the bar never practiced (before the modern era) because of the discrimination they encountered within society and in the courts. Those women who did manage successful law careers practiced civil rather than criminal law. The most spirited campaigns against this prejudice were conducted in the nation's capital following the Civil War.

Belva Lockwood applied to Columbian College (later George Washington University) for admission to its law school in the autumn of 1869. The institution turned down her application with the following rationale:

> Madam:
>
> The Faculty of Columbian College have considered your request to be

> admitted to the Law Department of this institution, after due consideration, have considered that such admission would not be expedient, as it would be likely to distract the attention of the young men.

The forty-year-old Lockwood was little flattered by this dismissal. She attended the National University Law School instead, and graduated in 1873. After winning the right to practice before the Supreme Court in her district in 1873, she was denied admission to practice before the Court of Claims. In 1876 the United States Supreme Court turned down her request to appear before the bench. She fought this discrimination, lobbying for a national bill to grant any woman lawyer the right to appear before the Supreme Court if she had practiced in the highest courts of her own state or territory for a period of three years. This statute passed Congress in 1879, and Lockwood became the first woman to be admitted under the law to practice before the Supreme Court, at a time when America could lay claim to fewer than sixty practicing women attorneys, with only thirty-one law school graduates in this select group.

In 1886 women students and graduates of the University of Michigan Law Department formed the Equity Club, an informal organization to promote "encouragement and friendly counsel" for women lawyers. A more ambitious national organization was launched in 1888—the Women's International Bar Association. This group had a four-point program:

1. To open law schools to women.
2. To remove all disabilities to admission of women to the bar, and to secure their eligibility to the bench.
3. To disseminate knowledge concerning women's legal status.
4. To secure better legal conditions for women.

The first objective in this reform campaign proved the most problematic.

Ellen Spencer Mussey became, by necessity, a champion of women's admission to law schools. In 1876 the Washington, D.C, woman took over her husband's flourishing legal practice when his health was failing. In 1892, when Mussey died without his wife being formally admitted to the bar, her livelihood was threatened. The widow was denied admission to the Columbian College Law School (as Lockwood had been a quarter of a century before). Lockwood had been admitted to the National University Law School, but the school changed its charter following Lockwood's graduation, specifically to keep out women. Thus, Ellen Spencer Mussey was unable to obtain admission to National or any other law school and was effectively barred from continuing her career. In 1893 several sympathetic judges conspired to allow Mussey to practice before them, ruling in favor of her admission to their courts based upon her proven ability and good character. Mussey was aware of the irony of continuing a career insured not by a degree and her own expertise and experience but dependent upon the charity of men in the profession.

Her anger and resentment led her to champion reform. In 1898, when six well-qualified women applicants were denied admission to Columbian, Mussey and another female attorney opened their own law school. Their institution admitted both men and women, gained in numbers and prestige, and eventually merged to become the law school of American University. Women in law, like women in academe who sought equal status within the profession, were often driven to establish their own institutions.

Although women in the ministry met with strong opposition, the "feminization of religion" in mid-century paved the way for female progress in this area. By 1880 many women were not only members but leaders of churches, with 165 accredited female ministers. The Universalist Church, with thirty-five women ministers, was the most "feminized" denomination in post-bellum times. Antoinette Blackwell earned a divinity degree from Oberlin College in 1850, to become America's first woman minister. Women had been popular evangelical preachers since before the Revolution, but Blackwell was the first to pursue a career through traditional channels, and to graduate from divinity school. Despite Blackwell's success, Oberlin's divinity school did not admit another woman for nearly forty years.

Women made enormous progress in journalism, literature, and reform in post-bellum days, all respectable professional accomplishments. Yet only in one field in which advanced degrees were required did women professionals make dramatic progress during the last quarter of the nineteenth century—medicine.

Many factors contributed to women's success in this field. Victorian values reinforced the concept that women physicians might be best suited to deal with women's gynecological disorders, sparing female patients the anguish of confessing embarrassing details to male doctors. So American society and the medical establishment were less threatened by those women who sought limited application of their medical education. Despite this Victorian rationale, men strongly opposed women's equal status in the medical profession. Male doctors might tolerate a female gynecologist or a woman practicing obstetrics, as long as females had limited access to established medical schools and were restricted to their own (presumably inferior) hospitals. However, women's goals and some of their achievements defied these limitations.

The unqualified support of feminists contributed to the marked success of women in the field of medicine. Lydia Folger, a cousin of feminist leader Lucretia Mott, attended the Central Medical College of New York at Syracuse, which was opened as a co-educational institution in 1849. Many of the male organizers were influenced by the feminism flourishing in upstate New York at the time. Indeed, this medical school was founded the year after the Seneca Falls convention. Some females were only able to attend medical schools founded with funds provided by feminist philanthropists during this time. Ann Preston, a Quaker activist in Pennsylvania, spent years collecting funds to provide for a women's medical college in Philadelphia, the first American medical school for women, which she established in 1850. As late as 1860 the Philadelphia County Medical Society still refused to recognize the school, withholding accreditation. The Quaker women of Philadelphia continued their campaign against prejudice despite all obstacles. In 1855 Preston sent Emmeline Cleveland, a promising candidate, to study at the Paris Maternité, where she completed an advanced course in obstetrics. Her European education was paid for by two women benefactors who wished to raise the standards of the Philadelphia school. Cleveland returned to head the obstetrics division of the school and became one of America's first female surgeons.

Individual women were instrumental in breaking down the barriers in all-male medical schools, as had been the case in men's colleges. In 1850 Harriot K. Hunt (after fifteen years of medical practice as a self-taught physician) applied to Harvard's medical school. Although the faculty granted permission for her to attend lectures, the male students rebelled, and the administration reversed its decision. (Hunt eventually received a degree, albeit honorary, from the Female Medical

College of Pennsylvania in recognition of her service to the medical profession.) In 1878, a quarter of a century and several hundred women doctors later, Marion Hovey offered Harvard $10,000 to admit women into its medical school. The funds were refused: the male bastion remained unsympathetic. However, a breakthrough into elite institutions came in 1883, when Mary Garrett offered the Johns Hopkins Medical School a generous gift, with the stipulation that it train female physicians, and the institution was finally open to women.

Female philanthropists attempted to bribe all-male institutions to break down the barriers, and had limited success. They were more successful in their campaigns to enlist younger women to continue pushing for reforms; they were mentors for women who wished to enter the profession. Scholarships for women to attend medical school, an expensive and unorthodox pursuit for women, came from private donors and from money collected by feminist organizations and societies. Women of talent and ability were supported financially and emotionally by a feminist network.

The first generation of women doctors who pioneered in all-male medical schools and established women's hospitals before the Civil War (Elizabeth Blackwell, Maria Zakrzewska, among others) eased the way for increasing numbers of women to enter medicine in the last half of the century. By the 1890s the growing number of women doctors constituted a dynamic force within the profession. Mary Putnam Jacobi, a woman doctor on the staff of the New York Infirmary and one of the outstanding women professionals of her day, wrote in 1890: "Women have always worked; but they demand now, and simply, some opportunity for a free choice in the kind of work, which, apart from the care of children, they may perform. The invasion of the medical profession is one of the more articulate forms of this demand."

By 1890 the University of Michigan had graduated eighty-eight women doctors, the Women's Medical College of New York Infirmary had produced 135 women doctors, and the Women's College of Philadelphia had trained 560. That same year women enrolled in medical schools in even larger numbers: the Medical College of Pennsylvania, 181; the Women's Medical College of the New York Infirmary, ninety; the Women's Medical College of Chicago, ninety; the University of California, eight; Cooper College of San Francisco, eighteen. Of course, even after these women graduated, there were barriers. Women physicians by necessity had to remind the public that they had their degrees. Female physicians almost always indicated in city directories their professional credentials by adding "M.D." after their names. Male physicians, with or without advanced degrees, could build up their practices. But a woman doctor had a difficult time establishing a career even if she could demonstrate her thorough academic and medical training.

Thus, women doctors were forced to create their own institutions and, eventually, their own positions. Female physicians demanded to be put on staff at newly created women's prisons and asylums. In 1890 a bill passed the New York State legislature providing for a woman doctor at each such facility. Other states followed suit. Even more important, women founded and staffed women's hospitals, where women physicians could practice. The New York Infirmary for Women and Children, founded in 1854, pioneered this effort. In 1862 Boston became the home of the New England Hospital for Women and Children. These institutions were the only ones in which women might admit and treat patients.

Before the establishment of women's hospitals, women were effectively banned from the serious practice of medicine in America. Dr. Annie Angell, a graduate of the Women's College of the New York Infirmary, served on the Mount Sinai staff in 1874, the first woman on record accorded this privilege. But in hospitals throughout the country, even as late as the 1880s (Mount Sinai in New York, Blockley Hospital in Philadelphia, and Cook County in Chicago), no more than two women were admitted to the staff of each institution. This was at a time when women physicians with medical degrees numbered nearly 2,500, and another 4,500, denied the benefit of medical school, practiced in spite of it.

At the turn of the century, the medical profession began to move against "irregular" medical practices and toward the professionalization of physicians. The standardization of medical curriculum and the formation of medical societies improved the profession. But during this critical time of medical reform, the number of women doctors was dramatically diminished. One cannot assume that this reflected an intentional weeding out of women from the profession, or that the standards of excellence and competence ignored questions of gender. The truth lies somewhere in between. In any case, by the outbreak of World War I, women had lost much of the momentum they had gained in the last quarter of the century. The status of women doctors in the city of Boston provides a case in point.

In 1850, the year Harriot Hunt requested admission to Harvard Medical School, only 2 percent of the physicians in Boston were women. During the next quarter century, the growth of female medical colleges and the development of women's hospitals fostered a generation of female physicians. Women had made great strides as professionals, and medical schools were welcoming ambitious females. By 1890 the proportion of women doctors in Boston had expanded to 18 percent. Boston had more female physicians (200) than America had women lawyers. Women doctors hoped, by the end of the century, that medical schools would follow the lead of enlightened institutions such as Johns Hopkins. Unfortunately, Boston University and Tufts medical schools instead substantially reversed their co-educational policies. These schools, formerly open, now limited the number of women.

This pattern was repeated throughout the country. Northwestern Medical School, without warning or public debate, closed its women's division in 1902. The percentage of women in the Michigan Medical School dropped from 25 percent of the total in 1890 to a little over 3 percent in 1910.

This regression was the result of a backlash against feminism. The status quo was threatened by women's bold strides into all-male domains at the end of the century. When women pressed to enter elite institutions and turned all-male institutions and establishments into sexually integrated ones, male conservatives lashed back, characterizing women's admittance into previously exclusive realms as "feminizing," which reflected diminished quality.

Men began to reestablish barriers against women. Male educators reasserted their dominance in academic and intellectual spheres which had been infiltrated by women. Colleges which had been co-ed for decades, such as Wesleyan, suddenly refused to admit women students: in 1910 this college returned to its all-male status after nearly half a century of co-education. Many co-educational institutions established quotas rather than a ban. But women's opportunities and choices were curtailed.

The progress women had made was not a quantifiable accomplishment from which we can add or subtract. The generation of women who invaded exclusive male fields demonstrated women's capabilities and talents, and their strong commitment to achievement—against the mainstream male ideology of female inferiority. Despite setbacks and reversals, the pioneers in this radical redefinition of "women's place" had a permanent impact on the future of women in America, defying the notion of women's intellectual inferiority through an impressive record of achievement. The generation which followed may have been denied the benefits of these accomplishments and may not have appreciated the militance of their predecessors. But the late-nineteenth-century feminist reformers proved that women were, indeed, intellectual equals to men. Their struggles insured that women would be better prepared to contend with ongoing battles against discrimination.

8
Sexuality and Stereotypes

NO OTHER topic has generated so much controversy among historians of American women as female sexuality. The nature of eroticism and passion, prescriptive attitudes and actual behavior, reproductive rights and patterns of repression, advice literature, and medical practice have been explored extensively. Trying to probe the mysteries of nineteenth-century sexuality poses daunting challenges. Nineteenth-century Americans were extremely reticent on the subject. Yet that century saw enormous transformations in sexual awareness, sexual attitudes, sexual behavior, and sexual discourse.

In colonial America, it was widely accepted that women possessed the same sex drive as men, or greater. Numerous literary tales, divorce records, novels crammed with adultery and lust, testify to women's pursuit of sexual pleasure in the eighteenth century. Pregnant brides were common and generally accepted. But by the early nineteenth century society refined feminine ideals into new models of republican motherhood and "true womanhood." These changes placed a new emphasis on sexual purity.

The antebellum cult of domesticity emphasized woman's "softer" nature: her innocence, vulnerability, passivity, and tenderness. Male preceptors advocated that woman's "weakness" should be cherished. One commentator argued: "So long as she is nervous, fickle, capricious, delicate, diffident and dependent, man will worship and adore her. Her weakness is her strength, and her true art is to cultivate and improve that weakness." This emphasis on physical characteristics had a sexual component: woman's "weakness" signified her vulnerability to men.

Women were encouraged to cultivate "feminine" qualities; society could not leave women to their instincts. Women were warned to guard against impurity. Piety, propriety, and restraint protected a lady's virtue; fashion, temper, and vanity might spell her downfall. Christian morality and domestic ideology preached a hard line: women were the guardians of the family, the conscience of the household. Women were expected to fulfill the dictates of their domestic roles as well as provide the family with unimpeachable moral example. From birth, girls were tutored to deny sexual feelings and aspire to spiritual stimulation rather than physical fulfillment.

If a woman failed to adhere to this strict ideal, she forfeited respectability. In 1808 Thomas Branagan counseled his male reader in *The Excellence of the Female Character Vindicated* to test the virtue of the woman he wooed. He suggested that a young man make sexual advances (within reason, suggestions rather than assaults) toward the woman he was courting. If she failed to give the proper response—"becoming abhorrence"—the suitor was warned. Women who did not repress their sexual urges and refuse physical temptation were subject to severe reprisal. Thus were young women conditioned to new patterns of emotional expression. By the 1840s and early 1850s "passionlessness" became the very essence of femininity.

The emergence of Victorian attitudes, the virtual deification of feminine "passionlessness" increased women's influence in the home and conformed to male ideals. Many middle-class women believed asexuality would improve their status within the family and society, earning them moral and spiritual superiority. Historians have argued persuasively that since society designated women as the "the sex," women inverted this formulaic reduction for their own ends. This strategy provided women with a very limited, domestic power, but one on which genteel females readily fastened their hopes. By denying their own sexuality, middle-class matrons hoisted themselves up from the mundane into an unassailable spiritual domain, a sphere in which they ruled. Moral superiority allowed woman a larger voice in family matters.

Modifications of the ideal were made throughout the nineteenth century. Feminist attacks on fashion were calculated to loosen the shackles which restricted and, some held, maimed women. Dress was quite clearly related in the female mind to sexual allure and to attracting male admirers. Elizabeth Cady Stanton railed at the slave to fashion: "She is the hopeless martyr to the inventions of some Parisian imp of fashion. Her tight waist and long, trailing skirts deprive her of all freedom of breath and motion. No wonder man prescribes her sphere. She needs his aid at every turn." Under the guise of dress reform, feminists continued their attacks on male "sexualization" of women.

The debates concerning dress reform reveal acute ambivalence on the part of males as well as feminists. An 1878 editorial in *The New York Times* held that "woman's madness about Clothes, as it seems to men, is born of her sex and seems absolutely incurable." The editorial went on to encourage women to "rise above" their degradation. Although male critics might deride fashionability, many of these same men opposed dress reformers, labeling them radical extremists. Although males might, in the abstract, object to their daughters and wives following the dictates of European couture, those women who strayed too far from mainstream fashion were labeled deviant and dangerous. Clothing reflected the status and propriety of ladies, and men demanded that the women in their families observe the rules of decorum.

Perhaps no other element of the feminist campaign attracted such scathing attention from the press: cartoons and editorials, brimming with ridicule and barely repressed rage. Women in trousers, even when they wore the attractively modified Bloomer costume popular at mid-century, were publicly hounded and scorned. Men feared that the "loosening" of dress codes might reflect female immorality. Males lambasted women whose dress, they suggested, reflected that they wished to "wear the pants" (serve as surrogate males), and, they repeatedly warned, with such conduct, men would soon be reduced to "petticoats." The sexual subtext of this debate is complex and contradictory. But males passionately protested this aspect of the movement which so threatened definitions of masculinity.

Women were not as much concerned with altering "masculinity" as they were with reforming definitions of femininity. Feminists concerned themselves more and more with questions of health and delicacy. Middle-class women were overwhelmed by the demands of childbearing and domesticity, the stresses of rearing a family and running a household. Exhaustion and anxiety drove many homemakers to the brink of collapse. Some women suffered emotional as well as physical breakdowns, and nervous disorders became common if not epidemic for middle-class American women by late nineteenth century.

Physicians as well as women patients had conflicting opinions concerning prescriptions for women's health. Most of the ailments attributed to women were rooted in educated guesses as much as medical knowledge. Antebellum physicians understood little about sex, reproduction, or even physiology. When women fell ill and the cause of illness was not easily detected, many doctors assumed (and then proceeded on the assumption) that these illnesses stemmed from gynecological disorders. The entire structure of medical specialization reflects this bias: gynecology developed to deal with women's "special" concerns, because standard medical practice failed fully to incorporate the treatment of women. Physicians promoted the idea of women's inferior constitution and delicate nature, which required vigilant safeguards.

These safeguards included strict medical supervision and sexual surgery. The response of the medical profession, overwhelmingly male, to women's problems has been a subject of scrutiny. Historian G. J. Barker-Benfield has demonstrated the ambivalence of male attitudes toward female sexuality. He has argued that "assertion of a women's natural sexlessness was wishful thinking of males scared spermless, as it were, by women's potential appetite." Barker-Benfield and others suggest that doctors responded with dramatic and detrimental cures for women's problems. It must be noted that female doctors as well hailed sexual surgery as an improvement in medical practice.

Cures ranged from cosmetic to radical. During the antebellum years females sought restorative treatment for various illnesses. This led to numerous movements, including a craze for water cures. Since Roman times the weak and infirm have sought revitalization in natural springs. Many simply bathed in the mineral waters, others drank it, and some made excursions into the sea (saltwater bathing). A number of individuals established institutes and training centers to promote various homeopathic cures: Rachel Gleason's Elmira Water Cure in upstate New York; James Jackson's Hygienic Institute in Dansville, New York; and Dio Lewis's Normal Institute for Physical Education in Boston. Women as well as men flocked to these establishments. Most of the hydropathic advocates promoted physical exercise and preventive medicine. These therapists believed, as Gleason argued, that no woman was "inherently weak or delicate, only restricted by fashion, sedentary domesticity, constricting dress and bad diet." Women were therefore resocialized to active and envigorating routines. The hydropathy cures included hot and cold baths, massages, wet compresses, diet, and daily gymnasium sessions.

Feminists and physicians alike believed that many infirmities could be overcome by regimens that rejected Victorian notions of female frailty. Women, they thought, had been systematically debilitated by stereotypes and need no longer be slaves to ill health. Feminists linked this campaign to their crusade to limit the size of families, arguing that women were crippled by repeated pregnancies. Feminists campaigned not only to revitalize women's health but to afford women a choice. Their campaign included what today we call sex education.

This feminist view was countered by conservative members of the medical community. Male physicians at mid-century were preoccupied with female nervous disorders. Whether these illnesses were real or imagined, doctors treated them with increasing frequency and unfortunate consequences in the latter half of the century. The diagnosis and treatment of hysteria is a case in point.

Although both men and women of all classes were subject to the conditions which might trigger hysteria, physicians expected large numbers of women, and for the most part upper- and middle-class women, to become hysterics. In the antebellum era, physicians diagnosed hysteria only after a patient's seizure. Although nausea, headaches, loss of sensation in parts of the body (loss of taste, smell, hearing, and vision in particular), and pains in the spine might be present in some cases, doctors often hesitated to diagnose hysteria unless the patient suffered a telltale seizure. But by the end of the century doctors developed new attitudes toward these symptoms.

Neurology was a growing field, and psychology was in its infancy. Doctors blended these sciences to diagnose women hysterics. Medical experts argued that hysteria preyed on women of the genteel classes because they were more egocentric, narcissistic, and impressionistic—an unflattering portrait promoted in the medical literature of the period. Physicians claimed that hysteria generally followed miscarriage, a death in the family, or financial setbacks which forced women into self-sufficiency. When doctors found women of the lower classes suffering from identical illnesses, they suggested that the exhaustion and sensuality of working-class life made poor women prey to this disease as well. These psychosocial explanations of hysteria do not address the important dynamic of gender. Scholars have suggested that hysteria was one way in which conventional women expressed dissatisfaction with their lives. Family obligations and women's confining domestic role stimulated "passive aggression." In this way, we can view hysterical women as both the product and the indictment of their culture.

The male medical establishment met this health crisis with drastic measures. Backaches, headaches, nearly all ailments in women were attributed to the uterus. One medical professor in 1870 proclaimed that it was as if "the Almighty, in creating the female sex, had taken the uterus and built up a woman around it." The womb was believed to be the source of various if not a majority of illnesses. Many doctors responded with "local treatment": a range of practices from leeching to injections to cauterization. Leeches might be placed on the vulva or neck of the uterus, with physicians cautioned not to let any escape into the vagina. If this process failed, a series of injections might follow: milk, water, linseed tea, or chemicals might be forced into the uterine cavity. Even more painful and dangerous, cauterization with a white-hot instrument was advocated in extreme cases. By the 1880s this very painful treatment (the operation was performed without effective anesthetic—only opium or alcohol to alleviate the pain) had been discredited.

Leading medical figure S. Weir Mitchell condemned these "primitive" practices. He and other prominent physicians introduced "rest cures," severe regimens of absolute immobility. Women were removed from their homes and daily routines, transferred to institutions which provided peace and absolute quiet. But these prolonged periods of rest could prove trying. Women were not only relieved of labor and responsibilities, they were isolated—often confined to their beds for six weeks at a time.

It is difficult to assess the nature and extent of women's diseases, and today it is almost impossible to evaluate past medical treatment. We do know that by the 1860s doctors might recommend surgical procedures for sexual disorders. In 1859 British gynecologist Isaac Baker Brown advocated clitoridectomy, surgical removal of the skin hood above the clitoris. This operation was performed to relieve women of nervous or sexual disorders. In 1866 Brown was expelled from the London Obstetrical Society for his part in this revival, and died shortly thereafter, a shunned figure. Unfortunately, American practitioners who followed Brown's lead met with no such ostracism. From 1867 until well into the first decade of the twentieth century we find evidence of clitoridectomies.

Dr. Robert Battey of Rome, Georgia—a leading exponent of clitoridectomy—also championed the use of "normal ovariotomy" or "oophorectomy" to treat women's disorders and breakdowns. The removal of ovaries for hysteria and neuroses increased during this era. Female castration thrived well into the 1890s, until medical authorities attacked this practice in large numbers.

Some scholars have charged that physicians needlessly inflicted pain and disfigurement on women. Historical accounts assessing medical opinion, physicians' care, and women's responses to treatment are diverse and controversial. Medical knowledge as well as therapeutic remedies are bound up with the culture. However, some treatments might have reflected the prevailing values which allowed abuse of women. Ignorance may have been the most significant element, but certainly it was not the only factor which fostered these practices.

One of the major transformations of the century can be attributed to women's exercising greater control over reproduction. The average birth rate of 7.04 per married female in 1800 was dramatically cut in half by 1900—to 3.56. This was achieved in the midst of enormous obstacles to birth control. Women knew very little about the process of sexual reproduction and even less about conception. Physicians seemed to advise with little more than pragmatic guesswork. A leading medical figure of the post-bellum period, Dr. J. Marion Sims, like many of his peers believed that menses was an indication of "an aptitude for impregnation." Thus, Sims and the majority of the medical profession advocated a "safe period," which today we calculate through scientific evidence to be the time when conception is most likely. Some doctors provided the opposite advice, however. The rhythm method was advocated with little hope of effectiveness, considering the primitive state of medical knowledge.

Some physicians thought that conception was directly related to female orgasm. This idea was disproven with a doctor's experiment involving a married woman who could not endure intercourse without excruciating pain. The physician prescribed a drug which rendered her unconscious while her husband performed his marital duty. The woman eventually gave birth, impregnated while comatose.

Contraceptive knowledge in late-nineteenth-century America was limited. By the 1850s rubber condoms were advertised and sold in eastern cities. Although the diaphragm had been invented, this device was not widely available in the United States before the 1920s. As early as 1864, Dr. Edward B. Foote's *Medical Common Sense* referred to "a womb veil," advocating use of a pessary to prevent conception. Some combined these methods with withdrawal; these methods proved effective in the aggregate, but were hardly reliable on an individual basis.

Evidence indicates that middle- and upper-class women tried numerous methods to prevent conception, especially in the late nineteenth century, when feminists publicly advocated limiting family size. This movement, the crusade for "voluntary motherhood," sprang from women's concerns over health and family. In order to increase a woman's capacity to rear and nurture all her children, many women wished to limit the number of their offspring. Many middle-class husbands supported their wives on this sensitive issue. Men and women argued "birth control" was potentially detrimental to women's status. But many feminists hoped that it might eventually strengthen women's position within society. Women's crusade for "voluntary motherhood" and "planned parenthood" reflected a collective bid for female self-control rather than a movement for sexual freedom. Since the majority of women were dependent on their families for emotional as well as marital support, many were unwilling to undermine their position. Feminist advocates of family limitation hoped that fewer children would allow women a new status within the household. Many advocated abstinence instead of contraceptives, for fear that they might be tainted with the hostility the "free love" crusaders attracted.

However, a handful of feminists were sexual radicals, attempting to divorce issues of sexual relations from reproduction. A few, such as Victoria Woodhull, championed birth control as a means to freedom. They believed the separating of sexuality and procreation was necessary to women's autonomy. This was a natural, however extreme, course for feminism to follow. The majority of feminists feared the repercussions of this radicalism and steered the birth-control movement along more conservative lines. The very language used reflects the fears of its advocates: "voluntary motherhood" appealed more to the general public than any call for "freedom" or "control."

Some have dismissed these less radical elements of the birth-control movement—calling the voluntary-motherhood crusaders conservative. A more sympathetic interpretation emerges in recent revisionist scholarship. The connection between women's lack of economic options and the advocacy of family limitation is apparent. The voluntary-motherhood movement focused on questions of family and reproduction, but sought to reform rather than demolish institutions which kept women confined. After redefining the female role model in the antebellum era with the cult of domesticity, middle-class women made considerable impact. They hoped to further their cause with campaigns that were also anchored to women's role in the home.

Many men cooperated in the effort to control reproduction. Contraceptive practices were more effective, if not widespread, among the educated classes. The different birth rates of white and other ethnic groups would indicate that values as well as technology played a role in reducing the birth rate. The ideal of a smaller middle-class family influenced this trend. The educated couple who were financially comfortable, but not wealthy, aspired to upward mobility; these couples realized that too many children were a burden. They also limited family size because children were no longer economic assets. Of course, large families were found among the rich, who could afford several children, or the poor, who needed the support of their offspring in their old age. But the majority (neither well-off nor poor) attempted to regulate and reduce reproduction.

Opposition to birth control persisted. Many religious leaders opposed any movement which divorced the sex act from religious purpose: as humans were enjoined to be fruitful and multiply, traditional church views condemned any attempt to interfere with procreation. The male establishment perceived that a crusade to limit family size would free women to leave their designated sphere and assume new roles. In the upper classes, women and men joined ranks against birth control because they felt threatened by the waves of immigrants coming into the nation. Theodore Roosevelt was outspoken on the question of "race suicide." He preached the doctrine that native white women must remain prolific to prevent the country from being overrun by "hunger-bitten hoards." In the South this ideology was equally popular among upper-class whites, who feared the booming black birth rate.

This countermovement was not brought about by simple disapproval of birth control. Rather, the opposition organized and in a sense triumphed during the last quarter of the century. In 1868 contraception was banned in New York, and in other states thereafter, prohibiting free access to birth-control information and devices. In 1872 the New York YMCA launched a program to enforce this prohibition. They hired Anthony Comstock as a special investigator dedicated "to prosecute, in all legal forms, the traffic in bad books, prints and instruments."

In March 1873 Congress passed a measure which provided "for suppression of trade in and circulation of obscene literature and articles of immoral use." Both advertisements and information were subject to prosecution, and Comstock also was hired to be a special agent of the U.S. Post Office. The legislative doctrine known as "the Comstock law" became notorious, especially after the first arrest.

Perhaps not unexpectedly, the first person prosecuted was Victoria Woodhull. Woodhull was influenced by the sexual hypocrisy of Victorian moralists and as well by the political intrigues in which she was involved. In 1872, she published an account of the adulterous affair of Henry Ward Beecher (perhaps the most famous minister of his day) and Elizabeth Tilton, the wife of his best friend, Theodore Tilton, a fellow reformer. Rumors of the affair had circulated privately in New York for many years. To the public, the fact that the charges were true perhaps was not as shocking as Woodhull's bold contempt for propriety, her unmasking of pillars of respectability. She later argued that she was not persecuted merely for her role in bringing the Beecher–Tilton scandal to light, but that her arrest was the first step in a government campaign to suppress freedom of the press, most especially journals edited by radicals and feminists. Whether or not Woodhull was the victim of a conspiracy, the decline of her fortunes paralleled the rise of Anthony Comstock. Although some members of the medical profession challenged Comstock's right to regulate their practice, by the 1890s the law and public opinion combined to suppress the free circulation of contraceptives and birth-control information.

The birth rate was reduced—cut in half—by more than contraception. Birth control was achieved in large part through abortion. This issue perhaps more than any other contributed to passionate conflict within the women's movement. The morality of the issue, many feminists argued, was secondary. They were primarily concerned with the circumstances which made abortion necessary. Many attempted to shift the debate to the question of safe and effective contraception. Radical women emphasized that abortion was a woman's last resort, one to which women were driven by the lack of effective contraceptive methods. In addition, many emphasized that most abortions were performed not, as stereotype would have it, on unwed women suffering the consequences of promiscuity, but rather the remedy was sought as often by married women, and the majority mothers.

The legal movement to prohibit abortion was first directed not at women who sought such radical means of birth control but at doctors who performed the operation. New York was the first state to enact an antidoctor statute, in 1829, and most northern states followed suit in the next two decades. By the Civil War, physicians decried the falling birth rate, and many blamed the decline on the prevalence of abortion.

During the 1870s the Comstock campaign and public opinion combined to promote a national crackdown. Abortion had been fairly secret before the war, but not so rare as one might suppose. Experts estimate one abortion for every thirty live births from 1800 to 1830. By mid-century this figure had escalated to one abortion for every six live births, showing an enormous upsurge despite statutes against the practice. Equally common, advertisements for abortifacients filled periodicals. The manufacture and sales of "female pills" flourished in nineteenth-century America, and if these medicines failed, women might resort to surgical means. The cost varied from decade to decade and region to region, but most women could find a doctor willing to perform an abortion for $100. A study of doctors' cases in mid-century shows that two-thirds of the women who sought abortions were married, and 60 percent of them had at least one child, confirming feminist claims that married mothers were a large proportion of abortion seekers in the nineteenth century.

During the 1850s abortion parlors began to flourish in eastern cities. Madame Restell was a notorious practitioner in New York City who did hundreds of abortions a year following the opening of her office in 1838. After the Civil War, because of mounting public protest and concern about repopulating after the devastations of war, states began to enact stricter legislation. Despite these restrictions and prohibitions, women continued to have abortions.

Unfortunately, some women could neither find nor afford proper medical care. Working-class women were especially prone to take matters into their own hands. In 1873 the *American Journal of Medical Science* reported the tragic consequences to which such action could lead: "She had stated that during her pregnancies she had suffered so much discomfort that she had determined to bear no more children. She procured a piece of steel wire as long and as large as an ordinary knitting needle...She had laid herself upon the bed and passing the wire up the vagina, pushed it, as she thought, very gently, into the uterine canal. Suddenly it slipped up and disappeared." The woman died shortly thereafter. Doctors were confronted with hundreds of botched abortion cases every year. In some cases the women survived, but more often they did not. We have no statistics on self-induced abortions, but a survey in the 1920s reveals that one of every two pregnancies ended in abortion. Despite dangers and obstacles, women were determined to control reproduction and would often do so by drastic means.

Some historians maintain that abstinence played an important role in family limitation. Because of the "passionlessness" which middle-class women cultivated, Victorian values finally created the climate which allowed women the power to say no. The "sexlessness" which males imposed upon women was turned back against men by many Victorian wives. This veto power was reluctantly accepted by males. Marriage was an institution in which males ruled paramount according to law. Yet women were able to manipulate ideology to protect themselves against unwanted pregnancies.

The availability of data on this subject is limited by the modesty which dictated sexual discourse. However, contemporaries argued that if husbands did not want to subject their wives to unwanted advances or if women denied them their marital rights, many men looked outside the home for sexual gratification.

The postwar era marked a flourishing of prostitution. During the 1870s some reformers suggested licensing the trade. Prostitution was regulated in parts of Europe, but, except for a period of four years in St. Louis, no American city registered prostitutes during the nineteenth century. With the failure to regulate prostitution, most reformers turned to a "social-purity crusade." This group became vocal in the late nineteenth century.

Concerned about prostitution in American society, feminists were divided over the best method to attack the problem. Many held that all prostitutes were victims. Most women with Victorian values believed that a woman did not choose "a life of shame" but was seduced, drugged, abused, or forced into the role. Many of these bourgeois feminists were remarkably unsophisticated in their analysis. One innocent suffragist reflected what many believed: "How long would any city government that is responsible for imprisoning honest girls in brothels hold its power, if its reelection depended in any degree on the votes of women?" However, it is not fair to characterize the entire feminist movement as naïve on this issue. Indeed, many provided informed insight. As Caroline Dall succinctly asserted: "Lust is a better paymaster than the mill owner or the tailor."

It is too simplistic, however, to argue that prostitutes sold sex because they had no other alternative. We know, of course, that domestic service and the needle trades were open to semi-skilled women. But many women realized that they could earn more as prostitutes. Wage-earning women realized, for example, that working temporarily as a prostitute, they could earn enough cash to dress better. With a better wardrobe, they hoped to move out of the most exploited work (domestics and pieceworkers) and into positions as shopgirls. However, too few were able to make prostitution any other than a dead-end proposition.

Popular misconceptions about prostitutes abounded: that most prostitutes were kidnapped by white slavers or trapped into the trade by fraudulent marriages, or that all prostitutes died of syphilis or became madams. Most Americans believed prostitutes were ruined women who could never move into respectable society. These myths were all grounded in some aspects of reality. Victorian America fostered an active white slave trade, even participating in an international traffic in young girls. Pimps often hung out at the docks or train stations to "take in" women new to the city and unschooled in urban vice. Large numbers of women were involved in prostitution. To assume that managing a brothel or dying from venereal disease was the fate of former prostitutes is highly imaginative. Rather, many women moved from this sexual subculture into domestic roles as wives and mothers. Indeed, some prostitutes were wives and mothers even while plying their trade. In addition, prostitutes could move into respectability merely by abandoning their trades and moving to a new community.

Reformers not only drew attention to the inequities that created the economic attractiveness and viability of prostitution for working-class women; feminists joined the popular campaign against the white-slave trade. Periodicals trumpeted the evils of this criminal activity. Muckraking authors scoured the red-light districts, revealing the evils which flourished openly there. Popular novels exploited the theme; two of the most prominent examples were Stephen Crane's *Maggie: A Girl of the Streets* (1893) and Theodore Dreiser's *Sister Carrie* (1900). Unfortunately, much of the literature tended to romanticize these women. But sensationalism also led to reforms.

Many social-purity crusaders sought to raise the age of consent for women to twenty-one, a vain hope. But many laws were abusive, and reforms remedied outmoded statutes. In 1880 Maine had an age of consent of ten; in Arkansas it was twelve. Following the social-purity campaigns, many states raised the age of consent to eighteen. Reformers put through a national statute, the Mann Act (1910), which prohibited the transportation of girls across interstate lines for immoral purposes. But the contribution of the social-purity campaign was much greater than mere legislation.

This movement provided women with a forum for discussion of the formerly forbidden subject, sex. The advocates of social purity, however, were not all the prudish fanatics of stereotype. Many were active feminists fighting social hypocrisy and sexual caricature. By the turn of the century, women not only were challenging the Victorian double standard which promoted prostitution but were openly questioning the very premises of Victorian morality. The level of sexual discourse was heightened enormously during the early years of this crusade.

Historical documents and traditional methodology shed little light on either sexual attitudes or sexual activities. Women's sexuality in the Victorian era cannot be divined from prescriptive literature, since accounts differ concerning prescribed behavior and prescriptions might well have been disregarded in matters of private choice. Very likely, moral standards may have been established by those who saw eroticism as undesirable; yet that which was condemned or taboo might have become the most attractive within an array of sexual choices. Indications are that women's sexual practices in the nineteenth century challenged the prim stereotype. Just as with the abortion issue, the majority of American women may well have ignored what authority stipulated and what experts preached.

The feminist critique of society allowed educated women to develop alternative views of themselves and their roles in society. These ideological reconstructions touched on private as well as public spheres. Stereotypes of inferiority and frailty projected in the popular culture were not only false but detrimental. After women addressed the moral, intellectual, and physical shackles society imposed, some were willing to tackle the emotional—or in modern terms, psychosexual—problems women faced.

Feminist critics derided the false and crippling images Victorian society promoted concerning women's sexuality. Only a minority of radicals supported "free love," a doctrine which advocated open and unregulated sexual relations between consenting adults. When put into practice, these attitudes usually resulted in a serial monogomy rather than a group marriage. But many more feminist reformers favored a revolutionary reinterpretation of women's sexual nature. Stanton, for one, attacked men who were "apparently ignorant of the great natural fact that a healthy woman has as much passion as a man." Some feminists held that it was the man's clumsy or rough performance during intercourse which led to women's passionlessness.

With the public persecution of Victoria Woodhull, and with the attacks on birth control and abortion, however, feminist theorists and strategists realized that many middle-class women were alienated by frank and open debates on sexuality. Any link with "free lovers" and advocates of sexual Utopia became a liability during the 1870s. Most feminists jettisoned any association with radicals rather than jeopardize broad-based support. Some simply suspended the demand for sexual reforms, channeling their energies into the fight for suffrage. Most feminists, realizing they could win more support by avoiding controversy, favored more popular crusades such as temperance or even divorce reform. The public campaign to redefine the nature of sexuality slackened considerably for a time; but the impact on women's private lives remains relatively unknown.

Some evidence suggests that the redefinition of women's sexuality led to striking departures from the cultural norms promoted in many contemporary texts and sermons. Departures in attitudes and behavior are found primarily among educated women, those who articulated their attitudes to provide us with records. Evidence from a late-nineteenth-century study by Dr. Clelia Mosher indicates that the sexual beliefs and practices of upper-middle-class women diverged radically from the image projected by both contemporaries and modern historians. Data from the Mosher survey, however small a sample (forty-five women), has been used to open up debate on this closed topic.

One-third of these forty-five women were born before the Civil War; another third were born from 1860 to 1870; and the other third were even younger when Mosher began her investigation in 1892 (it was concluded in 1920). Thirty-five of the forty-five women expressed their desire for sex independent of any wish to fulfill their husbands' desires.

Most saw sex as an integral part of their lives. One woman commented: "I consider this appetite as ranking with other natural appetites and like them to be indulged legitimately and temperately." However, Mosher's study indicates that many women were having intercourse more often than they would have wanted, had it been subject to their desires rather than those of their husbands. There is some indication that the frequency and timing of sexual intercourse were increasingly determined by mutual consent.

One aspect of sexual attitudes is dramatically illuminated by this study. Dr. Mosher asked the women how often they experienced orgasm—a phrasing that indicates that Mosher, a doctor familiar with women's sexual habits and concerns, expected the women to report the frequency of orgasm, rather than merely if orgasm was ever achieved. A significant 35 percent responded, "Always"; 40 percent answered, "Sometimes, but not always"; the others did not answer the question. The fact that 75 percent of these women at some time experienced orgasm is rare evidence of patterns of female sexuality. We cannot draw conclusions for a wider group, but we can speculate that educated wives of elite men believed female orgasm was a significant component of sex and (at one time or another) they experienced sexual climax.

This experience must be put into a larger context. The evidence of female orgasm cannot suggest completely the extent of women's sexual pleasure, but it affords insights into female expectations and sexual activity within marriage. Mosher's evidence partially challenges stereotypes of Victorian women. If the most cultivated and educated of American women rejected the prevailing attitude, perhaps middle-class and working-class women also deviated from prescribed norms.

One matter of enormous importance has yet to be touched on: same-sex affection, romantic friendship and love among women. This topic has attracted widespread interest in recent years. These relationships did not just sustain spinster females; married women cherished female friendships as much if not more than their relationships with men. Some wives had more intimacy with women confidantes than with their husbands. This female bonding was a direct result of the cultivation of separate spheres and the creation of a women's culture. Crushes between schoolgirls developed into lifelong friendships. The passion of these women is reflected in letters between female friends and in journals—as many friends kept diaries for confidantes and then exchanged them.

The language cannot be dismissed as rhetorical flourish, since other evidence demonstrates these were substantial and sustained relationships.

Most women believed that romantic friendships could co-exist comfortably with marriage. They maintained that heterosexual love was a different thing altogether. Affection between females was, as Margaret Fuller described, "purely intellectual and spiritual, unprofaned by a mixture of lower instincts, undisturbed by a need of consulting temporal instincts." Such affection was cherished by middle-class women.

Spinsterhood, which was becoming increasingly economically viable in late-nineteenth-century America, was more and more often a positive choice, instead of status by default. Some women held that they were simply not suited for marriage. However, those who did not marry did not always choose to spend their lives without affectionate companions or sexual partners. In Victorian America, most spinsters chose women companions. Few wished to risk illicit liaisons with men, and many perhaps preferred female mates.

Many spinsters experienced their first love as schoolgirls. Young women developed "flames" or "raves" and became passionately attached to one another while in school. Many pupils displayed enormous affection toward individual teachers as well. A study published in 1897 indicated that younger girls and older pupils, as well as students and teachers, followed courtship patterns. These rituals and the resultant relationships could blossom into passionate love, sexual intimacy, and perhaps lifelong associations which excluded men.

A small group of single women who carved careers for themselves lived as female couples, as "Boston marriages." Spinster couples would live, work, and travel together, much as heterosexual couples. Author Sarah Orne Jewett spent her life with companion Annie Fields; actress Charlotte Cushman had romantic involvements with two younger women before she initiated a twenty-year liaison with sculptor Emma Stebbins; and Alice James (sister of novelist Henry James) had a close and fulfilling intimacy with Katharine Loring. Indeed, Henry James developed a popular archetype of this romantic friendship in his novel *The Bostonians*. Although in James's novel the young protagonist, Verena Tallant, is swept away from her relationship with a charismatic older woman, Olive Chancellor, James hints that this solution might prove unfulfilling for Verena. Popular culture condoned these romantic friendships as long as they did not interfere with heterosexual relations. Women who shunned relationships with men or traditional marriage were thought to be asexual. In nineteenth-century America these liaisons did not provoke controversy because the general public assumed that there was no sexual component.

With the influence of European sexology and modern psychology, many female couples explicitly condemned homosexuality to protect their position. Scholars suggest that the survival of these Boston marriages may have been dependent upon women's public denunciation of sexual love between women. In 1892, when a young woman in Tennessee, Alice Mitchell, slit the throat of her female lover, Freda Ward, a spectacular scandal erupted, and Mitchell was quickly locked away after being declared insane. Eventually, the authorities became more suspicious of female friendships, and women couples were forced to deny their sexuality and, if lesbians, remain in the closet.

It is nearly impossible to delve behind the defenses these women built to protect their privacy and integrity. When Jeanette Marks, a student at Wellesley, fell in love with her professor, Mary Wooley, it was the beginning of a lifelong relationship. When Wooley assumed the presidency of Mount Holyoke from 1901 to 1937, Marks taught there. For the ten years following Wooley's retirement until her death in 1947, the two women were inseparable. Marks and Wooley lived together for fifty-two years. This close and passionate attachment, so obviously an imitation of a legal union, caused comment but no scandal. Wooley and Marks publicly condemned lesbianism, although their private lives might have suggested otherwise. In this, as on other matters of sexuality, public opinion and private practice might well have been at odds.

Despite the difficulty of determining the nature of these relationships, a study of sexuality is rewarding. If we look behind cardboard caricature, reality sharply reveals the flimsiness of our previous estimations of women's private lives. However, stereotypes are not easily dismissed; they exert tremendous influence over our lives. The power and importance of Victorian codes, whether or not these codes were observed, had a major impact (if only negative) on women's choices.

At the beginning of the nineteenth century women's lives, it is clear, were rigidly circumscribed. Most women became wives and mothers. Fulfilling biological roles consumed the majority of women's time and attention. By the end of the century, women had made great gains toward female autonomy. Many important battles had centered on sexual concerns.

Men rightly argued that women's entrance into the public sphere would transform their contributions in the private domain. Many women inventively refashioned arguments concerning women's role to allay men's concern. At the same time they steadily carved out more and more territory as their own. Despite proclamations of domesticity's primacy and the florid rhetoric of the voluntary motherhood movement, women slowly gained power by limiting the size of their families. Females played a larger role in determining sexual matters. Some women even excluded men entirely from their lives, without denying themselves a sexual partnership.

These social transformations were met with strong resistance from both men and women. Conservatives often painted feminists as immoral or loose women, brandishing sensationalist headlines which proclaimed a link between women's independence and their sexual downfall. Men instituted a sheltering system as much for their own aggrandizement as for women's protection. Women who rejected this protection, opting for freedom, were subjected to disrespect and antagonism. Unfortunately, rumor was as powerful a weapon as fact. Many women were sexually threatened or slandered to keep them in submissive roles. But feminists remained faithful to their cause in the face of severe opposition. The resolve of moral reformers, the energies of feminist activists, and the example of radicals pushed the debate over women's sexuality onto the public platform and paved the way for the modern movement toward sexual freedom.

9
Networks and Reform

FROM the very founding of the nation, informal female networks and organizations promoted female kinship and by the late nineteenth century became the basis for many social institutions. The exclusivity of middle-class membership and the "high moral tone" of many ladies' clubs created a "society page" atmosphere. Their popularity was phenomenal, especially in metropolitan centers. Chicago could boast of a burgeoning women's literary enclave, the Fortnightly Club, founded in 1873. Its members held discussions on popular literary works such as George Eliot's *Middlemarch*, and also had guest lecturers. The ladies' clubs were sex-segregated lyceums, emulating the movement popular earlier in the century.

Female intellectual circles thrived not only in urban centers but throughout the country. Many well-educated women could not get enough cultural stimulation from their domestic routine or the occasional diversions of town life. From the Shakespeare Society of Rockland, Maine (1889), to the Thursday Literary Club of Selma, Alabama (1890), and the Women's Reading Club of Walla Walla, Washington (1892), females banded together to improve their minds and pursue mutual interests.

Women's clubs did not originate during the post-bellum era. But the intellectual and feminist orientation of many of these groups was new. As early as 1866, Friends in Council, a gathering of local women, met regularly in Quincy, Illinois. Boston women founded the New England Women's Club in 1868. Perhaps the most notable of these "new" all-female organizations, the grandmother of women's clubs, was New York City's Sorosis. As the name suggests, this group represented a departure from the cultural and domestic circles which preceded it. The women of Sorosis chose to institutionalize their independent sisterhood: they formed a club based on feminist consciousness and dictated by male-imposed segregation.

The club was founded as a protest. The first group of women professionals following the Civil War naïvely believed that their status as pioneers, as women who had earned success despite the handicaps which society imposed, would topple barriers. They were mistaken. Indeed, in numerous cases, women's acknowledged and increasing excellence in previously all-male fields stiffened resistance. Many New York women were sadly disabused when the New York Press Association refused noted journalist Jane Croly admittance to a banquet held for Charles Dickens. Croly and her supporters were appalled by this indignity and vowed to form their own club. In March 1868 this band of irate feminists (originally called the Blue Stockings) launched an exclusively female society. Sorosis, as Croly explained, offered "a system of rewards, of recognition of merit in women." She went on: "Every boy born in America looks forward to the possibility of personal distinction . . . But women have nothing of this sort to anticipate. The household is their only acknowledged sphere and in it there is neither reward nor promotion." The founders, Jane Croly, Charlotte Wilbour, and Alice Cary, hoped Sorosis would counter this injustice.

The club boasted a number of prominent women. By 1870 membership included thirty-eight writers, six editors, twelve poets, six musicians, four professors, nine teachers, two artists, one historian, ten lecturers, three philanthropists, and two physicians. Sorosis provided professional women with recognition and offered a mutual support system. In addition, these middle- and upper-class women took it upon themselves not only to endorse suffrage and other radical solutions to discrimination in their social class but also to investigate conditions for working women.

Many of these "ladies' associations" wished to shed their genteel outlook and to increase their influence in public affairs. They realized they must abandon their polished image of refinement in favor of more feminist and political positions to achieve maximum impact. By the 1890s nearly one hundred thousand women were club members; by 1910 this number was eight hundred thousand. The era of the progressive woman reformer was at hand.

The climate of female supportiveness and the need to combat male exclusion encouraged many women to launch reform crusades. Just as there were many pathways to feminism, so there were many roads to progressivism. But we cannot discount the impact of female networks on the campaign for social justice and municipal reform. It is hard to disentangle late-nineteenth-century reformers from their feminist roots.

To chronicle one example: in 1876 twenty-one middle-class women formed the Chicago Women's Club. The group rather ambitiously organized itself into six departments: reform, philanthropy, home, education, art and literature, philosophy and science. Membership doubled in the first year. By 1886 there were over two hundred members; growth of the organization during its first decade was phenomenal. But this was only the beginning. By 1892 membership had doubled once again, and in 1900 the club was forced to set a limit of one thousand members. In addition, the orientation of the club membership shifted over the years. Whereas members were originally divided equally among the six departments, by the 1890s nearly two-thirds of the members were affiliated with the most progressive and activist branches of the organization: education, philanthropy, and reform. The Chicago Women's Club took an active role in the founding of other reform movements within the city such as the Legal Aid Society, the Public Art Association, and the Protective Agency for Women and Children. The club successfully championed the appointment of women physicians to the Cook County Insane Asylum, and contributed time and money for poor relief during the devastating depression of 1893.

Before, during, and after the depression they provided cheap lodgings for women as part of their ongoing crusade against exploitation. These women were not concerned solely with women's issues. Club members recognized that poverty and crime were larger problems with which feminists needed to grapple, and they sought to deal with these increasing urban ills with concrete actions as well as calls for reform. The Chicago Women's Club raised money for an industrial school for boys, and continued financial support for this venture.

Their financial and moral commitment to reform improved urban conditions. The women of this organization were decidedly activist, and many, if not most, were feminists. However, the group never officially endorsed women's suffrage. They were certainly open to the ideas of the National Suffrage Association and the American Suffrage

Association. Indeed, not only did the club entertain Susan B. Anthony and other suffrage leaders during their visits to Chicago, but the leadership also forbade the Home Department from forming an antisuffrage group. Some members complained that this prohibition violated the spirit of non-partisanship which the club cherished. Pro-suffrage advocates argued that although they would not call the issue to a vote within the club (it might divide the membership and damage their reform efforts), they also would not stand for any overt antisuffrage activity within the club.

Chicago supported one of the largest, most active and powerful of women's clubs. But most towns and even villages had similar organizations. The Women's Club of Cripple Creek, Colorado (founded in 1896), grew in one year from thirty-five to 135. Community pride counterbalanced resentment of their isolation. Women, in even relatively spartan areas, organized female societies.

In an effort to harness and direct the tremendous energy generated by women club members, Sorosis called a national convention in 1889. The Ladies' Social Science Association, established in 1873, had been the forerunner of the effort to bind together a national network of women. The earlier group, however, limited itself to questions of moral education, such as holding frank and open discussions on marriage and sexual relations. Despite the popularity of these "consciousness-raising" groups (combining the dissemination of information with sisterly support), the branches of this "national" organization were clustered in the Northeast, primarily in the coastal corridor (from Massachusetts to Washington), with the exception of Chicago affiliates. By contrast, following the call by Sorosis, delegates from over sixty organizations from all over the nation convened to found the General Federation of Women's Clubs. When the organization first drew up its bylaws, the founders outlined modest goals for the group. The 1890 constitution advocated a network of clubs dedicated to literary, artistic, or scientific purposes. Within a year, however, the goals of the organization began to shift dramatically.

From the beginning, women's clubs branched out into civic activity, not merely token activity, but deep commitment to reform. By the early twentieth century, these women were the backbone of the "municipal housecleaning" movement sweeping the country. Staunch activists insisted that the principles of their organization include the promotion of practical reform. The women's clubs generated kindergartens, libraries, and other valuable improvements. The women perceived that they must provide "housekeeping for the cities" as well, and their crusades improved the quality not just of their own neighborhoods but of the metropolis. By 1896 the federation amended its bylaws to reflect these fundamental aims.

However, even at the national level, suffrage was too controversial a topic for the federation to entertain. Not until 1904, when the dynamic Sarah Platt Decker became its president, did pro-suffrage advocates dominate the leadership. Decker made a lasting impression when she announced in her inaugural address:

> Ladies, you have chosen me your leader. Well I have an important piece of news to give you. Dante is dead. He has been dead for several centuries, and I think it is time that we dropped the study of his Inferno and turned our attention to our own.

Decker appointed more energetic and radical women to committees. But it still took more than a decade's work to convince the membership to endorse women's suffrage.

The Young Women's Christian Association (YWCA) was established in New York City in 1858. A Boston affiliate sprang up in 1866, and by 1873 over thirty-six branches flourished throughout the country. These institutions were not organized to provide charitable social services; rather, the YWCA fostered, in large measure, self-help for women. In 1874, when Charlotte Drinkwater was hired to head a YWCA with nearly two hundred women in residence, her superiors counseled her: "Build it up by your own originality; no one can tell you how to do it, and the men's prophecy of women's failures must not be fulfilled."

The YWCA provided single women in the cities with respectable boardinghouses. These facilities, by and large, were, like their residents, self-supporting. In addition, the YWCA met the needs of females in the urban underclass by offering vocational courses to enhance their prospects of employment. Training in domestic and other traditional female occupational skills may have channeled poor women into jobs that offered few opportunities for economic mobility. Yet these programs were welcomed by both immigrant greenhorns and rural migrants new to the sprawling urban jungle. In addition, the YWCA provided women with job-placement services.

Despite the conservatism of many of the organization's founders, later generations of YWCA leaders resisted attempts to restrict membership to members of Protestant churches who could demonstrate good standing in a sponsoring congregation. The YWCA programs, activities, and services were open to women regardless of creed or class. However, the organization was less than radical on the question of race. The national leadership buckled under pressure from southern affiliates and refused to integrate their local residences. Black women could join branches of the organization open to "coloreds only."

Ironically, this position was perceived as enlightened in its day, because the YWCA did not refuse black women membership—as did many national organizations, including the General Federation of Women's Clubs, which denied credentials to black women's organizations. Black women derided white women's hypocrisy. They openly challenged the double standard whereby white women, after suffering male exclusion, would turn around and impose similar prohibitions on black sisters. Black clubwoman Fannie Barrier Williams attacked this prejudice in an address at the World Columbian Exposition in 1893: "I regret the necessity of speaking to the question of the moral progress of our [black] women because the morality of our home life has been commented on so disparagingly and meanly that we are placed in the unfortunate position of being defenders of our name..."

Racism subjected black women to the demeaning stereotype of "easy virtue." In response, many black middle-class women became vociferous champions of female moral purity. To escape the curses of both sexual and racial slander, most black women embraced conservative tenets of asexuality which many white feminists found oppressive. Because only white females could embody fully ideals of American womanhood in the racist climate of the late nineteenth century, the sources of oppression for black and white women often differed.

Another black middle-class spokeswoman, Josephine St. Pierre Ruffin, expressed her contempt for racially segregated federations: "Year after year southern women have protested against the admission of colored women into any national organization on the grounds of immorality of these women... The charge has never been crushed, as it could and should have been at first." Following several failed attempts at integration, black clubwomen pressed for national affiliation of their organizations. In 1895 *The Woman's Era*, a black paper published in

Boston, supported this campaign. Shortly thereafter, the National Federation of Afro-American Women—active in sixteen states—merged with the Colored Women's League of Washington (by far the largest black female organization in America) to form the National Association of Colored Women (NACW).

The group elected Mary Church Terrell, a model of black female achievement, its first president in 1896. Born in 1863 in Tennessee, the daughter of slave parents, Terrell earned a degree from Oberlin College in 1884. She moved to Washington, where she married and enjoyed a career first as a teacher and then as a member of the District of Columbia Board of Education—the first black woman to hold such a post. Under her leadership, NACW membership grew to nearly fifty thousand. The organization sponsored kindergartens, seminars in child care and home economics, mothers' clubs, and many other activities. Northern clubs were especially geared to the needs of black migrants from the South. Terrell forged links with the all-white National American Women's Suffrage Association. She addressed their 1898 convention on "The Progress of Colored Women." Terrell became a speaker of international reputation following her appearance in Berlin in 1904 as a U.S. delegate to the International Congress of Women. She impressed her audience by delivering her address in French and German as well as in English. Despite her skills and renown, she was unable to convince white clubwomen and suffragists to abolish the color line, to desegregate national organizations.

Although most white clubwomen were insensitive to issues of racial equality, many middle-class matrons were increasingly preoccupied with class oppression. Female reformers struggled to bridge the gap between classes through sisterhood, if only for whites. Since many among the membership of these clubs fancied themselves "ladies bountiful," the stereotypical portrait of these women's organizations was surely unflattering. The most egalitarian among clubwomen attempted to break down class lines among whites.

As early as 1863, in New York City, middle-class reformers organized the Working Women's Protective Union to coordinate assistance programs for poor women in the city. Middle- and upper-class women sought to use their talents and skills to rescue women—their "less fortunate sisters"—from brutal and exploitive men (pimps as well as employers) who preyed on working-class females.

Despite the patronizing attitude of many union founders, reformers struggled against class divisions, trying to unite all under a feminist banner. During its first decade the union found jobs for twenty-seven thousand women seeking work in the city, and collected more than $10,000 to provide needy females with financial assistance. A similar society was founded in Boston at mid-century by a former Lowell "mill girl," Jennie Collins. She established a home for "needy women" and managed a non-sectarian employment agency at a time when the thirty thousand young working girls in Boston constituted 10 percent of the city's population.

Groups specifically committed to the protection of women emerged in most if not all urban centers throughout the country. Traveler's Aid Societies met incoming ships and directed immigrant women to YWCA homes to protect them from the white slave trade. By steering women into protected environments, the associations hoped to reduce the number of prostitutes and destitute women roaming city streets. Most women welcomed the opportunity to settle in the local YWCA boardinghouses, where they might find a home for a mere $3–$4 per week. Once these girls secured shelter and employment, social-service agencies provided them further assistance. The protective agency established by the Chicago Women's Club heard over 156 complaints by women in its first year. Problems with employers' totally unjustified withholding of wages constituted nearly one-third of the cases.

This was a recurring problem for women alone in the city. When the New York Union was founded in the winter of 1863–64, working-class women specified their most pressing and paramount concern: "Oh, if we could always get paid for our work, we could get along." Through protests lodged with these societies, a few wage-earning women were able to obtain back pay and fairer treatment from their employers. The middle-class reformers faced issues of economic justice as well as tending to philanthropic works.

Many working-class women with too little cash coming into the household also had family obligations which prevented their working outside the home. A number of city clubs established a Women's Exchange; any woman could join for a $5 fee. The exchange would collect 10 percent of the price of any item sold. This system provided home-bound women a source of income. Females confined to the domestic sphere found a reasonable and convenient outlet for commodities. A woman might support herself through the sale of home-made goods while still in school or while kept at home by infants and toddlers.

One of the most successful, the Women's Educational and Industrial Union, was launched by the New England Women's Club in 1877. These relatively sheltered reformers struggled to find common ground where women might meet "not purse to purse or talent to talent, but 'heart to heart.'" The Boston club members organized a subsidized lunchroom where women from the middle and working classes might mingle. In addition, evening classes offered working-class women training to improve their skills, as well as fostering contact with middle-class benefactors. By 1890 the union founded by the New England Women's Club had attracted 1,200 participants. The Boston organization was but one of a host of similar organizations thriving in the late nineteenth century.

Many clubwomen were active in feminist or proto-feminist organizations as well as in their own clubs. Paulina Wright Davis, in addition to participating in Sorosis (serving as its president during her long and active feminist career), was a member of the National Women's Suffrage Association, a founder of the National Association for the Advancement of Women, and editor of its journal, *New Century*. Model clubwoman Lucretia Longshore Blankenburg is another fine example. The daughter of Philadelphia's first woman physician, she was named after a woman her mother greatly admired, Lucretia Mott. After attending a local commercial college, Lucretia married a German immigrant and gave birth to three infants, all of whom died in childhood. In the late 1870s, seeking an outlet for her talents, she helped to found the New Century Club, a women's organization committed to civic as well as social purposes. The New Century Club offered night courses to wage-earning women; Blankenburg taught bookkeeping. She also started and sponsored the New Century Guild, a club exclusively for working women. Blankenburg campaigned for the use of police matrons, in response to the problems and working conditions of her women pupils and friends. She also crusaded for the appointment of women to the Philadelphia school board and eventually became president of the Philadelphia Women's Suffrage Association. She was an active member for sixteen years and eventually became an officer of the General Foundation of Women's Clubs. A respected clubwoman, she resigned her suffrage post to work full-time on getting the Women's Federation to endorse the vote for women, a long and hard battle which resulted in federation support of women's suffrage in 1914.

Although many clubwomen supported suffrage, the federation resisted supporting a national amendment. Another major reform movement of the era, temperance, met with less difficulty obtaining official endorsement. This crusade was not new in post-bellum America, but it escalated to unprecedented dimensions in the last quarter of the century. The temperance movement derived in part from women's lack of power over their lives. Women temperance advocates sought more control within the family and expanded influence in the larger society. For most women, the effects of liquor were doubled, because of the problems created when the men in the family drank. By the end of the century a swelling tide of women contended that liquor endangered their family's and their own happiness. Alcohol was an evil to be stamped out.

Women promoted what was commonly called "the white life," commitment to the moral regeneration of the American family. Most female temperance supporters embraced their domestic roles. Although some historians have suggested that temperance promoted cultural antagonism between the sexes, others argue that for most female temperance advocates the family, and not women, was their main concern. Revisionist scholars suggest that temperance women unwittingly contributed to their own repression; the majority of the "cold water warriors," as temperance advocates were called, accepted male dominance as a given fact.

Despite ongoing debates over the feminism or non-feminism of this campaign, the female temperance movement was during its heyday one of the largest reform movements of the century. Over two hundred thousand dues-paying members and thousands more sympathetic to the cause contributed to the strength of this campaign. In November 1874, at a meeting in Cleveland, over two hundred women representing organizations in seventeen states met to form the Women's Christian Temperance Union (WCTU). They argued that the saloon was a direct challenge to woman's domain, and as a threat to the family and a cause of social disorder and human misery, it must be destroyed. At their second national convention, the delegates resolved:

> That since women are among the greatest sufferers from the liquor traffic, and realizing that it is to be ultimately suppressed by means of

> the ballot, we the Christian women of this land, in convention assembled, do pray Almighty God, and all good and true men, that the question of the prohibition of the liquor traffic should be submitted to all adult citizens, irrespective of race color or sex...

The movement attracted not only women opposed to alcohol but other female reformers as well.

None was more dynamic and visionary than longtime WCTU president Frances Willard, who served as head of the organization from 1879 until her death in 1898. Willard's parents, graduates of Oberlin, were transplanted New Englanders who settled in Wisconsin with their teenage daughter. After completing her education, Willard worked her way from college teacher to college president, heading the Evanston College for Ladies. But she drifted out of her career in education and into reform. Clearly, Willard was committed to women being a moving force and she saw temperance as a means to an end. This inspirational leader, heralded as "St. Frances" by her followers, felt that temperance was the key to women's militance, a stepping stone for improving women's political status. In 1876, even before her election as head of the WCTU, Willard championed women's suffrage openly on the floor of temperance conventions.

The techniques and strategies of the temperance crusade were similar to those of other, earlier campaigns. But temperance was a cause which harnessed the energy of hundreds of thousands. The petition drive was particularly effective. In 1878 Willard led a "Home Protection" campaign, collecting 180,000 signatures in her home base of Illinois for support of the local option to prohibit the sale and consumption of liquor (known as the Maine Law, after the first state to implement it). The cross-class appeal, the tireless efforts of the women crusaders extended into every state by the 1880s. And, most important, Willard made the explicit connection between temperance and women's suffrage. She forged a bond between the two movements.

Willard's linkage was not welcomed by all suffrage advocates. Especially in the West, where temperance was less popular with state leaders, many suffrage leaders opposed any connection between the two issues. But most suffrage advocates welcomed the large numbers of women who advocated suffrage through their affiliation with the WCTU. Willard not only led her followers into the camp of women's suffrage but campaigned as well for a spectrum of reforms.

In 1881, after she obtained endorsement of women's suffrage from her following, Willard established an amazing number of departments for the WCTU—thirty-nine in all. Social purity, child-labor reform, and everything from prison reform to homes for unwed mothers were included in Willard's aims. Her enthusiastic efforts to turn the union into a broad-based feminist movement was ambitious, to say the least. She pioneered liaisons with the Patrons of Husbandry, the Knights of Labor, and other important national associations. She certainly raised the consciousness of temperance advocates concerning the importance of women's role within a modernizing American society. Willard summed up her philosophy in 1884 when she said: "Were I to define in a sentence, the thought and purpose of the Women's Christian Temperance Union, I would reply: *It is to make the whole world* HOMELIKE." She went on to proclaim that, to attain her goals, "a woman will enter every place on this round earth."

Her scope and vision were spectacular, but the union was unable to measure up to Willard's dreams of influence. Even the modest gains achieved under her aegis were dissipated after Willard's death in 1898. When the WCTU lost Willard, it reverted to a single-issue organization. By 1900 the WCTU rescinded its commitment to suffrage. The new leaders concentrated on their original aim of temperance.

However, the feminist ranks of the crusade were overflowing with another branch of the women's movement by the last decade of the century. The progressive woman reformer was a product not only of the clubwomen movement and the temperance crusade but of social activism. With the introduction of settlement houses, idealistic social workers opened up new professions for themselves in urban slums. Committed young American college graduates borrowed the idea of the settlement house from England, after they saw its impact on Britain.

Although the first settlement house in the States was founded by a man, Stanton Coit, who established the Neighborhood Guild in New York City in 1886, women's involvement in settlement work rapidly outstripped that of men. Quite independent of Coit, in 1887 a group of Smith College alumnae (headed by Vida Scudder, who was teaching English at Wellesley at the time) met to formulate a plan to put their education to better use. Late-nineteenth-century America offered the ambitious woman professional a long, hard road to a career, but most middle-class women college graduates had no outlets for their talents after earning a degree. And even the more successful, such as Scudder, were discouraged by the limitations imposed on them by gender discrimination.

In 1889 Scudder, her Smith classmates Jean Fine and Helen Rand, and four other young women rented a tenement on the Lower East Side of New York City. These newcomers were immediately approached by the local cop on the beat, who did not much care what plans they had in mind for the house they rented, as long as he received a monthly contribution. These naïve college women were rather rudely introduced to the harsh realities of urban life. Once the police and the women's neighbors discovered the group planned a settlement house, there was local skepticism. "Seven Lilies have been dropped in the mud, and the mud does not seem particularly pleased," is how one journalist put it.

These Smith graduates were the forerunners of the movement. In the same year, Jane Addams and Ellen Gates Starr established a similar institution in Chicago, Hull-House. They hoped to provide career opportunities, and also to change the community. Two years later there were only six settlements in the United States, but there were over seventy by 1897, and within three years, by 1900, there were over one hundred settlement houses.

The number of settlement houses grew steadily during the first decade of the twentieth century. By 1910, over four hundred such institutions had been founded. Some groups were incorporated, others not. Some of the settlements had religious affiliations and held church services on weekends, but most were sensitive to the diversity of the community they served and were non-sectarian.

Because many settlement workers lived in the houses (hence the term "settlement house"), relations between the reformers and their neighbors often went from acquaintance to affection, from suspicion to admiration. In 1906, when there were nearly two hundred residences throughout the country, over eight hundred workers lived in the settlement houses which they staffed. An additional three thousand settlement workers participated in programs but chose to live elsewhere. The overwhelming majority—three out of four—of these workers were women.

The profile of these urban reformers suggests a striking departure from earlier crusades. The average settlement-house resident was young, with a median age of twenty-five. The majority were not married. Almost 90 percent had attended college, and over half had done graduate study. In 1902 Columbia Teachers College used philanthropic funds to establish the Speyer School of Social Work, the first such school in the country. Many settlement workers were trained in this pioneering program in New York City. The settlement house met the needs of the age. As Jane Addams wrote in 1892: "Young people hear constantly of the great social maladjustment, but no way is provided for them to change it and their uselessness hangs about them heavily."

Urban reform appealed particularly to educated women with aspirations to contribute to their society. One Chicago reporter commented in 1908: "Twenty years ago . . . a young woman who was restless and yearned to sacrifice herself, would have become a missionary or married a drinking man in order to save him. Today she studies medicine or goes into settlement work." Social workers were attracted to the crusade by both the individualist and the communitarian appeals of the settlement house. Young, middle-class students seemed eager to commit themselves to self-sacrifice. Resident workers were sustained spiritually by actually living in the neighborhoods they sought to transform. Being able to affect the daily lives of those they served, settlement workers achieved modest but significant gains. Despite the small scale of the campaign, the personal and uniquely flexible nature of the operation (each worker contributing individually) rendered it effective. These pioneering groups were, as historian Allen Davis describes, the "spearhead for progressive reform."

In 1892 the leaders of women settlement workers (graduates of Smith, Wellesley, Vassar, Bryn Mawr, and Radcliffe) formed a College Settlement Association. These women could proudly claim the establishment of the University Settlement in New York, Denison House in Boston, and the College Settlement in Philadelphia. New York City boasted the largest number of settlements before 1900. In addition to Coit's Neighborhood Guild and the University Settlement, in 1893 Lillian Wald founded the Nurses' Settlement, and in 1895 the Hudson Guild was formed in Chelsea. Other cities joined in this movement with Kingsley House in Pittsburgh (1893) and Hiram House in Cleveland (1895), and similar establishments in Hartford (1895) and Louisville (1897).

In 1894 Susan Chester, a Vassar graduate, went into the upper South, where she founded her Log Cabin settlement outside Asheville, N.C. She wanted to transplant the formula for reform into a new environment. Just as young idealists had brought the London experiment to American cities, she wanted to apply urban reform to a rural setting. She determined "to maintain clubs for girls and women, to revive the weaving industry, and to provide a good library for the community." These seemingly modest goals were monumental for the community she served. The enthusiasm with which local residents supported and indeed flocked to her Log Cabin is testimony to Chester's success. Some library members walked eleven miles to use the precious facilities. And her attempts to revive weaving among mountain women sparked pride as well as accomplishment. However, the majority of settlement workers confined their efforts to urban areas.

Even within cities, settlement workers also struggled to create a "romantic revival" of handicrafts. As newly arrived European immigrants were rapidly absorbed into menial and debilitating factory labor, they generally abandoned traditional skills to put the Old World behind them and assimilate as rapidly as possible. Social workers who tried to preserve some of these skills through neighborhood fairs and exchanges were fighting a losing battle. Settlement residents had some success instilling in European-born Americans a sense of pride in their ethnic heritage, but in the long run, the romanticism of the revival could not compete with the realities of city slums.

Settlement workers also began to jettison some outmoded cultural baggage of their own. They began to realize that lectures and classes were not enough to cope with the serious social problems which the urban poor faced in their daily struggle. Jacob Riis's sketches of the ghetto, in *How the Other Half Lives: Studies Among the Tenements of New York*, had an influence on urban reform. Settlement workers organized exhibits of his photographs in fashionable galleries and salons, in the hope that such a powerful visual display might move city leaders to pay more attention to the plight of the poor.

During this same era of transformation, most settlement houses structured their operations to match the needs of their working-class clientele. Practical programs and services, such as child-care centers and kindergarten classes, were given top priority. Next in order of importance, social workers offered manual training and industrial education. While in residence, settlement workers developed a greater sensitivity to the deteriorating urban landscape which the working poor were helpless to improve.

In 1887 New York passed a Park Act requiring land to be set aside for grass, trees, and playgrounds throughout the city. Developers ignored the law, and city administrators failed to enforce it. In an effort to make the city honor its commitment, a Society for Parks and Playgrounds was formed. This group championed environmental issues and in 1906 launched a national movement for their cause, along with the National Playground Association. Jane Addams and other influential reformers served on the board.

Agitation for day care and parks was not enough for many of the new breed of settlement workers. As an example, in 1896 Hull-House residents responded to the plight of striking textile workers by collecting money to feed them. They even collected travel funds to send blacklisted workers to other cities. Participation in this and other protests was not sponsored by the settlement organization but was the choice of individual social workers. Although Jane Addams did not picket (she said she was too busy with other reforms to get herself locked up in jail), a fellow resident of Hull-House, Ellen Starr, favored direct action. When Starr joined employees of a Chicago restaurant picketing to protest long hours and low wages, she was arrested for interfering with the police. She proved her commitment to the working poor and argued to her comrades: "If one must starve, there are compensations in starving in a fight for freedom that are not found in starving for employers' profits."

Urban women reformers, especially settlement residents, saw very clear connections between prostitution and poverty, deviance and deprivation, and other, more subtle, dimensions to the "criminality" of the lower classes. Earlier in the century, in antebellum Massachusetts (where the first reform school for girls was established in 1857), a spirit of tolerance had prevailed for women offenders, especially juvenile delinquents. But by the latter part of the century, penal institutions were more concerned with classification and confinement, with isolation from society as much as rehabilitation.

Early attitudes concerning criminals championed the "reform" of women as an especially rewarding task, for as one superintendant of a female reform school put it: "It is sublime work to save a woman, for in her bosom generations are embodied, and in her hands, if perverted, the fate of innumerable men is held." In antebellum America, youthful female offenders were trained to fit into the domestic sphere, but by the turn of century notions of hereditary criminal tendencies and the concept of "irredeemable deviance" hampered prison reform.

The classification of juvenile female criminality was, not surprisingly, influenced by social as well as legal definitions. Male inmates were quite clearly charged with crimes stemming from their alleged proclivity for violence, for damage to personal or public property. However, young women in reformatories could just as easily be confined because of alleged immorality, charged with crimes ranging from "wantonness" to prostitution.

By the middle of the nineteenth century, authorities preached that girls in trouble should be locked away from temptation, placed in institutions and taught domestic skills. Reformers hoped they could change juvenile character and redeem fallen women. Female institutions began to segregate women by age and crime. By century's end, the emphasis was on confinement of the female criminal, not reform.

Once women were categorized and imprisoned, the state sought to keep them occupied and perhaps to teach them skills which might serve them when they left the institution. Most reformatories and prisons only allowed women to learn housekeeping. But by the end of the century, prison officials began to experiment with other programs. For example, in 1876, the state women's prison in Indiana established a laundry. Authorities imported consultants from Troy, New York, to advise concerning this facility. The superintendent condemned this labor as tiring, routine drudgery, but it fitted women for a trade after their prison term. The program continued despite objections to the back-breaking apprenticeship.

In 1879, Massachusetts initiated an even more ambitious enterprise. Prison officials established an indenture system within a year of the founding of the women's reformatory at Framingham. Women inmates were provided conditional early release if they had served three-fourths of their sentences and had a good record in prison. These female prisoners were found work as domestics in nearby homes. It was hoped that if women reentered society in semi-rural communities (the outskirts of Boston, in this case), they at least temporarily might avoid the temptations of an urban environment. Fewer than 10 percent of these early-release inmates returned to prison, a record which impressed advocates of the indenture program. Because these prisoners returning to the outside world did not undercut men's work, and because the indenture system channeled women back into the economy, the experiment was heralded as a success.

Prison reformers had many other battles to wage. Discipline for prisoners varied from state to state, but most institutions punished unruly inmates with solitary meals, handcuffs, or in extreme cases prolonged confinement in the "dungeon." At New York's Hudson House of Refuge in 1899 women rioted against the dungeon and abusive corporal punishment. But this is one of the few instances of organized resistance to prison authority.

Separate prisons for women were a significant demand in the late nineteenth century. Females were meted harsher treatment in mixed prisons. For example, at Sing-Sing, women were subjected to gags, straitjackets, hair croppings, and solitary confinement in cells without windows or light. These and other indignities led feminists to champion the rights of female prisoners, to help their sisters, indeed to be, as historian Estelle Freedman describes, "their sisters' keepers." By the turn of the century, conditions were much improved for women inmates at female prisons. In addition, female superintendents were more likely to use merit and demerit systems rather than the threat of punishment to control women prisoners. This and similar programs reflect the "maternalistic attitude" of women superintendents toward their charges.

Despite the maternalism women reformers might occasionally manifest, the great drive for reform generally provided for innovative rather than imitative roles for women. These new models appealed to women with both individualistic and communitarian ideals. The individual woman might dedicate herself to any movement which threatened family interests. Females could and did launch campaigns to promote their own private concerns, reforms which were attuned to a woman's need for autonomy, such as the settlement-house movement. At the same time, women joined forces in united efforts which provided females with a collective identity and sought to improve conditions for women as a group, such as the purity campaign and the clubwomen unions.

The success of these campaigns cannot be measured solely in terms of goals sought and aims achieved. Rather, we must analyze the ways in which these multifaceted crusades converted masses of women not only to the cause of reform but to awareness of their talents and capabilities. Clubs, networks, and associations created a climate for women in late-nineteenth-century America which led to transformations in women's image and status. Perhaps the contrast between women's involvement in the Philadelphia Centennial Celebration of 1876 and in the Columbian Exposition of 1893 partially demonstrates the changes.

In 1872, when the Centennial Board of Finance needed funds for its exposition, women's support was sought. Elizabeth Duane Gillespie, Benjamin Franklin's great-granddaughter, headed the effort. Gillespie organized a nationwide fund-raising campaign along the lines set for state suffrage campaigns, appointing captains for rural counties and city wards in every state in the Union. In return, women were guaranteed space in the main hall of the exposition. By June 1875, the women had collected $125,000.

Their jubilation was short-lived when the Centennial Commission informed them that the space intended for the women's exhibits had been allocated instead to foreign countries. Exposition organizers granted the Women's Department permission to set up an adjacent building for their exhibits. But since they were offered none of the funds they had raised, the offer was an empty gesture. Nevertheless, Gillespie and her associates collected more money, assembled booths in a separate building, and represented as well as reflected women's prodigious accomplishments with their exhibitions in the Woman's Pavilion.

The Women's Medical College of Philadelphia submitted a *materia medica* of over 150 specimens for display. Other booths highlighted female inventions, new sewing innovations, as well as an impressive collection of labor-saving housekeeping devices. Women artists from the Cooper Union, the Lowell School of Design at MIT, the Pittsburgh School of Design, and the Cincinnati School of Design sent contributions. Harriet Hosmer, the American woman sculptor, sent her work from Rome. Dress reformers had booths, and pioneers of nursery schools also set up exhibits. Such a wide range of material featuring new ideas and inventions both for women and by women was an important breakthrough. "Kindergartens" were featured at the Woman's Pavilion—a relatively new phenomenon; within four years, three hundred had been established, in nearly thirty cities across the country.

Stanton, among other radical feminists, opposed the Woman's Pavilion. She said: "Upon its walls should have hung the yearly protests of Harriot K. Hunt against taxation without representation . . . framed copies of all the laws bearing unjustly upon women—those which rob her of her name, her earnings, her property, her children, her person . . . Women's most fitting contributions would have been these protests, laws, and decisions, which show her political slavery. But all this was left for rooms outside the Centennial grounds."

Feminist leaders were disappointed that the Centennial Board denied them their request to present to dignitaries—as part of the Fourth of July celebration—a Declaration of Rights of Women. Despite male objections, Susan B. Anthony startled the gathered platform speakers by marching from her seat in the grandstand up to the Vice President of the United States on the platform to offer him the document. Including the feminist manifesto in the published proceedings did little to satisfy feminist critics.

Women of the Centennial Executive Committee planned their own style of protest: Woman's Day was held on election day, November 7. However, the ceremonies featured only polite speeches and social entertainments, with little political content and few references to women's suffrage. Women's involvement in the Philadelphia Centennial is interesting in contrast with events leading up to the Columbian Exposition.

When in 1889 Chicago was selected as the site of the 1893 Columbian Exposition, Myra Bradwell, a lawyer and a leading feminist in Chicago, met with the executive committee of the fair to secure official recognition for a women's auxiliary for the event. Over two thousand women attended a public meeting to demonstrate their interest in participating. Many Chicago feminists joined the Queen Isabella Society, an organization which wanted to feature—in a separate forum such as a "women's building"—the prodigious contributions of women to the growth and development of the New World.

From the outset, Bertha Palmer, elected head of the Board of Lady Managers, knew that the segregation of women's industries from the rest of the exhibits might disrupt feminist unity. This was a burning question on which everyone had strong opinions, with forceful feminist arguments on both sides of the issue. Those who favored a separate exhibit believed that the extent and variety of the contributions of women would not be appreciated unless they were displayed in a separate building. Others countered that the exhibit should not be one of sex but of merit, that women could compete side by side with men. The integrationists asserted that segregation on the basis of sex was sentimental and was detrimental to women's future progress. Although this fundamental difference was never fully resolved, most women worked out their differences for the "good of the fair."

When the Lady Managers finally agreed to a pavilion for women, they agreed that the building should have a woman architect—notwithstanding the fact that only eight women in America had graduated from architecture schools. The board held a competition in March 1891 and thirteen women entered. The winning design was submitted by Sophia Hayden. Born in 1868, she had earned her degree from MIT. The managers also insisted on numerous open competitions for the exterior and interior decoration of the building. Hayden was disturbed by the way in which the Columbian ladies solicited uneven and eclectic contributions, with little consultation on the overall design; she did not want the building "to look like a patchwork quilt," she said. Her criticisms wounded many female supporters who had favored the separate exhibit in hopes that the widest range of women's contributions might be displayed. However, the Lady Managers met Hayden's high standards when they invited Harriet Hosmer to design sculpture and Mary Cassatt to paint murals for the building.

In October 1892 an official dedication celebrated the completion of the project, and on May 1, 1893, the Woman's Building was officially opened. This ceremony dramatically differed from the activities which heralded the Woman's Pavilion at the 1876 Exposition. Bertha Palmer, director of the Board of Lady Managers, delivered a lengthy and impassioned speech on women's role in society, which included the following indictments:

> Of all existing forms of injustice there is none so cruel and inconsistent as is the position in which women are placed with regard to self maintenance—the calm ignoring of their rights and responsibilities which has gone on for centuries . . . the theory which now exists among conservative people that the sphere of woman is her home—that it is unfeminine, even monstrous, for her to wish to take a place beside or compete with men in the various lucrative industries—tells heavily against her . . . producers take advantage of it to disparage her work and obtain her services for a nominal price, thus profiting largely by the helplessness of their victim. . . .

Palmer went on to celebrate the role of the Woman's Building in helping to stem this tide of injustice: "We now dedicate the women's building to an elevated womanhood—knowing that by doing so we shall best serve the cause of humanity." The feminists used as their symbol a globe of the world, encircled by a banner which read: "Not for herself—but for humanity."

This may seem rhetorical flourish, but it represents a subtle departure from the women organizers of fair activities two decades earlier. At the Philadelphia Exposition most women were happy to contribute side by side with men—to demonstrate their accomplishments in celebration of the nation's one hundredth birthday. They were cheated by their male co-workers, rewarded with exclusion and marginal recognition. During the decades following the Centennial, social progress allowed women to compete and in many cases hold their own with men: in the professions, in reform, and in other previously exclusive male domains. Despite these gains, many upwardly mobile women forged a separatist ideology. As long as men continued to discriminate against them, many women who wanted equality sought status and recognition which, whenever possible, circumvented sexism. These independent women did not want to remain at the mercy of discriminatory male criteria. These self-imposed female separatists, however small a minority they were, represented a radical departure for women in nineteenth-century America.

Many women, not just feminists, believed that their interests which differed from those of men would be ignored by those in power. Female activists of many political stripes focused on their distinctive—and now legitimate—female concerns. Feminist radicals wreaked havoc, by sometimes integrating male domains and sometimes insisting on separate female institutions. These hardy pioneers promoted their own interests within and outside the social mainstream. Male hegemony was rocked by their persistent assaults. Besides drawing attention to women's particular concerns, many feminist activities captured the support of the majority of middle-class women. Female reformers thus harnessed a tremendous source of energy and strength, a resource which would enable them to continue their struggles for women's rights and equal justice.

10
Divided and United

BY THE end of the nineteenth century, women were not merely involved in their own political struggles; many females joined male comrades in protests and campaigns of mutual interest. Emma Goldman, Jane Addams, and Victoria Woodhull—to name three outstanding figures—each established a reputation within movements which, if not male-dominated, were oriented equally to men's concerns. Women did not play passive roles in these crusades. Indeed, women activists were often able to influence the goals of these organizations to reflect feminist as well as other radical demands.

Several socialist movements sprang up in the late nineteenth century in response to economic upheavals. Masses of women sustained these organizations. Collectivist social schemes appealed to women, and women's participation shaped many of these radical groups.

American Socialists debated feminist issues from the beginning. In 1872 an American representative at the first International in The Hague—in defiance of the party line—claimed: "The labor question is also a women's question, and the emancipation of woman must precede that of the workers." This placed feminism squarely at the center of socialist concerns (which is doubtless why Victoria Woodhull was closely associated with this movement during her early political career).

Leftist politicians have always been divided on a variety of issues, and "the woman question" proved no exception. When controversy over women's suffrage erupted in New York during the 1870s, the Socialists declared: "Universal suffrage cannot free humanity from slavery . . . The gaining of the vote by women is not in the best interests of the workers." Although the Socialists attempted to avoid feminist controversy (and the great railroad strike of 1877 gave the American movement other preoccupations), in 1883 theorist August Bebel expanded on an idea Marx had only hinted at: the progress of humanity could be measured by women's condition. Unlike most German thinkers, Bebel rejected the notion of woman as a timeless symbol. His analysis disputed the scientific explanations of women's inherent inferiority and the Darwinian justifications of female confinement to the household. He argued that women could and should be calculated as part of the work force and further that females were the first humans subjected to bondage.

This radical interpretation came at a time when the American work force was undergoing dramatic change. The rate of capital investment doubled between 1880 and 1890, coupled with an equally wrenching shift in the ratio of machine to hand labor. American industry's demand for unskilled labor increased, and an influx of millions of immigrants met this need. At the turn of the century the majority of the unskilled labor force was foreign-born. Many American Socialists during the 1870s and 1880s had been born in Germany. They brought their radical politics with other cultural baggage when they left the Old World. When German Socialists worked toward a broad-based reform movement in America at the end of the century, they mistrusted many of the native brands of radicalism, especially the bourgeois suffragists. Most of these foreign-born Socialists contemptuously attacked middle-class feminists as "agents of the capitalist class sent to dupe working women by offering meaningless aid." The paternalism of many matrons who wanted to "rescue urban urchins"—in many cases from their own parents—offended some immigrant and wage-earning women. Socialist men convinced many working-class women to turn their backs on the temptations of bourgeois reformers, to reject the folly of an independent feminist movement. These women formed their own Socialist organizations, "ladies' branches" affiliated with those of their male comrades. This, in conjunction with other political complexities, undermined women's status within American Socialism. In 1901, when the Socialist Party of America was founded, only eight of the 128 delegates were women. Although the Socialist platform endorsed equal political and civil rights for women, party leaders gave low priority to feminist concerns.

Despite setbacks, a thriving crop of Socialist women emerged at the turn of the century. Kate Richards O'Hare, a popular lecturer, spent her honeymoon on the speakers' circuit. She confessed: "I would prefer to be at home, but a sense of duty forces me to do something to improve the conditions of women in the industrial struggle for existence." The Socialist leadership commended females' selfless devotion to the cause. Ironically, this praise undermined one of the goals of the new generation of activist women: to defeat the romantic image of women as saints. American Socialist women wished to smash sentimental and restrictive images of wives and mothers, to pose the alternate view of women as partners in the struggle for political and economic justice.

Rose Pastor Stokes's life was a testimony to this cause. Born in Poland in 1879, she immigrated with her family and settled in Cleveland. In her first job she worked, as many immigrant girls did, in a cigar factory to help support her several siblings. In 1903 she moved to New York City to pursue a career as a journalist, writing for a Yiddish paper. Within three years she married a millionaire reformer, and the press called her the "Cinderella of the Sweatshops." However, this American fairy tale had a rather different ending when in 1906 the couple joined the Socialist Party. Stokes organized garment workers, hotel workers, and spearheaded a legal defense campaign after the 1913 Paterson strike. As revolutions erupted, Bolshevism became her goal. In 1918 she was indicted for antiwar activity and put on trial with Eugene Debs. She was prosecuted again in 1922 for her role in the founding of the Communist Party. Throughout her involvements with both the Socialist and Communist Parties, she disdained "purely feminist" causes. Stokes advocated separate women's committees only to spread radicalism among all the proletariat; she and other party women were advocates of equality but no friends of American feminism, which they labeled "bourgeois" and "elitist."

Feminists did have socialist allies with the growth and development of the Nationalist movement. When Edward Bellamy's *Looking Backward* appeared in 1888, it became one of the century's best-selling novels and initiated a political movement. Bellamy's Utopian vision included blueprints for reform of special interest to women. In *Looking Backward* the hero awakens in the year 2000 to discover a world vastly different from the one in which he had fallen asleep in the 1880s. Feminists marveled at the role of women in Bellamy's futuristic vision: women were accorded political parity. In addition, all adult citizens participated equally in the economy. Pregnant women were supported by the state, thus being liberated from dependency on their mates. Even more revolutionary but still relevant to women's concerns in late-nineteenth-century America, domestic work was state-supported as well. This Utopia included public kitchens and dining rooms, as well as day schools and nurseries. Bellamy's work had profound implications for the division of labor within society.

When Frances Willard finished the novel, she proclaimed the book a "revelation." Bellamy's ideas had a similar effect on other feminists such as Lucy Stone and Jane Croly. Many reformers, "repelled" by foreign-dominated Socialism, comfortably embraced Bellamy's Nationalism. His proposition that changes for good might come about through cooperation and the electoral process rather than bloodshed appealed to those bourgeois radicals who feared proletarian revolution. Many feminists, preferring Bellamy's "Americanization" of socialist ideology, joined the Nationalist crusade. It is not surprising that the young Charlotte Perkins Gilman became a lecturer for the movement.

Gilman, the grandniece of Harriet Beecher Stowe, is one of the most complex and important figures of the turn of the century. Her childhood and adolescence were plagued with unhappiness: her father deserted his family when Charlotte was seven. She had very little education; her brother earned a degree from MIT, but Gilman spent only a short time at the Rhode Island School of Design, which concluded her formal studies. She married in 1884 at the age of twenty-four, and after the birth of a daughter a year later, she suffered a severe breakdown. She fought her way out of her depression through writing; and in 1892 she published her first novel, *The Yellow Wallpaper*, "a bitter story of a young woman driven to insanity by a loving husband-doctor..." She divorced her husband and later, when he remarried, she gave him custody of their daughter, Katherine. Freeing herself of family and domestic impediments, she became a prominent lecturer, touring Europe and America.

Bellamy's influence is clear in Gilman's first major political study, *Women and Economics*, published in 1898. In this brilliant theoretical attack on conservative interpretations of the political economy, Gilman posits that society confused women's sexual and economic roles: women's oppression was the legacy of a patriarchal past, an anachronism in modern, industrial America. She championed reorganization of the economy: "The road to improvement was to permit women to participate equally in all affairs outside the home... By this means would women become full developed and independent human beings rather than creatures of sex, and would make distinctive and valuable contributions to society." Gilman asserted that because women were denied access to wage-earning jobs, they were forced to use sex to earn their keep, just as men sold their labor in exchange for a living. Her bold and radical critique expanded on this theme with her next book, *The Home: Its Work and Influence*, in 1903.

Gilman charged that the single-family home was economically wasteful and isolated women from the larger world. She advocated "French flats," or apartment dwellings, rather than the detached, nuclear households in which most Americans lived. In addition, Gilman proposed that household labor be professionalized: housecleaning and upkeep should be a paid occupation for wives, not domestic servants. She urged her middle-class readers not to settle for the acquisition of mechanized household gadgets, which still held women chained to the household; housewives should organize and get professional services for laundry, diapers, food preparation, and other tasks usually done in the home.

Gilman went on to write several Utopian novels, including *Herland* (1915), which was serialized in the magazine she founded in 1909, *The Forerunner*. For its fifteen years, Gilman's periodical contained spirited feminist attacks on law, education, fashion, and sports, and dozens of other subjects which attracted her attention. Women's work and the economics of domestic labor were the topics on which Gilman made a major contribution.

Advocates of socialized housework and movements for cooperative housekeeping predated both Bellamy and Gilman. Although most cooperative activity earlier in the century was part of the formal division of labor in an isolated social community (such as the Shaker village system), by mid-century many feminists advocated alternative arrangements to cope with household work. Melusina Fay Peirce delivered her critique of women's situation in a series of articles in the *Atlantic Monthly* in 1868–69. This Cambridge housekeeper, the wife of a Harvard professor, based her plan for women on radical ambitions:

> But two things women must do somehow, as the conditions not only of the future happiness, progress and elevation of their sex, but of its bare respectability and morality. 1st They must earn their own living. 2nd They must be organized among themselves.

Peirce outlined a plan to insure both goals. She urged women to band together to do housework cooperatively through associations which could then charge husbands for domestic services. Wages would be paid to cooperative houseworkers on a scale similar to that for men who did skilled work. Further, Peirce proposed cooperative stores, kitchens, laundries, and bakeries to tackle collectively tasks that were economically oppressive to women.

Most husbands resisted having their wives "make other men comfortable," as one critic put it. But the settlement-house movement paved the way for proliferation of public kitchens and cooperative dining facilities in the late nineteenth century. Single women in the cities, those least hampered by family demands and household drudgery, were best able to put these Utopian schemes into practice. However, recent research has uncovered an impressive record of cooked-food delivery services, cooperative dining clubs, and communal bakeries and laundries, testifying to housewives' attempts to address their economic problems. Cooked-food delivery services cover a surprising range in one scholar's chronicle: from Evanston, Illinois, to Palo Alto, California, from 1869 until the 1920s, ventures lasting anywhere from six months to thirty years (with a median lifespan of two years), using modes of transport from horse-drawn carriages to automobiles. The spirit of cooperation which women demonstrated in this allegedly "private sphere" of the household was equally important to political developments during these years.

Farm women were well aware of the need for cooperation when tasks required more hands than were available. The rural housewife was expected to join her husband in the fields if necessary. However, rigid gender divisions of labor existed on farms as well as in cities, and husbands rarely tackled "women's work." Yet, because of women's critical contribution to agricultural production, the majority of farm wives had a larger role in rural political culture—in a manner denied to all but a minority of their urban sisters.

With the founding of the Patrons of Husbandry (the Grange)—a fraternal society—in the late 1860s, women's equal participation was institutionalized. Local charters for the organization were granted when four women and nine men convened to establish a branch. Females had full voting rights, access to any office, and special posts designated to manage female affairs. The lecture coordinators for the Grange throughout New England and the Midwest were quite often women. Only in southern assemblies were women token members, with minimal participation in political affairs. In the Midwest, evidence suggests that Grange women were able to persuade many male members to endorse women's suffrage and support temperance.

By the mid 1870s, 25,000 Grange chapters counted 750,000 members. Kansas, which had been a battleground for women's suffrage following the Civil War (the referendum campaign of '67), became a field of combat once again when Grange members launched their most spirited agrarian attack on capitalist monopoly. Kansas produced two of the most outspoken female agrarian radicals, Annie Diggs and Mary E. Lease, who was remembered for her remark that farmers should raise more hell and less corn. Diggs, Lease, and many other female Grange lecturers with national reputations, such as Marion Rodd and Sarah Emery, were not lifelong residents of farms, although all but Lease were reared on homesteads. Lease was a daughter of the plains, starting her career as an organizer in Wichita.

The majority of the women in this movement were not orators but rather dedicated members who gave enormous support to the agrarian crusade. The average female Granger was drawn into the movement when her husband joined. But many women developed activities and interests which were not merely extensions of those of their husbands. Women within farmer alliances believed that their roles were "supportive" rather than, in any sense, secondary. Katie D. Moore urged her rural sisters to remember:

> We may feel we are silent factors in this work; we know we constantly need something to lean upon, like the honeysuckle upon the tree or fence. Let us so entwine ourselves around our brothers that should we be taken away they will feel they are tottering and can hardly stand. Let us be ready to consider, advise with, and listen to every arrangement they may feel interested in . . .

Moore went on to assert that her agrarian brothers should also be willing to consult with their sisters as well.

Michigan Grange leader Mary Ann Mayo was a teacher before she married and settled on a farm. When her friend Jennie Buell became an editorial assistant for the *Grange Visitor*, the Michigan Patrons journal, Mayo began in 1882 to write up reports of meetings for her local branch. Her contributions grew to include columns on health and "domestic arts." In 1884 she was invited to lecture on horticulture and housekeeping in local townships, first making appearances with her husband in attendance. Later, having had to "pluck up courage and go alone," she toured her home state of Michigan as well as parts of Ohio and Indiana. Mayo only undertook these assignments for the Grange after her children were grown, since she believed that a mother's first obligation was to her family. Despite her domestic concerns, Mayo endorsed measures to insure that "our girls as well as our boys are admitted into all of our Agricultural Colleges." Women Grangers with equal rights within the organization often pressed for reform in the larger society.

Many rural women were radicalized by participation in the agrarian revolt. Cassie Kemp rallied the women within her alliance, urging: "Stand firm if we can't vote. We have but one thing to fight with, and that is our tongues, and we must use that as best we can." Another woman in the North Carolina Alliance in 1891 (at a time when women constituted one quarter of the membership) looked to her work as a welcome challenge: "Our brothers . . . are giving us grand opportunities to show them, as Frances Willard says, that 'Drudgery, fashion and gossip are no longer the bounds of woman's Sphere.'"

The agrarian crusade, however, failed to stand by its commitment to female equality. This democratic farmers' crusade concentrated on reforming government money policy and attacking railroad monopolies. Populists had their own Utopian bible, *The Golden Bottle*, written by Ignatius Donnelly in 1892. In this popular indictment of capitalist greed, the heroine, Sophie Benezet, pleads: "Not charity, but justice. Not stealing from the poor and giving them back part of it, with many airs and flourishes and ostentation; but stopping the stealing, and permitting industry to keep the fruits of its own toil." When the Grange movement evolved into economic and political organizations—the Farmers' Alliance and the People's Party—membership failed to secure for women the equal rank they had enjoyed in the early groups. Populists accorded women an inferior role within their organizations once the group became a full-scale national political crusade. Nevertheless, at the local level, women's continuing participation prevailed.

Rural women established separate societies when they suffered male exclusion. In September 1891, Fannie McCormick, an organizer for the Kansas Knights of Labor, and Emma Pack, a women's club leader from Topeka and the editor of *The Farmer's Wife*, started the National Women's Alliance. This group's declaration of principles included endorsement of women's suffrage and a proposal for women's admission as equals to all political organizations. Some radical agrarian women even managed to preserve their sense of irony when men subjected them to the indignity of political inequality. Following the formation of the People's Party in 1892, Mary Lease lashed out at male comrades: "Thank God we women are blameless for this political muddle you men have dragged us into..." However, she and other feminists in the agrarian movement were outraged that Populists refused to endorse either women's suffrage or temperance. Lease's feminist commitment never wavered, and she proclaimed: "Ours is a grand and holy mission, a mission as high and holy as ever inspired the heart, fired the brain or nerved the sinew... ours is the mission to place the mothers of this nation on an equality with the fathers."

The depression of 1893 caused many political radicals to retreat—including the beleaguered Populists. Hampered by its regionalist image and politics, the People's Party was unable to effect a coalition between its membership and the urban working classes ripe for political organization. With William Jennings Bryan's defeat in the Presidential election of 1896, the movement dwindled even further. In fact, some might see the seeds of failure in the fact that Populists allowed race as well as gender to split their movement.

The great crusade against the capitalists and the monopolies kept to a color line despite the fact that the tenant-farm system (and sharecropping) exploited blacks and whites equally. White women within the Populist campaign, especially in the South, were accomplices in this discrimination. It would seem that until the twentieth century the great majority of white women in America were unwilling to acknowledge and resist racial oppression, even though it was similar to discrimination that in many ways held them to an inferior status. It is even more ironic that "white womanhood" was an excuse for racial violence in the postwar South. White women became symbols to the defeated Rebels; they were the unsullied, alabaster icons of Confederate mythmakers. Although the war was a lost cause, the celebration of the southern lady became a crusade which southern gentlemen cherished above all, thus, in a sense, carrying on the battle against the Yankees.

This had its darker side, however. The inflated imagery imprisoned white women behind stereotypes of chastity and purity. Even more damaging, black women were excluded from formal conceptualizations of "womanhood," a fact which continues to oppress black women. At the same time, white men projected their worst fears of revenge: the fear of rape of a white woman by a black man became a singular obsession of white males after the Civil War. Many white southern men believed it was a crime against them—violation of their domain—if a woman not only in their family but of their race was assaulted by a black. Thus, interracial rape (of a white by a black) was judged a crime against all whites for which all blacks were guilty. The actual violation of women became, in a social and political context, secondary to the symbolic meaning of the act. Allegations were as damaging as evidence, and in many cases, the white man's fantasy substituted for fact. Indeed, racism played such a distorting role that it is impossible in many cases to determine if rapes were committed when whites charged blacks with assault.

The southern crusade to "protect" white women which developed in the late 1860s was, in fact, a campaign by white men to maintain their racial superiority through paramilitary roles. The Knights of the White Magnolia and other fraternal orders grew into vigilante associations. The most powerful of these groups, the Ku Klux Klan, became a full-fledged terrorist organization. Sheets protected the identity of the organized outlaws, and lynching was their trademark. Lynching was a brutal ritualistic device employed by white gangs to keep blacks submissive and exploited. If whites simply wished to punish blacks who defied them, they could have manipulated the legal system or have used some less visible means of elimination (in the manner, for example, that underworld figures "disappear"). But the spectacle of public execution, often conducted in a carnival atmosphere, and sometimes combined with barbaric mutilation and cruelty, symbolized white power in the South. Lynching was, in the most ghastly sense, a form of social control.

The evil grew in the last decades of the century. America witnessed an average of fifty-seven black deaths by lynching a year during the 1880s, which grew to 116 per year by the 1890s, with 162 recorded deaths in the peak year of 1892. To give some idea of the regional dynamic of the phenomenon, in 1892 only four of 162 blacks were murdered by lynch mobs outside the South. Although southern demagogues defended the practice as an effective means of safeguarding white women, critics pointed out that only a minority of the lynch victims were even accused of rape, and, for example, in 1892 five of the murdered were women.

As lynchings became increasingly commonplace, southern blacks fought back. A courageous southern black woman led the campaign. Ida Wells was born the child of slaves in Holly Springs, Mississippi, in 1862. After she attended the local school established by the Freedman's Aid Bureau, Rust College, Wells became a teacher at the age of fourteen. She taught in Holly Springs before moving to Memphis in 1884. She was fired from her Memphis teaching post when she wrote editorials criticizing the local school board's inadequate facilities for black children. The former teacher devoted herself to a writing career and became co-owner of the *Memphis Free Press*, the local black newspaper. When one of her friends, a successful black businessman, was lynched in 1892, Wells exposed the crime in the pages of her paper. She rightly charged that white business competitors had manufactured misdeeds with which to smear the innocent. Blacks were executed with only the mock pretense that they had committed any offense; Wells knew her friend had been guilty of his color and success, not crime. The brave young editor directed her attack against both those who participated directly in lynching and those whose silence abetted this injustice.

After her editorial, Wells's office was vandalized and her press destroyed. When her own safety was threatened, Wells abandoned Memphis and the South. She moved North and began to lecture and write about mob violence and the murder of innocent blacks. Her pamphlet *Southern Horrors* chronicled the extent and acceptance of lynching in the South. Wells harped on the fact that most of these murders had nothing to do with the honor of white women, but were brutal, racially motivated executions.

Wells established antilynching committees in northern cities, mobilizing black women's clubs. She spread her gospel abroad as well, with successful tours of England in 1893 and 1894. Even after her marriage in 1895, when she settled in Chicago with her husband, Ferdinand Barnett, Wells-Barnett (as she then called herself) continued her activism. In 1895 she published *A Red Record*, giving grisly details of southern lynchings in the previous three years. She was part of a delegation to President William McKinley in 1898 which demanded official action in response to the lynching of a black postmaster in South Carolina.

By the turn of the century, Wells-Barnett was involved in a host of reform campaigns, not just the antilynching crusade. An early critic of Booker T. Washington, she was active in the Niagara movement (radicals who joined W.E.B. Du Bois in the struggle for racial equality) but did not support the National Association for the Advancement of Colored People (NAACP) because she found their policies too compromising. Wells-Barnett always supported women's roles in her various campaigns and many times led the parade during women's suffrage demonstrations. She was a leader whose career challenged both racism and sexism, an outstanding example of the power of the individual to challenge injustice.

Women figured prominently in many of the great political crusades of the late nineteenth century: Populism, Socialism, Nationalism, and the struggle for black civil rights. Yet their greatest impact was with a campaign one might call "a movement of their own": woman's suffrage.

The momentum of the Seneca Falls crusade had been interrupted by the Civil War, and the splits within the feminist movement following Reconstruction contributed to the failure to recapture this spirit. By the 1880s the suffrage movement was in the doldrums, and leaders remained divided over tactics and strategies. Alice Stone Blackwell, the daughter of Henry Blackwell and Lucy Stone (co-founders of the American Woman Suffrage Association), in 1887 initiated a merger of her group with the rival organization, the National Woman Suffrage Association. After three years of negotiations, the competing groups combined into a united front, the National American Woman's Suffrage Association (NAWSA), with Stanton as president. In 1892 Susan B. Anthony took over as NAWSA head, but she continued to face a membership divided over the best method to achieve the vote for women.

Anthony and her lieutenants wanted NAWSA to concentrate on a federal suffrage amendment, while rivals advocated local campaigns in the states. These state mobilizations were continually disappointing. Of the 480 campaigns between 1870 and 1910, only seventeen resulted in referenda. Even more crushing, suffrage supporters won in only two of the seventeen states where the question went to the polls.

By 1900 Anthony resigned her post, worn out by half a century of suffrage activism. NAWSA elected Carrie Chapman Catt to replace her, a leader who blossomed much later in the campaign. Catt recognized the obstacles on the home front and campaigned more vigorously abroad. She worked for the establishment of the International Woman Suffrage Alliance, and stepped down from her NAWSA post to devote herself to the alliance in 1904. Anna Howard Shaw assumed the NAWSA presidency and served for the next eleven years, although Anthony was still the moving force of the crusade and the head of the movement in all but name.

When Susan B. Anthony died in 1906, suffragists were forced to reflect on the eroding influence of decades of defeat. One younger leader commented: "The suffrage movement was completely in a rut... It bored its adherents and repelled its opponents." Yet a new generation of suffrage supporters were not content to let the issue languish.

In 1907 a group of suffragists met in New York City, prepared to revitalize the crusade. Harriet Stanton Blatch (daughter of Elizabeth Cady Stanton), one of the "new blood," explained their dissatisfaction: "We all believed that suffrage propaganda must be made dramatic, that suffrage workers must be politically minded. We saw the need of drawing industrial women into the suffrage campaign and recognized that these women needed to be brought into contact, not with women of leisure, but with business and professional women who were out in the world earning a living. The result was the formation of the Equality League of Self-Supporting Women, later called the Women's Political Union." By 1909 the union had attracted over nineteen thousand members, including such luminaries as Charlotte Perkins Gilman and Rose Schneiderman. The radicals breathed new life into a tired campaign.

In 1910 they sponsored the first of what would become a series of large-scale demonstrations, the suffrage parades. These protests drew attention to women's rights and proved the broad-based appeal of political feminism. One journalist reported in 1912 on a New York event: "Women who usually see Fifth Avenue through polished windows of their limousines and touring cars strode steadily side by side with pale-faced, thin-bodied girls from the sweltering shops of the East Side... All marched with an intensity and purpose that astonished the crowds that lined the streets."

In 1913 younger women in the movement advocated even more militant protests. Alice Paul and Lucy Burns, who had apprenticed in

London with British suffragettes (as had Harriet Stanton Blatch), organized a suffrage parade in Washington the day before Woodrow Wilson's Presidential inauguration. They launched a campaign against "the party in power" (a strategy of holding the current Administration responsible), which they adopted from their counterpart in England. NAWSA leaders condemned this policy as counterproductive. In 1914 Paul broke away to form an independent suffrage wing, the Congressional Union. Meanwhile, Shaw retired as head of NAWSA and Carrie Chapman Catt returned to the helm, to reinvigorate the traditional lobbying effort in Washington and the West, where local campaigns had proven most effective.

By June 1916 women had won the Presidential vote in twelve states. The Congressional Union realized that females might constitute a sizable voting bloc for the coming election. The organization sponsored the formation of a National Woman's Party (NWP) to campaign for pro-suffrage candidates. Despite a spirited anti-Democratic campaign by NWP, Wilson was reelected.

In January 1917, NWP stepped up its opposition and picketed the White House, demanding the vote for women. These protests were received with courtesy and curiosity, until July 1917, when violence broke out. Banners held high by the NWP protesters challenged America's claims of democracy. At first the courts dismissed these women arrested for "committing a nuisance," the only crime with which the pickets could be charged. But when the protests persisted, picketing women were jailed. Over five hundred women were taken into custody, and nearly one hundred imprisoned. Many fought back while in jail with hunger strikes. Prison authorities retaliated with the indignity and abuse of forced feeding. These women became martyrs as the campaign wore on.

Media attention and sympathy for the cause forced the government to abandon its hard line. In March 1918 the District of Columbia Court of Appeals invalidated all prison terms and arrests to which these peaceful protesters had been illegally subjected. At this same time, President Wilson shifted his political influence to support women's suffrage. He joined with NAWSA and NWP, and advocated a federal statute, the Susan B. Anthony Amendment. In 1920 the Nineteenth Amendment was passed and women finally were granted the franchise.

* * *

Votes for women meant different things to different women. Most suffragists were glad the battle was over and settled in to recover from a lifetime of campaigning. Others saw the vote as the first objective on an agenda for women. They actively pursued other legislative remedies, such as the Equal Rights Amendment, introduced by Alice Paul in 1923. Still others believed that women should use their votes to insure special treatment for women and children, advocating child-labor laws and "protective legislation" (laws governing female wage-earners), a campaign which ironically reinforced women's separate status before the law.

But granting the vote to women marked the end of an era. Once suffrage was achieved, women no longer were drawn together with a single united goal. Activist females channeled their energies into movements which spoke to their many concerns—most notably, the peace movement. Some argue that this "victory" actually weakened the push for women's rights. Some claim the movement only lay dormant—waiting to reawaken in the 1960s with the "women's liberation" campaign. Others maintain that this brand of radicalism died in the wake of accomplishing its primary goal.

What has happened to feminism is the conundrum of modern American women—women whose expectations and opportunities are very much shaped by the efforts of the nineteenth-century advocates of women's rights. Women's lives today have been altered radically through the campaigns of their foremothers. The causes and concerns of nineteenth-century women have had a dramatic impact on modern America. As each new generation comes of age, it is faced with an ever-evolving set of choices: to survive or to flourish, to exist or to organize, to accept or to protest, to remember, to repeat, to regret. The future holds no answers for us unless we look to our past—filled with nothing so simple as victory or defeat but a struggle for justice, an ongoing process of which we remain a part.

Bibliographic Essay

THE explosion of literature in women's history over the past quarter century has made the writing of this book easier as well as more challenging. The large number of monographs and studies on particular phases of women's experience and neglected groups in our past, as well as the fine feminist work done during the 1970s and early 1980s, enabled me to learn in years much about women's history that otherwise would have taken decades to assemble. The essay below will not include all the works I have consulted to prepare this volume, because some of the text derives from notes made for course lectures which were assembled long before this project was underway. I cite those works which have influenced me, the books and articles from which I gathered most of my material, and refer readers as well to literature that will help in the exploration of issues which well deserve further attention but which, for reasons of space, are merely mentioned here. I have tried to list, too, the many valuable forthcoming publications to which I have had partial or full access.

The sins of omission weigh heavily on those of us in the field, and despite the lengthy essay which follows, I'm afraid I am no exception.

Anyone working in women's history can be grateful for the numerous bibliographic and encyclopedic guides to the field which have appeared recently. First and foremost, the volumes which have done so much to guide scholars in the past decade toward a rediscovery of neglected women are Edward James, Janet James, and Paul Boyer's (eds.) *Notable American Women, 1607–1950: A Biographical Dictionary* (Cambridge, Mass.: Belknap Press, 1971), and more recently, Carol Green and Barbara Sicherman's (eds.) *Notable American Women: The Modern*

Period (Cambridge, Mass.: Belknap Press, 1981). This four-volume set provides not only information but insight into women's lives.

Several useful guides to published work on women are available. Barbara Haber's *Women in America: A Guide to Books* (Urbana: University of Illinois Press, 1981) is a heavily annotated guide which examines work from several disciplines. Rayna Green's *Native American Women: A Contextual Bibliography* (Bloomington: Indiana University Press, 1983); Phyllis Klotman and Wilmer Baatz's (eds.) *The Black Family and the Black Woman: A Bibliography* (N.Y.: Arno Press, 1978); Eugenie Leonard and Sophie Drinker's (eds.) *The American Woman in Colonial and Revolutionary Times, 1565–1800* (Westport, Conn.: Greenwood Press, 1975); as well as Martha Jane Soltow's *Women in American Labor History, 1825–1935: An Annotated Bibliography* (East Lansing: School of Labor and Industrial Relations, Michigan State University, 1972) point to essential background for research on women in areas which remain relatively unexplored even in the expanding field of women's history.

Women's history owes a great deal to many pioneers. One of the outstanding intellectual forerunners in the field began publishing in women's history in 1915 with *Women's Work in Municipalities* (N.Y.: D. Appleton, 1915). Mary Beard launched an intellectual crusade to chronicle female contributions to the past, culminating in 1946, when her *Woman as a Force in History* (reprint ed.; N.Y.: Collier Books, 1962) appeared. Few recognized that it was simultaneously a book long overdue and one which was enormously ahead of its time. Only Gerda Lerner's *The Majority Finds Its Past: Placing Women in History* (N.Y.: Oxford University Press, 1978) has come close to replacing this essential text of women's history.

The uneven *Womanhood in America from Colonial Times to the Present* (3rd ed.; N.Y.: New Viewpoints, 1982) by Mary Ryan first appeared in 1975, providing the first comprehensive analysis of women's experience from European settlement until the modern era. Generalizations quite naturally abound, but Ryan manages to provide a sharp and sensitive reading of women's exploitation and their responses to change within society. Carl Degler's recent study, *At Odds: Women and the Family in America from the Revolution to the Present* (N.Y.: Oxford University Press, 1980) is an ambitious overview of major issues and trends, with special attention paid to kinship and reproduction. Degler presents a fluid and cohesive portrait of American females by concentrating on white, middle-class women. Nancy Woloch's *Women: The American Experience* (N.Y.: Alfred A. Knopf, 1984) is a very fine textbook which weaves together the lives of outstanding and representative women with the traditional narrative format. This book will most likely be the first of a series which will attempt to cover the whole of American women's experience while integrating much of the new research being completed in women's history. An interpretive yet straightforward study of the nineteenth century, Eleanor Flexner's *Century of Struggle: The Woman's Rights Movement in the United States* (1959) (reprint ed.; Cambridge, Mass.: Harvard University Press, 1975), affords insights into the suffrage movement and the intellectual origins of American feminism.

What women's history has lacked in surveys has certainly been partially compensated by the numerous and very fine anthologies. Nancy Cott's *Root of Bitterness: Documents of the Social History of American Women* (N.Y.: E. P. Dutton, 1972) is an excellent collection of documents showing women's responses to social change. Another valuable documentary history, Rosalyn Baxandall, Linda Gordon, and Susan Reverby's (eds.) *America's Working Women: 1600 to the Present* (N.Y.: Vintage, 1976), contains material on women neglected in traditional women's history: native American women, slave women, women of color, immigrant women, wage-earning women, militant women, and others. James Axtell's excellent reader, *The Indian Peoples of Eastern America: A Documentary History of the Sexes* (N.Y.: Oxford University Press, 1981), illuminates native American women. Gerda Lerner's *Black Women in White America: A Documentary History* (N.Y.: Pantheon, 1972) affords us a rich and eclectic resource for exploring these neglected figures in American history.

One of the earliest collections of historical essays, Jean Friedman and William Shade's (eds.) *Our American Sisters: Women in American Life and Thought*, originally published in 1973, has been markedly improved by revisions and additions. Currently in its third edition (Lexington, Mass.: D. C. Heath, 1982), the volume is a compendium of valuable articles. One of the most innovative studies to date is Carol Berkin and Mary Beth Norton's *Women of America: A History* (Boston: Houghton Mifflin, 1979). These editors sought to integrate fifteen original historical essays with primary material, providing lengthy introductions for each chronological period. An ambitious prospect, the volume fails to hold together, but the originality of many of the essays infuses new life into the tired anthology format. Nancy Cott and Elizabeth Pleck's *A Heritage of Her Own: Towards a New Social History of American Women* (N.Y.: Simon and Schuster, 1979) includes twenty-four previously published pieces, assembled in a chronological format. The editors have provided an introductory essay, but the varying quality and methodology of the articles make for an eclectic and fragmented overview. Nevertheless, the large number of excellent essays on essential topics are valuable.

The best anthologies are those which transcend the collections aspect of the format and present a well-integrated and focused study. Perhaps the most successful in the genre is Linda Kerber and Jane Matthew's *Women's America* (N.Y.: Oxford University Press, 1982). Although the book may suffer from other faults, the editors have skillfully woven together excerpts and articles which present a cohesive yet sophisticated analysis of women's roles and contributions.

Many other collections have been published which focus on particular subsets of American women. Two important volumes which add to our understanding with original and provocative articles are Milton Cantor and Bruce Laurie's (eds.) *Class, Sex and the Woman Worker* (Westport, Conn.: Greenwood Press, 1977) and Sharon Harley and Rosalyn Terborg-Penn's (eds.) *The Afro-American Woman: Struggles and Images* (Port Washington, N.Y.: Kennikat Press, 1978).

Many of the most important articles and essays in women's history have appeared in relatively new journals which sprang up in response to the need for a feminist forum. In the past decade, both *Signs: A Journal of Women in Culture and Society* and *Feminist Studies* have established a formidable record as publishers of pathbreaking research, critical essays, and essential data in the increasingly important field of women's history. These journals not only have advanced our understanding of women in the past but have given researchers hope for the future. Scholars are greatly in their debt. Indeed, the vast expansion of this scholarship has spawned *The Women's Review of Books*, published by the Wellesley Center for Research on Women.

1. EDGING TOWARD EQUALITY

Literature on women in colonial America remains relatively sparse. This is particularly true for native American women, who suffer even greater neglect than the African and European women who settled the North American continent. Rayna Green's recent work has done much to help us to explore this lost past. In addition to the aforementioned bibliography, she has published "The Pocohantas Perplex: The Image of Indian Women in American Culture," *The Massachusetts Review*, Vol. 16 (Autumn 1975), and an excellent review essay, "Native American Women," *Signs*, Vol. 6 (Winter 1980). Theda Perdue is currently at work on this significant topic. Her "Indian Women: Old World Perspective, New World Realities" (unpublished paper presented to the Organization of American Historians, April 2, 1982) will be incorporated into a larger study.

Afro-American women have been treated only sketchily in studies of colonial slavery, although recent work shows promise: Cheryll Cody's "Naming, Kinship and Estate Dispersal: Notes on Slave Family Life on a South Carolina Plantation, 1786–1833," *William and Mary Quarterly*, 3rd ser., Vol. 39 (Jan. 1982); and Alan Kulikoff's "The Beginnings of the Afro-American Family in Maryland," in A. D. Land, L. G. Carr,and E. C. Papenfuse's (eds.) *Law, Society and Politics in Early Maryland* (Baltimore: Johns Hopkins University Press, 1977). The lives of some slave women have been documented; for example, in Gary Mills's study of an eighteenth-century Louisiana woman, "Coincoin: An Eighteenth Century 'Liberated' Woman," *Journal of Southern History*, Vol. 42 (May 1976). But generally we know very little about black women's experiences as slaves.

Free black women do not fare much better. Some scholars have attempted an overview, such as Chester Gregory's "Black Women in Pre-Federal America," in Mabel Deutrich and Virginia Purdy's (eds.) *Clio Was a Woman: Studies in the History of American Women* (Washington, D.C.: Howard University Press, 1980). Others have provided carefully crafted case studies; for example, Debra Newman's "Black Women in the Era of the American Revolution in Pennsylvania," *Journal of Negro History*, Vol. 66 (1976). But the field remains underdeveloped.

There are very few general texts on women's experiences in colonial America. The seventeenth century has been well served by two volumes: Lyle Koehler's provocative interpretation, *The Search for Order: The "Weaker Sex" in 17th Century New England* (Urbana: University of Illinois Press, 1980), and Julia Cherry Spruill's *Women's Life and Work in the Southern Colonies* (Chapel Hill: University of North Carolina, 1938). Lois Green Carr and Lorena Walsh's "The Planter's Wife: The Experience of White Women in Seventeenth Century Maryland," *William and Mary Quarterly*, 3rd ser., Vol. 34 (1977), and Alan Watson's "Women in Colonial North Carolina: Overlooked and Underestimated," *North Carolina Historical Review*, Vol. 58 (1981), provide updated analyses of European women settlers in the southern colonies, mainly by focusing on legal records.

Eighteenth-century women have received relatively more attention with Mary Sumner Benson's *Women in Eighteenth Century America: A Study of Opinion and Social Usage* (N.Y.: Columbia University Press, 1935) and multiple volumes by historians such as Elisabeth Dexter and Alice Morse Earle. All this work has been superseded by Mary Beth Norton's *Liberty's Daughters: The Revolutionary Experience of American Women, 1750–1800* (Boston: Little, Brown, 1980)—on which I comment below.

Colonial New England has provided scholars in women's history with rich resources concerning the role of religion; for example, Laurel Ulrich's impressive *Good Wives: Images and Reality in the Lives of Women in Northern New England* (N.Y.: Alfred A. Knopf, 1982). Some of the most intriguing articles on this topic are G. J. Barker-Benfield's "Ann Hutchinson and the Puritan Attitude Towards Women," *Feminist Studies*, Vol. 1 (1972); Mary Dunn's "Saints and Sinners: Congregational and Quaker Women in the Earlier Colonial Period," *American Quarterly*, Vol. 30 (Winter 1978); Margaret Masson's "The Typology of the Female Model for the Regenerate: Puritan Preaching, 1690–1730," *Signs*, Vol. 2 (1976); and Cedric Cowing's "Sex and Preaching in the Great Awakening," *American Quarterly*, Vol. 30 (1968).

Witchcraft remains an enthralling subject for scholarly research. Paul Boyer and Stephen Nissenbaum's *Salem Possessed: The Social Origins of Witchcraft* (Cambridge, Mass.: Harvard University Press, 1974) has been replaced as the standard text by John Demos's prize-winning *Entertaining Satan* (N.Y.: Oxford University Press, 1982). Carol Karlsen's revised and expanded version of her 1980 Yale dissertation, "The Devil in the Shape of a Woman: The Witch in Seventeenth-Century New England" (forthcoming from W.W. Norton), promises to be an exciting new interpretation.

Women's legal status has been an equally intriguing topic of scholarship. Sophie Drinker's essay, "Women Attorneys of Colonial Times," *Maryland Historical Magazine*, Vol. 56 (Dec. 1961), emphasizes the relative autonomy women were able to carve out for themselves in colonial America. Comparative work on the topic has been valuable and enlightening. Marylynn Salmon's 1980 Bryn Mawr dissertation, "The Property Rights of Women in Early America: A Comparative Study," has provided us with several good articles in the field: "Women and Property in South Carolina: The Evidence from Marriage Settlements, 1730–1830," *William and Mary Quarterly*, Vol. 58 (1981); "Equality or Submersion? Feme Covert Status in Early Pennsylvania," in Berkin and Norton's *Women of America*; and "'Life, Liberty and Dower': The Legal Status of Women after the American Revolution," in Carol Berkin and Clara Lovett's (eds.) *Women, War and Revolution* (N.Y.: Holmes and Meier, 1980). Joan Gundersen and Gwen Gampel's "Married Women's Legal Status in Eighteenth Century New York and Virginia," *William and Mary Quarterly*, 3rd ser., Vol. 39 (Jan. 1982), suggests that married women's ability to operate freely was hampered by the increasing professionalization of law in colonial America.

Divorce petitions have provided scholars of women's history with clues about colonial female status and experience: D. Kelly Weisburg's "'Under Great Temptations Heer': Women and Divorce in Puritan Massachusetts," *Feminist Studies*, Vol. 2, nos. 2/3 (1975); Nancy Cott's "Divorce and the Changing Status of Women in Eighteenth-Century Massachusetts," *William and Mary Quarterly*, 3rd ser., Vol. 33 (1976); and Matteo Spaletta's "Divorce in Colonial New York," *The New-York Historical Society Quarterly*, Vol. 39 (Oct. 1955).

Demographic and reproductive studies, as well as work on marriage and the family, have rapidly multiplied in the past decade. Philip Greven's *The Protestant Temperament: Patterns of Religious Experience, Childrearing and Self in Early America* (N.Y.: Alfred A. Knopf, 1977) is an ambitious attempt to employ social psychology to understand attitudes in the past. Edmund Morgan has published two surveys: the modest *Virginians at Home: Family Life in the Eighteenth Century* (Williamsburg, Va.: Colonial Williamsburg, 1952), and the more impressive *The Puritan Family: Religion and Domestic Relations in Seventeenth Century New England* (N.Y.: Harper and Row, 1966). John Demos's *A Little Commonwealth: Family Life in Plymouth Colony* (N.Y.: Oxford University Press, 1970) imaginatively and sensitively interprets Plymouth households on the basis of legal records and evidence of material culture.

Especially valuable for students of colonial social change is Thad Tate and David Ammerman's (eds.) *The Chesapeake in the Seventeenth Century* (Chapel Hill: University of North Carolina, 1979); see particularly articles by Darrett Rutman and Anita Rutman and by Lorena Walsh. An erratic and highly selective portrait of southern families, Daniel Blake Smith's *Inside the Great House: Planter Family Life in Eighteenth-Century Chesapeake Society* (Ithaca, N.Y.: Cornell University Press, 1980), argues that changes in southern attitudes toward the family support Lawrence Stone's interpretation of the development of affective kin patterns within Anglo cultures during the eighteenth century.

Case studies remain an effective tool of colonial history. Russell Menard's "The Maryland Slave Population, 1658–1730: A Demographic Profile in Four Countries," *William and Mary Quarterly*, 3rd ser., Vol. 32 (1975), demonstrates the higher ratio of men and the scarcity of children in the slave community. John Faragher's "Old Women and Men in Seventeenth Century Wethersfield, Connecticut," *Women's Studies*, Vol. 4 (1976), posits that men's status within the community was more negatively affected by increasing age, whereas women could maintain or augment their role as they grew older. Tax lists, probate records, and population tables for colonial Woburn provide Alexander Keyssar with evidence for his "Widowhood in Eighteenth-Century Massachusetts: A Problem in the History of the Family," *Perspectives in American History*, Vol. 8 (Cambridge, Mass.: Charles Warren Center for Studies in American History, Harvard University). Daniel Scott Smith's "Parental Power and Marriage Patterns: An Analysis of Historical Trends in Hingham, Massachusetts," *Journal of Marriage and the Family*, Vol. 35 (1973), suggests that parents' influence over children can be measured in their control of offsprings' marital choices, and concludes that parental power over children decreased in the eighteenth century.

Several scholars have tackled other complex topics relating to marriage and reproduction. Sexual behavior and fertility have been illuminated by Daniel Scott Smith and Michael Hindus's "Premarital Pregnancy in America, 1640–1971: An Overview and Interpretation," *Journal of Interdisciplinary History*, Vol. 5 (1975); Lee Gladwin's "Tobacco and Sex: Some Factors Affecting Non-Marital Sexual Behavior in Colonial Virginia," *Journal of Social History*, Vol. 12 (1978); and Robert Wells's "Family Size and Fertility Control in Eighteenth Century America," *Population Studies*, Vol. 25 (1971). Marriage and childbirth are examined by Catherine Scholten in "'On the Importance of the Obstetrik Art': Changing Customs of Childbirth in America, 1760–1825," *William and Mary Quarterly*, Vol. 34 (1977); Robert Wells in "Quaker Marriage Patterns in a Colonial Perspective," *William and Mary Quarterly*, 3rd ser., Vol. 29 (1972); and Richard Wertz and Dorothy Wertz in *Lying In: A History of Childbirth in America* (N.Y.: Free Press, 1977). Currently, Judith Walzer Leavitt is at work on a full-length study of women and childbirth in America. For a comprehensive analysis of trends, consult Robert Wells's survey, *Revolutions in Americans' Lives: A Demographic Perspective on Americans, Their Families and Society* (Westport, Conn.: Greenwood Press, 1982).

Scholars have recently explored the meaning of the American Revolution for females. Two pathbreaking books which have advanced our understanding of the era tremendously are *Liberty's Daughters* by Mary Beth Norton and Linda Kerber's *Women of the Republic: Intellect and Ideology in Revolutionary America* (Chapel Hill: University of North Carolina Press, 1980). Although there is some overlap in Norton's and Kerber's analyses of women's experiences during the war, most often the two volumes manage to complement rather than to repeat or challenge one another. For example, while Norton concentrates on the effects of war on those women who remained at home, Kerber devotes a good deal of her attention to the women who traveled with the soldiers. Each in its own way provides a "complete" portrait of its subject. Norton's dynamic interpretation of women's mobilization for war (as individuals and in "ladies' auxiliaries"), her analysis of slave women as well as free, and her highly effective use of private documents to illuminate women's interior lives are vivid. Equally impressive is Kerber's delineation of women's growing political awareness and subsequent ambivalence toward roles and responsibilities in the new nation. Kerber argues that despite women's exclusion from public spheres following the Revolution, they were heirs to an enhanced ideological role as "Republican mothers." Raising "liberty-loving sons" became women's patriotic duty and civic responsibility. Both these books magnify our appreciation of women's roles and contributions.

The article literature for this dynamic transformation is considerably less than adequate. Of interest are Ruth Bloch's "American Feminine Ideals in Transition: The Rise of the Moral Mother, 1785–1815," *Feminist Studies*, Vol. 4 (1978), and Joan Hoff Wilson's "The Illusion of Change: Women and the American Revolution," in Alfred Young's (ed.) *The American Revolution: Explorations in the History of American Radicalism* (Northern Illinois University Press, 1976). What little work has been done on suffrage for women in New Jersey was completed before the modern resurgence of interest in women's history. See Edward Turner's "Women's Suffrage in New Jersey," *Smith College Studies in History*, I, no. 4 (Northampton, 1916).

2. WOMEN'S WORK AND THE COTTON REVOLUTION

Some of the recent scholarship on women and work has focused on domestic labor and unpaid work, such as Susan Strasser's ambitious and entertaining *Never Done: A History of American Housework* (N.Y.: Pantheon, 1982) and Ruth Cowan Schwartz's thorough and engaging *More Work for Mother* (N.Y.: Basic Books, 1983). But much of the literature has concentrated on wage-earning women, such as Susan Estabrook Kennedy's *If All We Did Was to Weep at Home: A History of White Working-Class Women in America* (Bloomington: Indiana University Press, 1979), which contains a good bibliography. Alice Kessler-Harris's *Out to Work: A History of Wage-Earning Women in America* (N.Y.: Oxford University Press, 1982) attempts to cover the colonial period and the nineteenth century, but two-thirds of the book is devoted to the twentieth century.

The story of the mill girls in antebellum New England is one of the most exciting chapters of women's history. Caroline Ware's *Early New England Cotton Manufacture* (Boston: Houghton Mifflin, 1931) has been superseded by Thomas Dublin's *Women at Work: The Transformation of Work and Community in Lowell, Massachusetts*, 1826–1860 (N.Y.: Columbia University Press, 1979). Several collections of primary material add to our appreciation of this experience. Benita Eisler's *The Lowell Offering: Writings by New England Mill Women*, 1840–1845 (Philadelphia: Lippincott, 1977); Philip Foner's *The Factory Girls: A Collection of Writings on Life and Struggles in the New England Factories of the* 1840s (Urbana: University of Illinois Press, 1977); and

Thomas Dublin's *Farm to Factory: The Mill Experience and Women's Lives in New England*, 1830–1860 (N.Y.: Columbia University Press, 1981) are highly recommended. Lucy Larcom's memoir of her days as a mill girl, *A New England Girlhood* (reprint ed.; N.Y.: Corinth Books, 1961), vividly illuminates the era. For another view of factory life, consult Barbara Tucker's "The Family and Industrial Discipline in Antebellum New England," *Labor History*, Vol. 21, no. 1 (Winter 1979–80).

Students interested in the history of white southern women should begin their research with Anne Firor Scott's *The Southern Lady: From Pedestal to Politics*, 1830–1930 (Chicago: University of Chicago Press, 1970). Articles supplement our understanding of the role of the plantation mistress, as, for example, D. Harland Hagler's "The Ideal Woman in the Antebellum South: Lady or Farmwife?" *The Journal of Southern History*, Vol. 46, no. 3 (Aug. 1980); Sudie Sides's "Southern Women and Slavery," *History Today* (Jan. 1970); and John Ruoff's "Frivolity to Consumption: Or, Southern Womanhood in Antebellum Literature," *Civil War History*, Vol. 18 (Sept. 1972).

Two of the more important recent additions to the field are Catherine Clinton's *The Plantation Mistress: Woman's World in the Old South* (N.Y.: Pantheon, 1982) and Suzanne Lebsock's *The Free Women of Petersburg: Status and Culture in a Southern Town*, 1784–1860 (N.Y.: W. W. Norton, 1983). Clinton focuses on the roles and experiences of plantation mistresses by examining women's diaries and the personal papers of plantation families in seven southern states, while Lebsock concentrates on women's urban experiences in her study of antebellum women in Petersburg, Virginia.

Carol Bleser's *The Hammonds of Recliffe* (N.Y.: Oxford University Press, 1981) is a pioneering study of southern family history. Bleser sheds light on a larger southern experience by concentrating on one family, tracing the roles and experiences of individuals from differing generations. Bertram Wyatt-Brown's *Southern Honor: Ethics and Behavior in the Old South* (N.Y.: Oxford University Press, 1982) includes valuable chapters on white southern family life and women's role in male ideology. Jan Lewis's *The Pursuit of Happiness: Family and Values in Jefferson's Virginia* (N.Y.: Cambridge University Press, 1983) illuminates an important chapter of southern history while tackling a critical topic. Recent dissertations on the planter class have focused on marriage and the family in the Old South. Ann William Boucher's "Wealthy Planter Families in Nineteenth Century Alabama" (University of Connecticut, Ph.D., 1978) contains an excellent chapter on women. Steven Stowe's study of southern ideology and courtship (forthcoming from Johns Hopkins University Press), Jane Turner Censer's work on wealthy North Carolinians, and Joan Cashin's work-in-progress on planter families on the frontier (Ph.D. candidate at Harvard University) will add to this growing literature.

Our appreciation of the experience of the vast majority of women in the nineteenth-century South, females in the yeoman class, remains severely limited. Scholars at work on this vital yet unexplored area are truly pioneers. Perhaps Victoria Bynum's assessment of yeoman life in nineteenth-century North Carolina (dissertation-in-progress at University of California at San Diego) and Elizabeth Fox-Genovese's research on Georgia will pave the way for future work, studies which can bring greater understanding of the complexity of class in both the Old South and the New.

Slave women remain shadow figures in women's history. The first major article on the subject appeared in 1971: Angela Davis's "Reflections of the Black Woman's Role in the Community of Slaves," *Black Scholar*, Vol. 3 (Dec. 1971). Davis has recently expanded on her views with *Women, Race and Class* (N.Y.: Random House, 1982). Essays have improved our understanding of black women's experiences under slavery, such as Darlene Hine's "Female Slave Resistance: The Economics of Sex," *Western Journal of Black Studies*, Vol. 3 (Summer 1979), and most especially Jacqueline Jones's "'My Mother Was Much of a Woman': Black Women, Work and the Family Under Slavery," *Feminist Studies*, Vol. 8 (Summer 1982). Our appreciation of the complexity of slave women's family role is advanced by Herbert Gutman's *The Black Family in Slavery and Freedom*, 1750–1925 (N.Y.: Pantheon, 1976). But a full-length study of slave women is lacking.

Two significant additions to the scholarship are the revised and expanded version of Deborah White's 1979 University of Illinois at Chicago Circle dissertation, "Ain't I a Woman: Female Slaves in the Antebellum South" (forthcoming from W. W. Norton); and a study of black women in American history from the antebellum era until the present, in progress, by Jacqueline Jones (forthcoming from Basic Books). These two works present diverging interpretations of slave women's role in the antebellum South and should generate scholarly debate as well as point historians in new directions for research.

The anthology edited by Harley and Terborg-Penn supplies important insights into free black women's experience, but woefully few pieces deal with the antebellum years. Suzanne Lebsock's perceptive and intriguing "Free Black Women and the Question of Matriarchy: Petersburg, Virginia 1784–1820," *Feminist Studies*, Vol. 8 (Summer 1982), shows careful research and pinpoints essential questions which are ignored by concentrating on slavery.

A very fine study which focuses on the post-bellum and modern era is Dolores Janiewski's "From Field to Factory: Race, Class, Sex and the Woman Worker in Durham, 1880–1940" (Duke University, Ph.D., 1979). As the title suggests, this is a far-reaching analysis which advances our understanding of wage-earning women in Durham but has implications for our appreciation of women workers all over the country during this period.

3. TIES THAT BOUND

When Barbara Welter's article on the "cult of true womanhood" appeared in 1966 it opened up decades of debate on women's roles and status in nineteenth-century America. This and other important pieces by Welter are collected in her *Dimity Convictions: The American Woman in the Nineteenth Century* (Athens: Ohio University Press, 1976). Any further investigation of the subject should begin with Ann Douglas's *The Feminization of American Culture* (N.Y.: Alfred A. Knopf, 1977), which offers a detailed analysis of ideology and movements and affords a portrait of a middle-class elite which reigned in this important era. The role of domesticity in the lives of nineteenth-century women is sensitively revealed in Harvey Green's *The Light of the Home: An Intimate View of the Lives of Women in Victorian America* (N.Y.: Pantheon, 1983). An impressive and engaging work, Nancy Cott's *The Bonds of Womanhood: "Woman's Sphere" in New England, 1780–1835* (New Haven, Conn.: Yale University Press, 1977), has become the standard volume on northern antebellum women.

Kathryn Sklar's *Catharine Beecher: A Study in American Domesticity* (New Haven, Conn.: Yale University Press, 1973) demonstrates the power of good biography—a work which not only sheds light on the individual but places the person within the context of her times. Full-length interpretive studies remain to be done for a host of notable women. This void will surely be amended by future work.

Women writers of antebellum America have received disproportionate attention in the cultural history of the period. Both their fiction and their personal records afford vast amounts of material of which many scholars have taken advantage. Mary Kelley has provided a sharp and sensitive reading of women writers with her *Private Woman, Public State: Literary Domesticity in Nineteenth Century America* (N.Y.: Oxford University Press, 1983). Susan Conrad's *Perish the Thought: Intellectual Women in Romantic America, 1830–1860* (N.Y.: Oxford University Press, 1976) is a thorough but less stimulating assessment of the subject. Judith Fryer's *Three Faces of Eve: Women in the Nineteenth Century American Novel* (N.Y.: Oxford University Press, 1976) presents an intriguing perspective by looking at women's roles in the major works of nineteenth-century fiction. Sarah Elbert's *A Hunger for Home: Louisa May Alcott and Little Women* (Philadelphia: Temple University Press, 1983) promises to be the first in a series of excellent revisionist monographs on American women writers. We should all be grateful to Nina Baym for her heroic study, *Woman's Fiction: A Guide to Novels by and about Women in America, 1820–1870* (Ithaca, N.Y.: Cornell University Press, 1978).

Unfortunately, there have been far fewer volumes on women artists. An especially fine piece is Jean Gordon's "Early American Women Artists and the Social Context in Which They Worked," *American Quarterly*, Vol. 30, no. 1 (Spring 1978). An excellent volume which provides stimulating visual material as well as an informative text is *Artist in Aprons: Folk Art of American Women*, ed. by C. Kurt Dewhurst et al. (N.Y.: E. P. Dutton, 1979). Rozsica Parker and Griselda Pollock's *Old Mistresses: Women, Art and Ideology* (N.Y.: Pantheon, 1982) treats women artists in a cross-cultural context.

4. ORGANIZATION AND RESISTANCE

Women reformers in antebellum America left voluminous records which scholars have only recently begun to mine. Some of the most valuable essays are Mary Ryan's "The Power of Women's Networks: A Case Study of Female Moral Reform in Antebellum America," *Feminist*

Studies, Vol. 5, no. 1 (Spring 1979); Carroll Smith-Rosenberg's "Beauty, the Beast, and the Militant Woman: A Case Study in Sex Roles and Social Stress in Jacksonian America," *American Quarterly*, Vol. 23 (Oct. 1971); and Regina Morantz's "Making Women Modern: Middle Class Women and Health Reform in Nineteenth Century America," *Journal of Social History*, Vol. 10, no. 4 (June 1977).

Full-length studies of women reformers have been less provocative and inspiring. For sturdy analysis, see Keith Melder's *Beginnings of Sisterhood: The American Woman's Rights Movement, 1800–1850* (N.Y.: Schocken, 1977). A rather unsatisfying study of urban reform is Barbara Berg's *The Remembered Gate: Origins of American Feminism* (N.Y.: Oxford University Press, 1978). One major exception to this rule is Mary Ryan's prize-winning *Cradle of the Middle Class* (N.Y.: Cambridge University Press, 1981), a sensitive and insightful study of class and gender in an upstate New York community which affords us a revisionist view of religion, reform, and community values.

A pioneering work on female abolitionists is Alma Lutz's *Crusade for Freedom: Women of the Antislavery Movement* (Boston: Beacon Press, 1968), which remains a valuable source. A recent addition is Blanche Hersh's *The Slavery of Sex: Feminist-Abolitionists in Nineteenth Century America* (Urbana: University of Illinois Press, 1978). We know shockingly little about the participation of free black women in this crusade. Some useful articles are Ruth Bogin's "Sarah Parker Remond: Black Abolitionist from Salem," *Essex Institute Historical Collections*, Vol. 110, no. 2 (April 1974), and Ira Brown's "Racism and Sexism: The Case of Pennsylvania Hall," *Phylon*, Vol. 37, no. 2. Although we have several studies of the Grimké sisters, including Gerda Lerner's *The Grimké Sisters from South Carolina: Pioneers for Women's Rights and Abolition* (Boston: Houghton Mifflin, 1967), few other women abolitionists have been accorded such scholarly study. Lydia Maria Child, Maria Weston Chapman, Sojourner Truth, Harriet Tubman, and Lucretia Mott, to name only the top leadership of the crusade, would be well served by new biographies.

Fanny Wright is another figure who merits attention. Abolitionism ignited her zeal for reform, but Wright branched out to join several reform campaigns, as Arnita Jones describes in "From Utopia to Reform: Frances Wright and Robert Dale Owen," *History Today*, Vol. 26, no. 6 (June 1976). Although several volumes have appeared on American

Utopias, women's special role within the antebellum movement has yet to be fully explored. Dolores Hayden tentatively outlines major issues in the opening chapters of *The Grand Domestic Revolution: A History of Feminist Designs for American Homes, Neighborhoods, and Cities* (Cambridge, Mass.: MIT Press, 1981) and tangentially touches on feminism in *Seven American Utopias: The Architecture of Communitarian Socialism, 1790–1975* (Cambridge, Mass.: MIT Press, 1976).

5. BATTLING WOMEN

Women's legal status in the new nation remains a relatively complex and misunderstood topic. Many of the debates from the colonial period carry over into the post-Revolutionary period. How closely were women bound into the circumscribed status prescribed by law? To what extent could women circumvent legal prohibitions and operate independently? What was the impact of statutory reform on women's position in antebellum America? Carol Elizabeth Jenson's "The Equity Jurisdiction and Married Women's Property in Ante-Bellum America: A Revisionist View," *International Journal of Women's Studies*, Vol. 2, no. 2 (1978), challenges and reinterprets Mary Beard's rather optimistic view of women's relative freedom in early America. Jamil Zainaldin's "The Emergence of a Modern American Family Law: Child Custody, Adoption and the Courts, 1796–1851," *Northwestern University Law Review*, Vol. 73, no. 1038 (1979), is rather dry but highly informative. In "Invisible Women: The Legal Fiction of Marital Unity in Nineteenth Century America," *Feminist Studies*, Vol. 5, no. 2 (Summer 1979), Norma Basch examines the subtlety and complexity of women's status as defined in the statutes vs. their experience before the law, an analysis she expands in *In the Eyes of the Law: Women, Marriage and Property in Nineteenth Century New York* (Ithaca, N.Y.: Cornell University Press, 1982).

Students of the suffrage movement should consult Mary Jo Buhle and Paul Buhle's *A Concise History of Woman Suffrage: Selections from the Classic Work of Stanton, Anthony, Gage and Harper* (Urbana: University of Illinois Press, 1978). Flexner's *Century of Struggle* offers an informative overview.

The work of Ellen DuBois revises and expands our understanding of women suffragists. Her *Feminism and Suffrage: The Emergence of an Independent Women's Movement in America, 1848–1869* (Ithaca, N.Y.: Cornell University Press, 1978) is a superb monograph. Her exacting and sensitive portrait of the struggles over suffrage is invaluable for a reassessment of the meaning of feminism in women's lives. DuBois's *Elizabeth Cady Stanton and Susan B. Anthony/Speeches, Writings and Correspondence* (N.Y.: Schocken, 1982) is another essential text. Her lengthy critical essays, which introduce the documents, illuminate the lives of two dynamic leaders while chronicling sisterhood and feminism during the second half of the nineteenth century.

The Civil War has produced tons of literature, but there are few studies of the contributions of women. The published memoirs and diaries afford important source material, especially C. Vann Woodward's prize-winning *Mary Chesnut's Civil War* (New Haven, Conn.: Yale University Press, 1981). Volumes of correspondence have become popular, such as Robert Manson Myers's (ed.) *Children of Pride: A True Story of Georgia and the Civil War* (New Haven, Conn.: Yale University Press, 1972). Great quantities of documents and letters from the Civil War were preserved and are available in archives, yet many of our most basic questions about women's experiences in the war and its aftermath remain unanswered.

The standard survey and single text on the topic remains Mary Elizabeth Massey's *Bonnet Brigades* (N.Y.: Alfred A. Knopf, 1966), which provides a wealth of detail but, published nearly twenty years ago, does not incorporate the new social history. Several other volumes fall into this category: Katherine Jones's *When Sherman Came: Southern Women and the "Great War"* (Indianapolis, Ind.: Bobbs Merrill, 1964); Francis Butler Simkins and James Welch Patton's *The Women of the Confederacy* (Richmond, Va.: Garrett and Massie, 1936); and Bell Irwin Wiley's *Confederate Women* (Westport, Conn.: Greenwood Press, 1975). The sentimentalization of the role of white southern women is a topic that calls for more attention; see especially Nancy Kondert's "The Romance and Reality of Defeat: Southern Women in 1865," *Journal of Mississippi History*, Vol. 35, no. 2 (Summer 1973).

Studies of women's mobilization for war, the U.S. Sanitary Commission, and civilian life (both North and South) are sorely needed. Nina Bennett's dissertation "The Women Who Went to War: The Union Army Nurse in the Civil War" (Northwestern, Ph.D., 1981) is a step in the right direction.

The teachers' crusade for black freed people has been sensitively treated in Willie Lee Rose's *Rehearsal for Reconstruction* (N.Y.: Oxford University Press, 1964) and explored in depth, with particular attention to women, in Jacqueline Jones's *Soldiers of Light and Love: Northern Teachers and Georgia Blacks, 1865–1873* (Chapel Hill: University of North Carolina, 1980). A good study which also deals with the postwar period is Elizabeth Jacoway's *Yankee Missionaries: The Penn School Experiment* (Baton Rouge: LSU Press, 1979).

We still have little idea of the meaning of emancipation for women slaves (although Jacqueline Jones's forthcoming study promises to shed light on this topic). Few of the voluminous studies of the impact of defeat on the South treat women seriously. Carol Bleser's forthcoming study of southern marriages may illuminate some aspects of this intriguing subject. But scores of other topics cry out for attention.

6. NATIVES AND IMMIGRANTS

Work on native women remains paltry; see Rayna Green's "Native American Women," *Signs*, Vol. 6, no. 2 (1980). Some evidence of women's roles is emerging from literature on the fur trade and western settlements; see especially William Swagerty's "Marriage and Settlement Patterns of Rocky Mountain Trappers and Traders," *Western Historical Quarterly* (April 1980).

Literature on women in the West and on the frontier has undergone a virtual boom during the past decade. Volumes of women's correspondence have appeared; see especially Joanna Stratton's *Pioneer Mothers: Voices from the Kansas Frontier* (N.Y.: Simon and Schuster, 1981). Several illuminating articles give a wide-ranging perspective on patterns of settlement and female experience in the West; see especially Sheryll Patterson-Black's "Women Homesteaders on the Great Plains Frontiers," *Frontiers*, Vol. 1 (Spring 1976); Christine Stansell's "Women on the Great Plains, 1865–1890," *Women's Studies*, Vol. 4 (1976); and Rex Myers's unscholarly but informative "An Inning for Sin: Chicago Joe and Her Hurdy-Gurdy Girls," *Montana: The Magazine of Western History*, Vol. 27 (Spring 1977).

John D. Unruh's *The Plains Across: The Overland Emigrants and the Trans-Mississippi West, 1840–1880* (Urbana: University of Illinois Press, 1979) is an authoritative and exhaustively researched study and includes important material on women. Glenda Riley's *Frontierswomen: The Iowa Experience* (Ames, Iowa: Iowa State University Press, 1981) is an informed and useful account. John Faragher's *Women and Men on the Overland Trail* (New Haven, Conn.: Yale University Press, 1979) provides important insight into life for emigrating families through careful analysis of over one hundred and fifty diaries and journals.

Julie Roy Jeffrey, in her *Frontier Women: The Trans-Mississippi West, 1840–1880* (N.Y.: Hill and Wang, 1979), follows her subjects through until they resettle in the West. Women were required to undertake additional, sex-stereotyped "male" tasks while on the trail and often continued these duties while on the frontier. She argues this expanded sphere of responsibility must have brought women higher self-esteem. Norton Juster's *So Sweet to Labor: Rural Women in America, 1865–95* (N.Y.: Viking, 1979) is a rather thin analysis of women's experiences on the land.

The debate over women's status in the West continues. T. A. Larson's "Dolls, Vassals, and Drudges—Pioneer Women in the West," *Western Historical Quarterly*, Vol. 3 (1972), suffers from a misleading title but sensitively explores suffrage in Wyoming and Utah, with some interesting insights into general issues.

Unfortunately, most studies of the frontier deal exclusively with white women, and indeed southern women are absent from the literature as well. An important exception is Nell Painter's excellent monograph *Exodusters: Black Migration to Kansas after Reconstruction* (N.Y.: Alfred A. Knopf, 1977), which deals with both freedmen and freedwomen. However, our understanding of black women—their roles and choices after emancipation—remains limited.

Studies of immigrant women and working-class women in urban cities in mid- and late-nineteenth-century America have multiplied in recent years. The collections by Milton Cantor and Bruce Laurie (*Class, Sex and the Woman Worker*) and by Rosalyn Baxandall, Linda Gordon, and Susan Reverby (*America's Working Women*) contain excellent articles and primary material. In addition, informative pieces on Irish women, Chinese women, Italian women, and other immigrant and working-class females appear in the volumes edited by Shade and Friedman, Berkin and Norton, Cott and Pleck, and Kerber and Matthew. The *Journal of Urban History* devoted an issue to "Immigrant Women and the City" (Vol. 4, no. 3, May 1978).

Philip Foner's *Women and the American Labor Movement: From Colonial Times to the Eve of World War I* (N.Y.: Free Press, 1979) is an ambitious text, as is Barbara Wertheimer's *We Were There: The Story of Working Women in America* (N.Y.: Pantheon, 1977). Both are superior to Cecyle Neidle's *American Immigrant Women* (Boston: Twayne, 1975). A specialized and insightful volume, Faye Dudden's *Serving Women: Household Service in Nineteenth-Century America* (Middletown, Conn.: Wesleyan University Press, 1983), is a valuable addition to the literature.

Two recent dissertations which expand our understanding of related topics are Christine Stansell's "Women of the Laboring Poor in New York City, 1820–1860" (Yale University, Ph.D., 1979), which is forthcoming from Alfred A. Knopf in a revised version, *City of Women*; and Susan Levine's "In Their Own Sphere: Women's Work, the Knights of Labor and the Transformation of the Carpet Trade, 1870–1890" (City University of New York, Ph.D., 1979).

7. PATHBREAKING AND BACKLASH

Thomas Woody's pioneering *A History of Women's Education in the United States*, 2 vols. (N.Y.: Science Press, 1929), is an encyclopedic text. Antebellum educational attitudes and patterns are analyzed in Kathryn Sklar's *Catharine Beecher: A Study in Domesticity*. Two excellent articles which provide valuable information on women's entry into the teaching profession during these years are Maris Vinovskis and Richard Bernard's "The Female School Teacher in Antebellum Massachusetts," *Journal of Social History*, Vol. 10, no. 3 (March 1977), and "Beyond Catharine Beecher: Female Education in the Antebellum Period," *Signs*, Vol. 3, no. 4 (Summer 1978). Especially valuable is Anne Scott's "The Ever-Widening Circle: The Diffusion of Feminist Values from the Troy Female Seminary," *History of Education Quarterly*, Vol. 19 (Spring 1979). Another fine volume which explores women's roles in nineteenth-century education, Nancy Hoffman's *Woman's 'True' Profession: Voices from the History of Teaching* (Old Westbury, N.Y.: Feminist Press, 1981), includes valuable primary material, lavishly annotated, with an excellent bibliography.

A steady stream of studies on women's role in college education has added to our knowledge of female education. Roberta Frankfort's *Col-*

legiate Women: Domesticity and Career in Turn-of-the-Century America (N.Y.: New York University Press, 1977) is an excellent monograph, as is Dorothy McGuigan's *A Dangerous Experiment: One Hundred Years of Women at the University of Michigan* (Ann Arbor: University of Michigan Press, 1970). Several other scholars have contributed enormously to our appreciation of the complexities of this issue: Mary Walsh and Francis Walsh's "Integrating Men's Colleges at the Turn of the Century," *Historical Journal of Massachusetts*, Vol. 10 (June 1982); Ronald Hogeland's "Coeducation of the Sexes at Oberlin College: A Study of Social Ideas in Mid-Nineteenth Century America," *Journal of Social History*, Vol. 6, no. 2 (Winter 1972–3); Patricia A. Graham's "Expansion and Exclusion: A History of Women in American Higher Education," *Signs*, Vol. 3 (Summer 1978); and Sarah Gordon's "Smith College Students: The First Ten Classes, 1879–1888," *History of Education Quarterly*, Vol. 14 (Spring 1974).

Turn-of-the century educators hotly debated the question of women's intellectual capacities. Rosalind Rosenberg's prize-winning *Beyond Separate Spheres: Intellectual Roots of Modern Feminism* (New Haven, Conn.: Yale University Press, 1982) weaves together biographical material on the first generation of women social scientists while offering an intellectual history of the period. Her portrait of pioneers during an important coming-of-age for women in academe provides us with an absorbing and informative account. She also examines debates on female intellect and innate sexual identity which raged during this important transitional period. Of special interest are Edward Clarke's *Sex in Education: or, A Fair Chance for the Girls* (1873) (reprint ed.; N.Y.: Arno Press, 1972), and Julia Ward Howe's *Sex and Education: A Reply to Dr. E. H. Clarke's "Sex in Education"* (1874) (reprint ed.; N.Y.: Arno Press, 1972).

The role of intellectual women in an expanding, consumer-oriented culture is vital to an understanding of the late nineteenth century. William Leach's *True Love and Perfect Union: The Feminist Reform of Sex and Society* (N.Y.: Basic Books, 1980) strengthens our appreciation of the many facets of feminism in the late nineteenth century. His creative analysis of the development of department stores, his interpretation of dress reform, and his assessment of the American Social Science Association are enormous contributions.

Women's roles in the professions are examined in Annie Nathan

Meyer's *Woman's Work in America* (1891) (reprint ed.; N.Y.: Arno Press, 1972). This compilation of essays on late-nineteenth-century women has not yet been updated or replaced by any new text in the field. The literature on professional women needs more biographical material and more studies of urban women before a comprehensive text can be written to surpass Meyer's volume.

For an excellent study of women in the medical profession, consult Mary Walsh's *"Doctors Wanted: No Women Need Apply": Sexual Barriers in the Medical Profession, 1835–1975* (New Haven, Conn.: Yale University Press, 1977). Although Walsh concentrates on Boston, she makes some sharp and provocative claims about women in the medical profession throughout America. Her controversial analysis opens up debate on the long-neglected subject of women physicians. Sarah Stage provides an interesting account of women and medicine in *Female Complaints: Lydia Pinkham and the Business of Women's Medicine* (N.Y.: W. W. Norton, 1979). Elizabeth Smith's "Heirs to Tortula: Early Women Physicians in the United States," *New York State Journal of Medicine*, Vol. 77 (June 1977), is full of fascinating data. Regina Morantz is currently at work on a full-length treatment of female doctors in the nineteenth century. An annotated bibliography, *Women in Medicine: A Bibliography of the Literature on Women Physicians*, eds. Sandra Chaff, Ruth Haimbach, Carol Fenichel, and Nina Woods (Metuchen, N.J.: Scarecrow Press, 1977), is useful for scholarly research on the topic.

Unfortunately, there is no comparable literature on women in the legal profession. A few biographies and articles supply useful information, but a major interpretive work is sorely needed. Those interested in pursuing the subject would be well served to consult Sophie Drinker's "Women Attorneys of Colonial Times," *Maryland Historical Magazine*, Vol. 56 (Dec. 1961); Anita Wallach's "Arabella Bobb Mansfield (1846–1911)," *Women's Rights Law Reporter*, Vol. 2, no. 1 (April 1974); Harold B. Hancock's "Mary Ann Shadd: Negro Editor, Educator, and Lawyer," *Delaware History*, Vol. 15, no. 3 (1973); and Kathleen Lazourou's "'Fettered Portias': Obstacles Facing Nineteenth Century Women Lawyers," *Women Lawyers' Journal*, Vol. 64 (Winter 1978).

There were female scientists in America since before the Revolution, as Joan Hoff Wilson's "Dancing Dogs of the Colonial Period: Women Scientists," *Early American Literature*, Vol. 7, no. 3 (1973), ably documents. Deborah Jean Warner's "Women in Science in Nineteenth Century America," *Journal of American Medical Women's Association*, Vol. 34, no. 2 (Feb. 1979), is a valuable study, but the leading text on the subject is Margaret Rossiter's prize-winning *Women Scientists in America: Struggles and Strategies to* 1940 (Baltimore: Johns Hopkins University Press, 1982).

Doubtless, future studies of women's colleges and professional associations in this era will shed further light on female progress. For now, our knowledge is limited, selective, and generally confined to New England and Middle Atlantic urban centers.

8. SEXUALITY AND STEREOTYPES

Literature on sexuality and stereotypes has multiplied rapidly during the past decade. We have had several useful studies which defy categorization but touch upon related topics. Karen Halttunen's *Confidence Men and Painted Women: A Study of Middle-Class Culture in America, 1830–1870* (New Haven, Conn.: Yale University Press, 1983) falls into this category—and offers a perceptive and lucid cultural history. Ellen Rothman's revision of her dissertation, "Intimate Acquaintance: Courtship and the Transition to Marriage in America, 1770–1900" (forthcoming from Basic Books) promises to be an important study. Lois Banner's *American Beauty* (N.Y.: Alfred A. Knopf, 1983) is another—an encyclopedic survey of attitudes toward facial fairness, fashion, and personal styles, which sheds light on nineteenth-century attitudes toward sexuality. But Banner's study and other work on "fashion"—for example, Jeanette Lauer and Robert Lauer's "The Battle of the Sexes: Fashion in Nineteenth Century America," *Journal of Popular Culture*, Vol. 13, no. 4 (June 1980)—demonstrate how murky and imprecise our definitions and typologies become in an area which encompasses manners, behavior, and sexuality.

Scholars are currently creating new vocabularies, new methodologies, and new conceptual frameworks to deal with the significant subjects of sex and sexuality. Scholars interested in this pathbreaking field should begin with *Women: Sex and Sexuality*, eds. Catharine Stimpson and Ethel Spector Person (Chicago: University of Chicago Press, 1980). Recent review essays are also helpful in sorting out the issues. See especially Martha Vicinus's article in *Feminist Studies*, Vol. 8, no. 1

(Spring 1982), and Estelle Freedman's creative as well as critical essay in the tenth anniversary edition of *Reviews in American History* (Vol. 10, no. 4, Dec. 1982), entitled "The Promise of American History: Progress and Prospects."

Some of the most fascinating research deals with women's roles and medical practice. Scholars should consult Carroll Smith-Rosenberg's "The Hysterical Woman: Sex Roles and Role Conflict in Nineteenth Century America," *Social Research* (Winter 1972); John S. Haller, Jr.'s "From Maidenhood to Menopause: Sex Education for Women in Victorian America," *Journal of Popular Culture*, Vol. 6, no. 1 (Summer 1972); and the especially fine *Horrors of the Half-Known Life: Male Attitudes Toward Women and Sexuality in Nineteenth Century America* (N.Y.: Harper and Row, 1976) by G. J. Barker-Benfield. John Haller and Robin Haller's *The Physician and Sexuality in Victorian America* (Urbana: University of Illinois Press, 1974) contains useful articles, although it is somewhat outdated.

Because of the lack of privately recorded reflections on sexuality, historians imaginatively have utilized published sources for their study of attitudes. Especially useful are Ronald Walters's (ed.) *Primers for Prudery: Sexual Advice to Victorian America* (Englewood Cliffs, N.J.: Prentice-Hall, 1974) and Barbara Ehrenreich and Deidre English's *For Her Own Good: 150 Years of the Experts' Advice to Women* (N.Y.: Anchor Press, 1978). Another creative way to determine sexual mores is by looking at those who challenge traditional values and patterns. Lewis Perry's "'Progress, Not Pleasure, Is Our Aim': The Sexual Advice of Antebellum Radicals," *Journal of Social History*, Vol. 12 (Spring 1979), provides sensitive insights.

Victoria Woodhull was one of the most enigmatic and engaging characters of postwar America, and a dynamic critic of Victorian morality and sexual repression. She is deserving of more attention and is certainly an important subject for a serious revisionist study.

In nineteenth-century America, women's attitudes toward sex and marriage were very much bound up with childbearing. Feminists opened up discourse on this critical topic and championed women's control over their own bodies. Whether they advocated abstinence or contraceptives, most middle- and upper-class women began to limit family size. We know very little about early-nineteenth-century practices, but some leads are offered in Nella Weiner's "Of Feminism and Birth

Control Propaganda, 1790–1840," *International Journal of Women's Studies*, Vol. 3, no. 7 (1979). One of the most enlightening books remains Linda Gordon's *Woman's Body, Woman's Right: A Social History of Birth Control in America* (N.Y.: Vintage, 1976), which places politics and sexuality squarely at the center of women's concerns. Another very valuable text is James Reed's *From Private Vice to Public Virtue: The Birth Control Movement and American Society Since 1830* (N.Y.: Basic Books, 1978). Those unfamiliar with the arguments of this literature would do well to consult Elizabeth Fee and Michael Wallace's "The History and Politics of Birth Control: A Review Essay," *Feminist Studies*, Vol. 5, no. 1 (Spring 1979).

Scholarly research indicates that one of the most effective means of population control in the past, and one quite commonly used, is abortion. We have few private records which discuss abortion, but evidence in the public domain is quite startling. We can look to medical evidence, legal statutes, and other published material to measure the attitudes toward and the extent of abortion in America. See P. S. Brown's "Female Pills and the Reputation of Iron as an Abortifacient," *Medical History*, Vol. 21 (July 1977), and James Mohr's authoritative *Abortion in America: The Origins and Evolution of National Policy, 1800–1900* (N.Y.: Oxford University Press, 1978). Those unfamiliar with the subject would benefit from Barbara Hayler's review essay, "Abortion," in *Signs*, Vol. 5, no. 2 (Winter 1979).

A long-neglected aspect of women's sexuality is same-sex love and lesbianism. An early article by William R. Taylor and Christopher Lasch, "Two 'Kindred Spirits': Sorority and Family in New England, 1839–1846," *New England Quarterly*, Vol. 36, no. 1 (March 1963), pointed to the affection and mutual support a genteel female couple afforded one another. Over a decade later, Carroll Smith-Rosenberg's "The Female World of Love and Ritual: Relations Between Women in Nineteenth Century America," *Signs*, Vol. 1, no. 1 (Autumn 1975), expanded on the theme and enriched our understanding of women's romantic experience. Smith-Rosenberg states that many if not most upper- and middle-class women, even those with husbands and children, had primary and passionate attachments to female peers. The implications are intriguing, especially if we allow that women might have acted on their desires and affections.

The lives of gay men and women in the past have been illuminated by a growing body of literature during the past few years. The American past has been examined by Jonathan Katz's *Gay American History: Lesbian and Gay Men in the U.S.A.: A Documentary* (N.Y.: Thomas Cromwell, 1976). But those who are primarily interested in women's experience should study Lillian Faderman's *Surpassing the Love of Men: Romantic Friendship and Love between Women from the Renaissance to the Present* (N.Y.: William Morrow, 1981). Faderman's work not only deals with lesbians but offers a detailed and sensitive portrait of female culture in nineteenth-century America. Her book provides an international context for same-sex love among women, replete with medical, social, literary, and intellectual sources.

Some of the most intriguing recent work focuses on women who were born in the nineteenth century but grew to sexual maturity in the twentieth. See, for example, Martin Bauml Duberman's "'I Am Not Contented': Female Masochism and Lesbianism in Early Twentieth Century New England," *Signs*, Vol. 5, no. 4 (1980), and especially Blanche Weisen Cook's "'Women Alone Stir My Imagination': Lesbianism and the Cultural Tradition," *Signs*, Vol. 4, no. 4 (1979).

Women who defied sexual norms continue to fascinate American historians. Yet few serious studies of prostitution have emerged. A revival in feminist scholarship has partially addressed this problem. Vern L. Bullough's *The History of Prostitution* (New Hyde Park, N.Y.: University Books, 1964) is a superficial survey. A better but still unsatisfactory treatment is Robert Riegel's "Changing American Attitudes Towards Prostitution, 1800–1920," *Journal of the History of Ideas*, Vol. 29, no. 3 (July–Sept. 1968). The field has profited from studies of immigrant women's involvement in the trade; see especially Yuji Ichioka's "Ameyuki-san: Japanese Prostitutes in Nineteenth Century America," *Amerasia Journal*, Vol. 4, no. 1 (1977), and Lucie Cheng Hirata's "Free, Indentured, Enslaved: Chinese Prostitutes in Nineteenth Century America," *Signs*, Vol. 5, no. 1 (Autumn 1979).

The leading authority in this growing scholarship is Ruth Rosen. Not only has she written a definitive and important study, *The Lost Sisterhood: Prostitution in America, 1900–1918* (Baltimore: Johns Hopkins University Press, 1983), but she has co-edited, with Sue Davidson, *The Maimie Papers* (Old Westbury, N.Y.: Feminist Press, 1977), the correspondence between a prostitute and a middle-class woman reformer. Her work explores the turn of the century and we look forward to more research which will expand our knowledge.

9. NETWORKS AND REFORM

Women's involvement in reform at the end of the century was dramatic. Allen F. Davis's *Spearheads for Reform: The Social Settlements and the Progressive Movement, 1890–1914* (N.Y.: Oxford University Press, 1967) remains an impressive analysis of the settlement-house workers, and women's role within the movement. Harry P. Kraus's *The Settlement House Movement in New York City, 1886–1914* (N.Y.: Arno Press, 1980) and John Rousmaniere's "Cultural Hybrid in the Slums: The College Woman and the Settlement House, 1889–1894," *American Quarterly*, Vol. 22, no. 1 (Spring 1970), are equally useful.

Temperance is slowly emerging as a subject of serious scholarly interpretation, breaking away from the stereotypical image of temperance advocates as ax-wielding fanatics. Barbara Leslie Epstein's *The Politics of Domesticity: Women, Evangelism and Temperance in Nineteenth-Century America* (Middletown, Conn.: Wesleyan University Press, 1981) has done much to advance our understanding of this important issue, as has Ruth Bordin's *Women and Temperance: The Quest for Power and Liberty, 1873–1900* (Philadelphia: Temple University Press, 1981). DuBois's work on Stanton and Anthony includes fresh insight into feminism and temperance. Frances Willard, one of the most dynamic leaders in the Women's Christian Temperance Union, is sensitively analyzed in Mary Jo Buhle's *Women and American Socialism, 1870–1920* (Urbana: University of Illinois Press, 1982), but a full-length biography is lacking.

The women's club movement has recently received some well-deserved attention with *The Clubwoman as Feminist: True Womanhood Redefined, 1868–1914* (N.Y.: Holmes and Meier, 1980) by Karen Blair. We need more work with attention to regional and class differences. Mary Elizabeth Massey's "The Making of a Feminist," *The Journal of Southern History*, Vol. 39, no. 1 (Feb. 1973), gives us some insight into one southern woman's life during this era, but the field demands additional study of individuals, as well as institutional studies.

Barbara Kuhn Campbell's *The 'Liberated Woman' of 1914: Prominent Women in the Progressive Era* (Ann Arbor: University of Michigan Research Press, 1979) defines trends and patterns from detailed biographical material on notable women. Its blend of statistical data and ideological analysis provides us with an engaging perspective.

Women involved themselves in numerous reforms in the nineteenth century. David Pivar's *Purity Crusade: Sexual Morality and Social Control, 1868–1900* (Westport, Conn.: Greenwood Press, 1973) is a very fine monograph. Estelle Freedman's *Their Sisters' Keepers* (Ann Arbor: University of Michigan Press, 1981) is a sensitive analysis of feminist involvement in reforming criminal systems. Barbara Brenzel's *Daughters of the State: A Social Portrait of the First Reform School for Girls in North America, 1856–1905* (Cambridge, Mass.: MIT Press, 1983) illuminates neglected aspects of the reform campaign.

Important shifts in the last quarter century are revealed in the contrast in women's participation in the Centennial Celebration of 1876 and the 1893 Columbian Exposition. The 1876 campaign is ably examined in Judith Paine's "The Women's Pavilion of 1876," *The Feminist Art Journal* (Winter 1975–6). Jeanne Weimann's recent volume, *The Fair Women* (Chicago: Academy Press, 1981), provides a wealth of data on the Chicago Fair, rather undigested, but still a cornucopia of literary and visual material.

10. DIVIDED AND UNITED

Literature on women's involvement in radical movements has been growing by leaps and bounds. Much of the work done covers the period 1870 to 1920, an important transitional phase for women's history. The only topic followed through until 1920 in this volume *(The Other Civil War)* is the suffrage issue, which is sketched only briefly in the text. In many of the works cited below, much of the material deals with the twentieth century as well as the nineteenth.

Women's involvement in Socialism is explored in depth in Mary Jo Buhle's *Women and American Socialism, 1870–1920* (Urbana: University of Illinois Press, 1982), a brilliant study which examines not only Socialist women but women's radical impulses and feminist influence on radicalism during this dynamic period, offering insights into women's involvement in the Populist crusade and the Nationalist movement as well. This excellent volume also suggests dozens of important topics for further exploration. Margaret Marsh's *Anarchist Women, 1870–1920* (Philadelphia: Temple University Press, 1980) is a provocative study of a group which has long been neglected by traditional historians.

An equally rich text, Dolores Hayden's *The Grand Domestic Rev-*

olution: A History of Feminist Designs for American Homes, Neighborhoods, and Cities (Cambridge, Mass.: MIT Press, 1981), provides not only an expansive overview of women's reforms in terms of their spheres and spaces but an exciting intellectual challenge to stereotyped views of women's roles in the culture.

General studies of the Populist movement tend to ignore women's contributions, despite references to outstanding leaders such as Annie Diggs and Mary Lease, who are without biographies. Donald Marti's "Woman's Work in the Grange: Mary Ann Mayo of Michigan, 1882–1903," *Agricultural History* (Winter 1982), provides limited appreciation of female involvement in the Grange and does little to advance our understanding of women within the larger context of rural reform. Julie Roy Jeffrey's more successful "Women in the Southern Farmers' Alliance: A Reconsideration of the Role and Status of Women in the Late Nineteenth Century South," *Feminist Studies*, Vol. 3 (Fall 1975), offers a perceptive view of women's participation in politics and the socioeconomic status of females within rural culture. Lu Ann Jones, candidate in the Southern Oral History Program of the University of North Carolina at Chapel Hill, has shared with me some of her as yet unpublished work on farm women in the late-nineteenth-, early-twentieth-century South. Dealing with agricultural periodical literature, Jones has creatively rethought women's role in this society and female contributions to changes in the South during this critical period. Her sensitive and innovative analysis is a much needed contribution.

Charlotte Perkins Gilman is a key figure in women's history at the turn of the century. A revived interest in Gilman has brought us reprints of her work as well as studies of her life and career. Those interested in this fascinating figure should consult Mary A. Hill's *Charlotte Perkins Gilman: The Making of a Radical Feminist, 1860–1896* (Philadelphia: Temple University Press, 1980), and for an alternative perspective, see Carol Berkin's "Private Woman, Public Woman: The Contradictions of Charlotte Perkins Gilman," in Berkin and Norton. Carl Degler's introduction to Gilman's *Women and Economics* (N.Y.: Harper and Row, 1966) provides us with yet another interpretation of this important figure. Ann Lane's scholarly rescue of Gilman's fiction has been an enormous contribution: *The Charlotte Perkins Gilman Reader: The Yellow Wallpaper and Other Fiction* (N.Y.: Pantheon, 1980) and *Herland: A Lost Feminist Utopian Novel* (N.Y.: Pantheon, 1979). We look forward to her completion of her current work-in-progress on Gilman as well.

Women's politics in late-nineteenth-century America focused on the struggle for the vote. The details of this campaign are examined in depth in Eleanor Flexner's *Century of Struggle: The Woman's Rights Movement in the United States* (1959) (reprint ed.; Cambridge, Mass.: Harvard University Press, 1975). An analysis of Alice Paul's pivotal role and the influence of the Woman's Party is revealed in Christine Lunardini's very fine dissertation: "From Equal Suffrage to Equal Rights: The National Woman's Party, 1913–1932" (Princeton University, Ph.D., 1981). Ruth Barnes Moynihan's *Rebel for Rights: Abigail Scott Duniway* (New Haven, Conn.: Yale University Press, 1983) is a compelling portrait of a complex leader of the suffrage crusade and other reform movements. Two other recent studies which shed light on essential aspects of this campaign are Rosalyn Terborg-Penn's "Afro-Americans in the Struggle for Woman Suffrage" (Howard University, Ph.D., 1977) and an intriguing analysis of female antisuffrage, Jane Jerome Cahmi's "Women Against Women: American Antisuffragism, 1880–1920" (Tufts University, Ph.D., 1973).

Other volumes which provide excellent primary and secondary material relevant to this movement are William O'Neill's *Everyone Was Brave: A History of Feminism in America* (Chicago: Quadrangle, 1971); Aileen Kraditor's *The Ideas of the Woman Suffrage Movement, 1890–1920* (N.Y.: Columbia University Press, 1965); and the authoritative source books, Elizabeth Cady Stanton, Susan B. Anthony, and Matilda Gage (eds.), *History of Woman's Suffrage*, 6 vols. (N.Y.: Fowler and Wells, 1881, 1922).

The commitment and dedication of several generations of feminist scholars made this bibliography of over 250 citations possible. We can only hope future work will both acknowledge this debt and, as tribute, match these important contributions.

Index